The Whole Chicken Cookbook

Jim Fobel

The Whole Chicken Cookbook

More than 200 Tantalizing Recipes for Serving Up Every Part of the Bird

Illustrations by Jim Fobel

BALLANTINE BOOKS ■ NEW YORK

Copyright © 1992 by Jim Fobel
Illustrations copyright © 1992 by Jim Fobel

All rights reserved under International and Pan-American Copyright
Conventions. Published in the United States by Ballantine Books,
a division of Random House, Inc., New York, and simultaneously
in Canada by Random House of Canada Limited, Toronto.

Library of Congress Catalog Card Number: 92-90077
ISBN: 0-345-36535-6

Cover design by Georgia Morrissey
Cover art by Charles Waller
Text design by Beth Tondreau Design/Mary A. Wirth

Manufactured in the United States of America
First Edition: October 1992
10 9 8 7 6 5 4 3 2 1

To my father, Jack,
for letting me keep Whitey
and all the other chickens,
ducks, turtles, lizards, frogs,
and stray dogs

Acknowledgments

I give special thanks to friends who have helped with the creation and production of this book: Tom Bernardin, Anthony and Betty (Fobel) Borge, Roger Bourget, Neil Chan, Joëlle Delbourgo, Rus DePriest, Ginny Faber, Denise Ferguson, Michael Kalmen, Michael and Monica McGlade, Julie Merberg, Jane Mollman, Jonathan Moor, Georgia Morrissey, James Paltridge, Mardee Regan, Elizabeth Schneider, Paul Sylvester, Lisa Thickitt, Chris Waller, and Mary Wirth of Beth Tondreau Design.

Contents

Contents

Introduction

I don't take chickens for granted. I give them all the respect they've earned as the most popular bird in the world. And that goes for the eggs that they lay, too.

When I was just a boy of six, in 1952, we had a small chicken farm in the countryside near Lake Erie, Ohio, where my parents raised hens to sell their eggs. I remember in particular one day when stacks and stacks of chirping boxes filled with new baby chicks arrived by truck. When we opened them, one chick, the "runt of the litter," seemed tired and weak and I wanted it for my very own. We separated it from the rest to be my pet. I named it Whitey.

Thriving on my care, Whitey soon became the biggest bird on the farm. I was happy and proud. But I shouldn't take all the credit: it turned out that Whitey was a rooster. The *only* rooster in the henhouse. Luckily for me (and for Whitey), he never ended up on our dinner table.

The chickens we raised were free range. Although most of the time they were kept in a yard fenced with chicken wire, we sometimes let them out to roam the farm. Mom and Dad said that their eggs tasted better that way. The chickens never wandered very far. At dusk they always headed back to the coop to roost. Occasionally we found a few perched high in a tree in the peach orchard, but they were easily retrieved.

So, my love affair with chickens and their eggs began at an early age. Since ours was an egg farm, we kept our chickens for laying, not eating. We bought chickens for cooking from the market just like anybody else. In those days, however, you always bought whole birds. If you wanted them cut into serving parts you did it yourself at home. Even today, buying chickens whole remains the best bargain. You can learn how to cut up a chicken in Chapter 1.

In the kitchen my mother taught me from the start that nothing should be wasted. If there were extra chicken backs and wings, she made soup. If there was leftover chicken from Sunday supper she made it into another meal. But of course on the days when she made her special chicken and dumplings, it was guaranteed that not a drop or a crumb would be left for any other purpose.

The most popular dishes of the day for using leftovers were chicken à la king, chicken divan, and chicken croquettes. They are dishes that I grew up eating and cooking, and I love them just as much today as I did back then.

When I began to plan this book I wanted to include recipes for some of those old favorites, but in deliciously updated fashion. When you sample my versions you will discover that they have more flavor than their blander ancestors. Chapter 9 is devoted entirely to recipes calling for leftover chicken.

Tastes vary, cooking styles change, and grocery budgets fluctuate. Nutritional needs and dietary concerns differ from person to person. But one thing is certain: chicken is the answer to everyone's needs. It is nutritiously low in fat, calories, and cholesterol, and is a good source of high-quality protein. It fits right in with today's healthful eating.

Because chickens are inexpensive to raise compared to other animals, they are a good value in the market. It takes just two pounds of feed to produce one pound of chicken.

Throughout history, chicken has nourished the poor during

lean years and at the same time, tickled the fancy taste buds of the rich. Broth made from chicken has always been elixir to heal the sick, rich or poor.

Chicken can be luxurious or down-home. It is versatile, easy to prepare, and tastes great. Its flavor and texture make it perfect for all kinds of seasoning and cooking techniques. In every cuisine around the world chicken is roasted, grilled, poached, barbecued, fried, stir-fried, sautéed, fricasseed, broiled, or microwaved. It can even be buried in salt and baked, or smoked over Chinese tea.

To change its personality further it can be stuffed, pounded, ground, pickled, shredded, sliced, diced, slivered, or minced. There are more ways to fix chicken than there are days in the year.

I found the most delicious chicken that I ever ate in a small town in the south of Mexico just a few years ago. I encountered the aroma of roasting chicken long before I actually discovered where it was coming from. I followed the trail of that fragrant scent to a small madre-padre chicken ranch. Out front there was a little shop with an electric rotisserie behind a glass wall, where a dozen plump golden hens revolved slowly in front of some red hot coils. A sign stated that the *pollos* were 8,000 pesos apiece (about $4.00 U.S.). I had to have one.

My timing was good. A man was just about to take the birds from the giant skewers. I carefully studied each of them and pointed to a well-rounded one. The vendor smiled proudly as he slid it onto a sheet of brown paper and put it into a bag for me.

Heading quickly back to my bungalow, I borrowed salt and pepper shakers from the hotel kitchen along the way. The exquisite tenderness of that fresh young chicken remains vivid in my mind. Each part had a distinct and different characteristic.

The wings were dark reddish-brown and quite crunchy from turning so close to the heat. The toasting enhanced the flavor of the skin the way a dark brown potato chip in a bag of paler ones shows how cooking can intensify flavor. The meat in the middle of the wing, a long thin morsel, was taken easily from the double bone. It was crisp around the edges but moist within from constant self-basting. The wing itself, when pulled from the bird, brought along a good chunk of juicy white breast meat.

As I tugged at one drumstick, the entire leg just fell off. I bent the joint backward and the thigh and drumstick divided in two with no effort at all. Taut skin, thin and crunchy, covered the drumstick. Much of its fat had melted away leaving it translucent. One good bite confirmed that the coarse texture and short grain of the dark meat tasted best with the crispy skin attached.

Long strips of juicy flesh, torn in ribbons from the thigh, had the deepest flavor of all the parts. It was as if a huge quantity of chicken broth had been reduced to concentrate the flavor, then used to saturate the meat.

As for the breast, the skin popped off the top like a thin brittle shell, which I crunched and folded into my mouth. The delicate white meat lifted off in layers while the tender fillet clung to the breast bone below. I tasted the warm, pleasant essence of chicken. I don't know how they kept it so moist. The tail and those two little "cheeks" of flesh on the back were all that was left. Perhaps they were the choicest parts of all, and they too soon disappeared. No salt or pepper was needed.

Chicken, whether plucked apart primitively and gobbled up over a sheet of paper in a hotel room, or served up whole under a silver dome and carved with finesse in a fancy restaurant, is still the same delicious bird that's nourished the world for more than 4,000 years.

Jim Fobel
New York City, 1992

The Whole Chicken Cookbook

A Chicken Primer 1

When it comes to handling and cooking chicken you've got to play by the rules. They are simple and straightforward and they are what this chapter is about.

The most important rules are the ones pertaining to handling raw chicken and the ones that teach you how to tell when the bird has cooked long enough (chicken is always served well done).

Also included here is much additional information that should be helpful. For example, by looking at a simple chart you can quickly find out how much stuffing it takes to fill a bird and how long to roast it. Or you can learn how to save money by skinning and boning breasts and thighs at home. A calorie chart gives you insight not only into the undoubted benefits of chicken to your diet, but also shows you how many fat calories (cholesterol!) you can trim by removing the skin. How to truss and carve is covered, too, with simple illustrations that are easy to follow.

You can learn how to cut up a raw chicken into serving pieces and find out how much meat there is compared to bone. You can even read up on freezing and thawing chicken, and find out how to judge a bird's age by its size.

Stuffing and Roasting Chart for Whole Chickens

This chart gives an initial roasting time at a high oven temperature (400°) and the duration at a lower (325°) oven temperature. It also tells you how much stuffing is needed. The easiest way to test for doneness is by pricking a fork into the thickest part of the thigh; the juices will run clear, not pink, when the bird is done. Also, the drumstick will move easily when jiggled. To play it safe, check the internal temperature of the chicken by sticking a meat thermometer into the thigh; when it is done the temperature will register about 180°. The temperature of the stuffing should register 165° on a thermometer. Small birds are generally overcooked by the time the stuffing is done, so choose birds over 4 pounds for stuffing.

CHICKEN SIZE	INITIAL 400° ROASTING	ADDITIONAL ROASTING AT 325°	APPROXIMATE AMOUNT OF STUFFING TO FILL MAIN CAVITY
2½ pounds	20 min.	About 30 min.	–
3 pounds	25 min.	About 40 min.	–
3½ pounds	25 min.	40 to 50 min.	–
4 pounds	30 min.	50 to 60 min.	2 to 2½ cups
5 pounds	30 min.	1 to 1¼ hrs.	2½ to 3 cups
6 pounds	30 min.	1¼ to 1½ hrs.	3 cups
7 pounds	30 min.	1½ to 2 hrs.	3 to 3½ cups
8 pounds	30 min.	2 to 2½ hrs.	3½ to 4 cups

When the chicken is done, remove it from the oven and let it stand for 20 minutes (to settle the juices) before carving.

NOTE: In general, an unstuffed bird will be done about 20 minutes sooner than a stuffed one.

A few precautions should always be followed when handling uncooked chicken. All surfaces that raw chicken touches, including your hands, should be thoroughly scrubbed before you go on to any other food preparation. Bacteria such as salmonella can be transferred to other foods very easily if this rule is not followed. (For example, a raw vegetable for salad that is cut on an unwashed board just used for raw chicken can carry such bacteria over to the salad.) This means scrubbing knives and utensils and hands with detergent and hot water and rinsing them well. The board you use should not be wood. Always use a plastic board reserved solely for chicken preparation. If you must use wood, or if you work on a wooden counter, clean once, and then clean again with chlorine bleach. Never put cooked chicken back on a platter or tray that held raw chicken, unless the platter has been thoroughly scrubbed first.

I sometimes rinse and cut up my chicken right in the sink, so I know exactly what the bird has touched; and the cleanup is easy, contained as it is to the sink.

Handling Uncooked Chicken

Remove the giblets (heart, gizzard, and liver) and the neck from the chicken, checking both the main cavity and the neck cavity. Set them aside. Rinse the chicken inside and out under cool running water. Pat dry inside and out with paper towels and place the bird on a plastic cutting board that you use only for chicken. Wash your hands with hot soapy water immediately after working with chicken.

How to Ready a Bird for Roasting

After you have rinsed and dried the bird, dab the inside with paper towels again to make sure it is very dry. Rub the inside of both the main cavity and neck cavity with either half a lemon

How to Stuff a Chicken

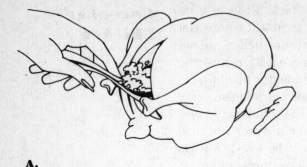

A.

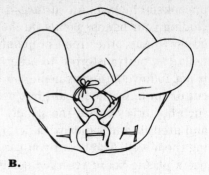

B.

or a little vinegar dabbed on with a paper towel. Always cook a chicken immediately after stuffing it.

You can stuff both the main and neck cavities. First spoon enough stuffing to loosely fill the main cavity (illustration A) without packing it (the stuffing will expand during baking). Push the tail upward to hold the stuffing and pierce it with a long skewer or several toothpicks (illustration B). Tie the drumsticks together with string. If there is enough stuffing for the neck cavity, slip your fingers under the loose skin (illustration C) and carefully work them toward the breast meat to partially separate the skin from the breast without tearing it (this allows room for more stuffing). Then spoon in the stuffing, pushing it toward the breast. Pull the skin over the stuffing and use a couple of skewers or toothpicks to attach it to the back of the bird. Place the chicken breast side up in a shallow roasting pan and bend the wing tips backward, forcing them under the chicken, as shown in illustration D. Proceed with a specific recipe, or rub it with butter or olive oil and sprinkle with salt and pepper and roast according to the chart.

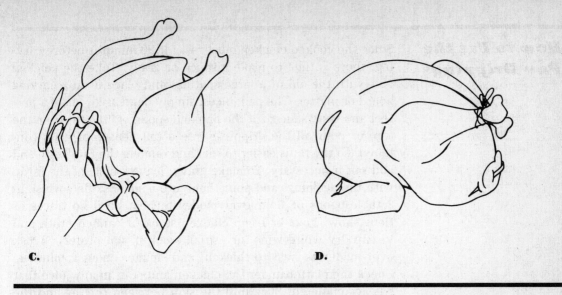

C.

D.

There are many ways to truss a chicken. All you really need to do is tie it up so it holds its shape during roasting. (If you already have a favorite way, ignore this and continue doing it your way.) This method is for those who don't want to mess around with a lot of string. All you have to do is pull the drumstick ends together so that they are slightly overlapped and tie them tightly together with string. Period. If you have stuffed the bird, follow the instructions about forcing the tail upward before tying. Sometimes I'm not in the mood to truss my bird, so I don't bother. It always tastes just as good.

Trussing a Chicken

How to Use the Pan Drippings

Since the cooked chicken must rest for 20 minutes before carving, there is time to make a sauce or gravy. Take the chicken out (with the aid of a large spatula) and place it on a carving board or platter. The pan juices, simply degreased, make a perfect and tasty sauce; tilt the pan and spoon off the fat from the top, or pour all the drippings into a tall heatproof glass container (so the fat is easier to see) and remove the fat. Taste and add salt if necessary. To make gravy, leave a little of the fat in with the drippings and pour them into a small skillet; whisk in 2 tablespoons of flour over moderate heat until no traces of flour show. Pour in 1 cup chicken stock or canned broth and ½ cup dry white wine (or use all stock if you prefer). Whisk over moderate heat to thicken, and simmer about 2 minutes. Check the platter under the chicken and pour in any juice that has accumulated. Slice into the skin between the leg and the breast on each side and let any juices there drain onto the platter, then add it to the gravy or sauce. Always taste for seasoning and add a little salt and a pinch of pepper to taste. Serve hot.

How to Carve a Chicken

If your bird is stuffed, spoon out the stuffing into a serving dish before carving. The chicken can be carved directly on the platter, but it is better to carve it on a board, then transfer the pieces to a warm platter and cover.

1. Insert a long fork into the top of the breast bone to hold the chicken steady as you work. With a long, sharp, slightly flexible knife, cut between the breast and thigh (illustration A), using your hand to push the thigh away from the bone; the joint will easily separate. Repeat with the second leg.
2. Pick up one leg and move it so you can feel the joint between the drumstick and thigh. Slice directly through the cen-

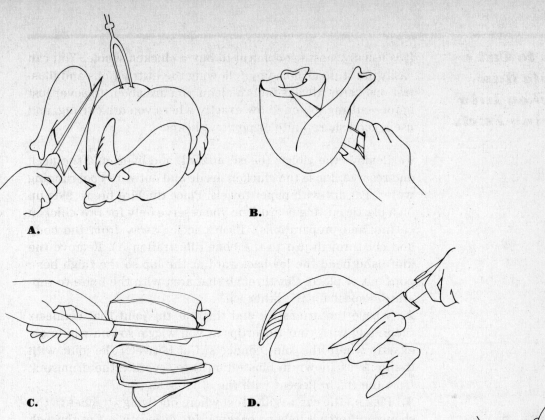

A.

B.

C.

D.

ter of the joint (illustration B). If desired, slice the meat from
the thigh as shown in illustration C, slicing parallel to the bone.
Usually drumsticks are served whole.

3. Bend the wings away from the chicken so you can feel the
joint where they are attached. Cut directly through that joint
as shown in illustration D.

4. Feel the wishbone at the neck base and cut around it with
a paring knife; pull it out to free it. Using a long fork to steady
the breast, slice down diagonally from the breast bone to the
wing joint (illustration E) and lift off the slices of breast as you
work. Arrange all the pieces on a warm platter and serve.

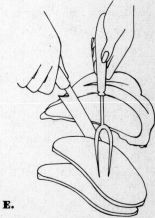

E.

How to Cut a Whole Raw Chicken Into Serving Parts

It is usually most economical to buy a chicken whole. You can easily cut it up at home by following the instructions and illustrations here. Always feel the joint you are about to sever just before cutting so you know exactly where you are cutting, and use a good sharp knife or poultry shears.

1. Remove the giblets (heart, gizzard, and liver) and the neck and reserve. Rinse the chicken inside and out with cool running water. Pat dry with paper towels. Place the bird breast side up on a plastic cutting board (one you reserve only for raw chicken cutting and preparations). Push one leg away from the body and cut through just to the bone (illustration A). Remove the knife and bend the leg backward at the hip so the thigh bone pops out of place. Cut through that area with the knife to separate. Repeat for the other leg.

2. Wiggle the drumstick and thigh at the joint that connects them; feel with your fingertips as you wiggle so you will know exactly where the joint connects. Cut between the joint with the knife as shown in illustration B to separate the drumstick from the thigh. Repeat with the other side.

3. Pick up the carcass and feel where one wing attaches to the shoulder. Force it to bend backward to dislocate it. Cut through at that spot (illustration C) to separate the wing from the carcass. Repeat with second wing.

4. Stand the carcass upright, with neck cavity on your cutting board. Cut through to separate the back section from the breast, letting them fall in opposite directions (illustration D). Whack through at the neck to sever.

5. Cut along the top of the breast bone and then let the knife slip just to one side (illustration E) and cut down through the bone, using strong pressure and a large heavy knife or cleaver, to cut the breast lengthwise into two pieces. (In some recipes, you will want to cut each breast half in half again, crosswise.)

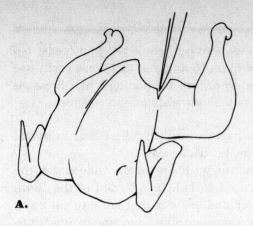

A.

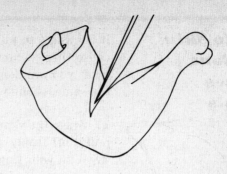

B.

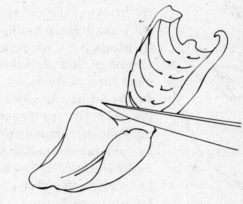

C.

D.

E.

How to Skin and Bone Chicken Breasts

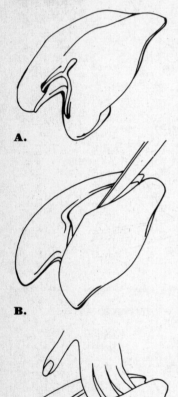

A.

B.

C.

It is easiest to pull the meat from a whole chicken breast because there is more to hold on to and you can more easily see what you are doing. The procedure for boning a half breast is the same, though there may be no wishbone to remove.

1. Grasp the skin with a paper towel (to get a better grip) and pull it off firmly as you peel it backward.

2. With your fingers, feel the wishbone at the wide end of the breast (where the neck used to be). It is buried in the flesh. Feel the shape of the bone and use a paring knife to cut away surrounding flesh. After the bone has been uncovered (illustration A), pull it out by the prong ends.

3. Using a sharp knife, cut along one side of the breast bone (illustration B), scraping close to the bone between the flesh and bone; you are not actually cutting bone, just freeing the meat from the bone.

4. With fingertips, reach between the meat and the bone (illustration C) until the meat is freed from the bone. With a paring knife, cut around any small bones or rib bones still attached to the meat and pull them out. Cut away any cartilage. On the underside of each breast half there is a fillet or tenderloin that looks like a flap of meat. If you are boning large quantities of breasts, consider saving these and freezing them for a separate dish (because they are so tender and tasty). Inside the fillet you will see a white tendon. To remove it, grasp it with a paper towel from the wide end and pull it slowly out while pressing hard against the surrounding flesh with a small knife.

In many supermarkets and butcher shops you can buy chicken thighs that have already been skinned and boned; you will pay extra for these, but remember that you lose about half the weight if you are skinning and boning them yourself; that is, 2 pounds of chicken thighs will yield 1 pound of skinless, boned thighs. (Theoretically, you will pay twice as much per pound for skinless boned thighs.)

1. Grasp the skin with a paper towel so you can get a good grip and pull it off firmly in one piece.
2. Place the thigh, meaty side down, on your plastic cutting board. With a sharp paring knife, cut lengthwise down to the bone (illustration A) from end to end.
3. Place the thigh with bone upright and scrape the meat down, scraping against the bone (illustration B). When you get halfway, turn it on the other end and repeat to free the meat from the bone.

How to Skin and Bone Chicken Thighs

A.

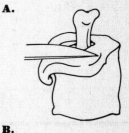

B.

When you trim chicken wings as shown here, you will lose about ½ pound per 3 pounds of wings. Not all recipes require chicken wings to be trimmed. Usually, the wing tips are cut off and reserved for stock. Sometimes the remaining double section is cut to make two pieces. When leaving them whole, it's a great idea to cut out the flap of skin at the "elbow" as shown in the illustration. You can do this with a sharp paring knife. It allows sauces and flavoring to penetrate.

Trimming Chicken Wings

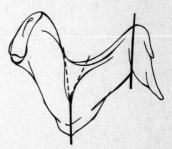

How Much Meat Will You Get from One Chicken?

You will get approximately half the weight of a chicken in meat. A 3-pound bird will yield about 1½ pounds of skinned, boneless, uncooked meat, which will be reduced to about 1 pound cooked. Remember, if chicken is $1.00 a pound, you are paying $2.00 a pound for just the meat. Of course you should use the bones and trimmings to make stock.

How to Grind Chicken

Ground chicken is becoming increasingly available in supermarkets these days. I cannot, however, predict if it will become a staple item at butcher counters or if it will disappear. Since an entire chapter here is devoted to recipes using ground chicken, here is how to grind it yourself.

The best texture and fat-to-lean ratio comes from a mixture of half thighs and half breasts. These should be skinless and boned. Cut the meat into 1-inch cubes and force them through the small round holes of a meat grinder. Alternatively, you can partially freeze the cubes, just to make them firm, and finely grind them in a food processor, using the pulse button.

How Long Will Chicken Stay Fresh?

Most chickens appear in retail stores just hours after being inspected and packaged. If kept under refrigeration the chicken will retain maximum quality for seven days from that period. Of course you do not know how long a store has had the chicken unless it is "open-dated," in which case the bird will have a "sell-by" dated label.

When you buy a chicken, plan to keep it in the coldest part of your refrigerator (usually the meat tray) for no more than 2 days. If you want to keep it longer, freeze it.

Chickens and parts should be rinsed, patted dry with paper towels, separated into portions, and repackaged in clean bags.

It goes without saying that chicken and chicken parts should have a fresh, clean aroma.

Calories of Chicken Parts

The calorie content of chicken varies greatly from part to part, and chicken with skin contains more fat and calories than without. Here is a general guide from the U.S. Department of Agriculture.

	WITH SKIN	WITHOUT SKIN
½ medium roasted breast	193 calories	142 calories
1 medium roasted drumstick	112 calories	76 calories
1 medium roasted thigh	153 calories	109 calories
1 medium roasted wing	99 calories	43 calories

1 cup cooked dark meat, chopped without skin	286 calories
1 cup cooked light meat, chopped without skin	242 calories
4 ounces raw ground light meat (breast)	125 calories
4 ounces raw ground dark meat (thigh)	135 calories
4 ounces raw chicken livers	142 calories
4 ounces cooked chicken livers	178 calories
4 ounces cooked chicken hearts	210 calories
4 ounces cooked chicken gizzards	174 calories
1 cup light or canned chicken broth or stock	approximately 20 to 30 calories
1 cup medium strength chicken broth or stock	approximately 30 to 40 calories
1 cup strong chicken broth or stock	approximately 40 to 50 calories

How to Freeze Chicken

Uncooked chicken may be frozen whole or cut up into serving parts. Use moisture-proof material such as aluminum foil, freezer paper, or plastic freezer bags. Press the air out of each package and seal it well. Frozen chicken kept at 0° will remain fresh for 4 to 6 months.

Cooked chicken should be frozen using the same techniques and materials as for uncooked. If the cooked chicken is in a sauce or gravy, use a rigid container with a tight-fitting lid. Cooked chicken may be kept in the home freezer for up to 2 or 3 months.

Thawing Frozen Chicken

It is best to thaw chicken in the refrigerator with the wrapping loosened. A whole chicken, 4 pounds or under, will require 6 to 12 hours to thaw in the refrigerator. It can be thawed more quickly by placing the wrapped chicken in cold water. It is not a good idea to refreeze either cooked or uncooked chicken once it has been thawed. Each successive thawing and refreezing lowers the quality of flavor and texture.

Chickens can be thawed in a microwave oven; consult your manufacturer's directions for timing.

How to Tell When a Chicken Is Done

Each of the recipes in this book gives specific times and guidelines for testing for doneness. In general, a chicken is cooked when the juices run clear, not pink, when the thickest part of flesh is jabbed with a long fork. Salmonella is heat-sensitive, and is destroyed at temperatures at or above 140°. The U.S.D.A. recommends cooking chicken to an internal temperature of 180°. Boneless parts should be cooked to 160°. Even though a chicken has been thoroughly cooked, you might on occasion find an unusual dark red color at the bone joints. This happens most frequently in birds that have been frozen. There is no cause for alarm. This is caused by a reaction within the bone structure during freezing.

A chicken is done, also, when the drumstick moves easily in its socket when lifted or twisted. The internal temperature at the thickest part of the flesh when cooking whole chickens or bone-in parts should register 180° when the bird is done; the internal temperature of the stuffing should register 165° when the chicken is done.

This list gives the names and weights of various chickens, starting with the smallest and increasing to the largest.

Poussin: A very young chicken 4 to 6 weeks of age. Generally they weigh between 1 and 1½ pounds.

Cornish hens (or Rock Cornish hens): Sold fresh or frozen, these are usually baby hens, just 5 to 6 weeks old, and weighing between 1 and 2 pounds.

Broiler fryer: The most popular size of bird, these are between 7 and 9 weeks old and weigh between 2 and 4 pounds. They are good for broiling, frying, roasting, grilling, poaching, and the like—just about any recipe not calling for a special bird (such as a fowl or roasting chicken, for example).

Roasting chicken: Weighing between 4 and 8 pounds, this type is usually stuffed and roasted; the birds are between 3 and 5 months old. (Often these are full-grown Cornish hens.)

Stewing hen or fowl: These tasty birds are a year or more old and generally weigh between 3 and 7 pounds. They require a long simmer to make them tender. They make exquisite stock or broth.

Capon: These are surgically castrated roosters, 4 to 5 months old, weighing between 6 and 9 pounds. They grow quite plump and tasty after their operation. They are perfect for stuffing and roasting.

How to Tell the Age of the Bird by Its Size

Generally speaking, free-range or kosher chickens taste better than those that are commercially produced. Trouble is, there are no specific guidelines about the precise definition of a free-range bird—for example, was it free to roam every day, pecking and foraging for food along the way, or was it simply let out of the coop into another fenced yard for an hour every day? If you use a reliable butcher or poultry shop, ask about their free-

Free-range versus Mass-produced Chickens

range and kosher chickens. If you live near Chinatown, they will most likely offer fresh-killed chickens daily.

All of the recipes in this book were tested with store-bought commercially raised (mass scale) chickens with exceptional results. The mass-produced birds seem to be getting better and better.

What Is the Best Kind of Salt to Use?

All of the recipes (unless otherwise specified) were tested with ordinary everyday table salt, because that is what most people have in their kitchen. My personal preference for cooking is flaky (coarse) kosher salt. Since it is fluffy, a teaspoon of kosher salt equals about ½ teaspoon of packed ordinary table salt. I also like sea salt. Neither kosher salt nor sea salt interferes with the flavor of food. Since most people cannot detect the difference, and since the table salt is so convenient, I used it for testing. When I am cooking for myself or other people (and not testing recipes for a book), I always choose the kosher salt.

What to Do with Wing Tips, Backs, Bones, and Trimmed Parts of Chicken

Of course the answer is to make stock. If you have a freezer, simply collect enough bits and pieces as they accumulate and freeze them for a future stock. When backs and necks and wings are inexpensive, buy a quantity and make a big batch of chicken stock. Since freezer space is usually at a premium, boil the stock down so it is reduced by at least half, or even three-fourths, then freeze it. It can be reconstituted when you use it. You can even boil it down to a glaze and pour it into ice cube trays. Keep a bag of the frozen cubes on hand and you can throw one into any soup or sauce; it will transform the dish. People will think you slaved all day.

Whole Chicken Preparations

2

Buying whole chickens in the supermarket or butcher shop is always the best bargain. You pay one price per pound, and you get both light and dark meat along with the giblets and the makings for a batch of broth or the bonus of pan-drippings to make gravy. The birds are available in small, medium, or large and are tagged as Cornish hens, broiler/fryers, roasting hens, capons, or stewing hens.

You can choose a recipe for rapid-roasting a small bird or stuffing a plump one to roast the old-fashioned way, slowly in the oven until it's golden brown and tender. There's even a recipe for a roasted rooster bursting with oyster stuffing that will fill your house with the most wonderful aroma long before it's done. Stuffed chickens make mouth-watering, homestyle dinners when served with all the trimmings.

There are some savory international stews here too; Mexican *pozole*, French *poule-au-pot*, and Mom's American chicken and dumplings. All of them will warm your heart, your home, and your tummy while they steam up your windows on a cold, rainy day. And, of course, everyone loves main dish chicken pot pies topped with delicate flaky pastry.

The versatile chicken can also be cooked the Chinese "white-cut" way, where it rests in a pot of boiling water and is then plunged into ice water and served with fragrant scallion-ginger sauce.

Golden Roast Chicken with Belly-band Potatoes

This is a simple roast chicken with sprigs of fresh rosemary and butter tucked between the skin and the breast meat. The herb permeates the meat and the pan juices. Belly-band potatoes—those little new potatoes with a band of skin pared from their middles—and carrots are roasted in the pan alongside the golden bird. You may substitute thyme, oregano, or tarragon for the rosemary.

MAKES 6 SERVINGS

18 small new red-skinned potatoes (about 3 pounds)
6 medium carrots, peeled and cut into 1½-inch lengths
5 to 6-pound roasting chicken
4 tablespoons (½ stick) butter, softened
4 large sprigs fresh rosemary or 2 teaspoons dried rosemary
2 medium onions, peeled and chopped
Salt and pepper
1 tablespoon all-purpose flour
½ cup chicken stock, canned broth, or white wine

1. Bring a large pot of lightly salted water to a boil over high heat. Using a paring knife, slice off a 1½-inch-wide band of skin from the center of each potato. Drop the potatoes and carrots into the water; partially cover and when the boil resumes, boil for 15 minutes. Drain.

2. Preheat the oven to 325°. Rinse the chicken inside and out with cold water. Pat dry. Loosen the skin over each breast half by inserting your fingers in between them. Tuck 1 tablespoon butter and 1 sprig rosemary under the skin on each side (if using dried, use ½ teaspoon in place of each sprig). Put 1 sprig rosemary or ½ teaspoon dried in the main cavity and tie the legs tightly together with string. Put the chopped onions in a large shallow roasting pan and place the chicken, breast side up, on top of them. Scatter the potatoes and carrots around the chicken. Melt the remaining 2 tablespoons butter in a small pot. Brush the chicken and vegetables lightly with some of the butter. Sprinkle with salt and pepper. Chop the remaining sprig of rosemary or crumble remaining ½ teaspoon dried and sprinkle over the potatoes, carrots, and chicken. Roast for about 20 minutes per pound, lightly brushing the chicken and vegetables with butter every 30 minutes. Turn the oven to 375° during the final 20 minutes, to brown lightly. A 6-pound chicken should be done in 2 hours. The chicken is done when the drumsticks move easily and the thigh juices run clear when pricked with a long fork or knife. Transfer the bird to a platter, letting any juice run from the cavity into the roasting pan. Scoop out the potatoes and carrots with a slotted spoon and arrange them around the chicken. Cover loosely with foil and let stand for 20 minutes before carving.

3. Place the roasting pan over two burners (if the drippings are very fatty, spoon off or blot away some with a paper towel). Stir in the flour with a fork or a whisk. Cook for a minute, stirring; pour in the stock and bring to a boil to thicken lightly. Add salt and pepper to taste. Serve hot, with the chicken and vegetables.

Spicy Rapid Roast Chicken

This is the kind of recipe that you just throw together. All you do is rub the chicken with butter or olive oil and sprinkle it with herbs. No need to truss or fuss. Pop it into a very hot oven and it's done in a hurry.

MAKES 2 TO 4 SERVINGS

2 to 3-pound whole chicken
1 tablespoon olive oil or soft butter
¼ teaspoon salt
¼ teaspoon black pepper
¼ teaspoon dried oregano, crumbled
¼ teaspoon dried basil, crumbled
¼ teaspoon paprika
⅛ teaspoon cayenne pepper (optional)

1. Preheat the oven to 450°. Rinse the chicken inside and out under cold running water. Pat dry with paper towels.

2. Put the chicken in a small baking pan. Rub with the olive oil or butter. Sprinkle with the salt, pepper, oregano, basil, paprika, and cayenne pepper. Roast for 20 minutes. Lower the oven temperature to 400° and roast until done, about 25 minutes longer for a 2-pound bird or 40 minutes more for a 3-pound bird. Let rest 10 to 15 minutes. Serve hot.

Caraway Chickens with Light Gravy

MAKES 12 SERVINGS

1 tablespoon plus 2 teaspoons whole caraway seeds
8 tablespoons (1 stick) butter, softened
2 whole large roasting chickens, about 6 pounds each
1 cup Basic Chicken Stock (page 47) or canned broth
3 tablespoons all-purpose flour
¼ cup dry white wine
Salt and pepper

1. Place 1 tablespoon of the caraway seeds in a mortar, spice grinder, or blender and pulverize. In a small bowl beat the butter until fluffy. Stir in the caraway powder to blend. On a square of waxed paper or aluminum foil, form the caraway butter into a log about the size of a stick of butter. Wrap tightly, twisting the ends of the paper or foil, and refrigerate until solid, at least 1 hour.

2. Preheat the oven to 350°. Place the chickens, breast side up, on a work surface. Beginning near the main cavity, carefully slip your fingers between the skin and breast meat and gently work apart to separate almost to the neck area of each bird; be careful not to tear the skin. Cut three-quarters of the chilled caraway butter into thin slices and slide them under the skin of each breast half. Toss 1 teaspoon of the remaining whole caraway seeds into the cavity of each chicken. Truss the chickens with string and place them breast side up on a rack in a large shallow roasting pan.

3. Melt the remaining caraway butter in a small saucepan over low heat. Lightly brush the chickens with half the melted caraway butter.

Savory and succulent, these buttery birds taste of the caraway butter that is tucked under their skins and in their cavities before roasting. The seeds enhance the light, flavorful gravy, too. Make the caraway butter several hours or even a day ahead of time so it can chill before you prepare the chickens. This is a good choice for a big family get-together. Be sure to note that Parsleyed Potatoes (page 363), the ideal accompaniment, will require a good bit of time.

4. Roast the chickens in the center of the oven for 30 minutes. Brush with the remaining caraway butter and continue to roast, basting with the pan drippings every 20 minutes, for about 1½ hours longer, or until the internal temperature reaches 180°. Transfer birds to a large platter to rest for 15 minutes while the juices settle.

5. Meanwhile, pour the pan drippings from the roasting pan into a heatproof bowl or large measuring cup. Carefully pour the juices from the cavities of the birds, and any that have accumulated on the platter, into the bowl. Spoon 2 tablespoons of the fat from the surface of the drippings into a medium, nonaluminum skillet. Skim off and discard any remaining fat. There will be about 1 cup of juice remaining. Add enough of the stock (and/or water) to make a total of 2 cups; reserve.

6. Add the flour to the chicken fat in the skillet and stir over moderate heat until bubbling. Cook for 1 minute to make a roux. Pour in the reserved chicken juices and the wine. Whisk constantly over moderate heat until the gravy boils and thickens slightly. Simmer, stirring constantly, for 3 minutes. Remove from the heat. Season with salt and pepper to taste. Serve hot, with the chickens.

Elizabeth Schneider's Tender-Juicy Roast Chicken

MAKES 2 SERVINGS

2 to 2½-pound free-range chicken
2 teaspoons soft butter
Salt and pepper

1. Take the giblets and neck from the chicken and reserve for another use. Rinse the chicken inside and out with cool running water. Pat dry inside and out with paper towels. Dry thoroughly. Place the bird breast side down on a small rack over a plate. Do not wrap; instead, drape a paper towel over the bird and refrigerate for 12 hours. Turn the bird breast side up and let dry on the rack 12 hours longer (if any liquid has accumulated on the plate, pour it off and discard).

2. Preheat the oven to 300°. Rub the bird all over with the butter. Place the bird, uncovered, on a rack in a small roasting pan, breast side down. Roast for 50 to 60 minutes. Turn the bird breast side up. Baste with the pan drippings. Sprinkle lightly with salt and pepper and roast until it is cooked through, 25 to 30 minutes longer. When done, the juices will run clear (not pink) when the thickest part of the thigh is pierced with a fork. Let stand 15 minutes before carving.

My good friend, food writer Elizabeth Schneider, author of *Uncommon Fruits and Vegetables: a Common-sense Guide,* told me about her favorite way to roast a young chicken. I tried it and the results were exceptionally tasty. The bird must air-dry in the refrigerator for 24 hours, so plan accordingly. The resulting dry skin roasts beautifully crispy. You might consider serving Roasted Shallots (page 373), new potatoes, and Creamed Corn (page 373) alongside. A green salad and vegetable are fine, too.

Roast Chicken with Hungarian Cracker Stuffing

This is a simple, homey dish. My "Aunt" Betty always made a double batch of this stuffing and used it to stuff a turkey. The stuffing reminds me of a cross between Jewish kishke and matzo balls. For dinner serve with buttered sweet peas and Mashed Potatoes and Gravy (page 364), or with Roasted Shallots (page 373), Fresh Stewed Tomatoes (page 374), and Creamed Corn (page 373).

MAKES 6 SERVINGS

- **4** to 5-pound roasting chicken
- **1/2** lemon
- Salt
- **2** medium carrots, peeled and halved lengthwise
- **2** medium ribs celery, halved lengthwise and crosswise
- **1** medium onion, peeled and sliced
- **2** chicken bouillon cubes
- **1** teaspoon paprika

Cracker Stuffing:

- **2** cups ground or finely crushed soda crackers (about 50 2-inch crackers)
- **5** tablespoons butter
- **1** small onion, peeled and grated
- **2** tablespoons chopped parsley
- **6** large eggs
- **1/4** teaspoon grated nutmeg
- **1/8** teaspoon black pepper

1. Preheat the oven to 350°. Rinse the chicken inside and out with cool water. Pat dry. Rub the inside of the cavity with the lemon. Sprinkle very lightly with salt. Arrange the carrots, celery, and onions in a shallow roasting pan. Add the bouillon cubes, paprika, and 1 cup hot water.

2. Put the cracker crumbs in a large mixing bowl. Melt 4 tablespoons of the butter in a small skillet over moderate heat; add the grated onion and parsley; sauté about 2 minutes. Add to the crumbs. Stir in 2 of the eggs to moisten evenly. Then stir in 2 more. Finally, stir in the remaining 2 eggs, nutmeg, and pepper. No salt should be needed, since the crackers are salted; if necessary, add a pinch more.

3. Spoon the stuffing into the cavity of the chicken. Tuck the wing tips under the bird by forcing them backward. Push the tail upward and hold in place with a skewer or toothpicks. Tie the drumsticks together with string. Place on the bed of vegetables in the roasting pan. Rub the chicken with the remaining tablespoon of soft butter. Cover tightly with a double layer of aluminum foil.

4. Roast for 2 hours. Uncover, baste with the pan drippings, and roast to brown and cook through, about 30 minutes longer. The bird is done as soon as the juices run clear when the thickest part of the thigh is pierced with a long fork, the internal temperature of the thigh reaches 180°, and the temperature of the stuffing reaches 165°. When done a drumstick will move easily at the joint. Let stand 20 minutes before carving.

Roasted Rooster with Oyster Stuffing

People are always asking, "What's a capon?" It's a rooster, though a plump, surgically castrated one. The big bird is especially delicious filled with oyster stuffing, so I have paired them here.

MAKES 8 SERVINGS

Oyster Stuffing:

- **1** loaf Italian bread or 5 cups toasted croutons
- **3** tablespoons butter
- **3** tablespoons olive oil
- **3** cups chopped onion
- **3** cups finely diced celery
- **2** large garlic cloves, peeled and minced or crushed through a press
- **1** pound lean ground pork
- **1** cup chopped fresh parsley leaves
- **1** teaspoon ground sage
- **1** teaspoon ground cumin
- **1/2** teaspoon dried basil, crumbled
- **1/2** teaspoon grated nutmeg
- **2** teaspoons salt
- **1/4** teaspoon black pepper
- **2** dozen (1 pint) raw oysters, 1/3 cup oyster liquor reserved
- **3** large eggs

Rooster:

- **1** large onion, chopped
- **8** to 10-pound whole capon, thawed if frozen
- **1** lemon, cut in half

1. Prepare the oyster stuffing: If starting with a loaf of Italian bread, preheat the oven to 350°. Cut the bread into 1/2- to 3/4-inch cubes and place on a large baking sheet. Bake, tossing and turning every 10 minutes, until deep golden brown, 30 to 40 minutes. Remove and let cool.

2. Melt the butter with the olive oil in a large heavy flame-proof casserole or dutch oven over moderate heat. Add the onion and celery; sauté to soften and lightly brown, stirring frequently, about 15 minutes. Add the garlic and cook 2 to 3 minutes longer. Add the toasted croutons, tossing to combine. Transfer to a large bowl. Crumble in the ground pork, then add the parsley, sage, cumin, basil, nutmeg, salt, and pepper. Coarsely chop the oysters and add them. In a bowl whisk together the 3 eggs with the reserved ⅓ cup oyster liquor (or white wine if lacking enough juice from the oysters). Add gradually to the stuffing, tossing so it absorbs evenly. The stuffing should be moist, neither wet nor dry. If necessary, this can be corrected with a little broth or water, or by adding a few more croutons. There will be about 8 cups of stuffing.

3. Stuff the rooster: Preheat the oven to 400°. Scatter the chopped onion in a large shallow roasting pan. Rinse the rooster under cold running water, inside and out, and pat dry with paper towels. Rub the cut sides of the lemon all over the bird, inside and out. Loosely fill the main cavity with stuffing (it will hold 4 to 4½ cups). Loosen the flap of skin around the neck (you can slide your finger between the skin and breast flesh to make the area for stuffing slightly deeper). Fill with 1 to 1½ cups stuffing. Put the remainder of the stuffing into a small buttered casserole and reserve in the refrigerator.

4. Secure the flap of neck skin to the back of the bird with skewers or picks. Tie the drumsticks tightly together with string and tuck the wing tips inward by forcing them under the bird. Place on the bed of onions and put in the center of the oven. Roast for 30 minutes. Turn the heat down to 325° and roast, basting with pan juices every 20 minutes, for about 20 minutes per pound (including the initial high-temperature roasting). A

9-pound capon will be done in about 3 hours. To test, the drumstick should move easily when grasped and the juices should run clear when the thigh is pierced with a fork or knife tip. Take from the oven, transfer the bird to a platter and cover with aluminum foil, and let stand about 20 minutes. Pour the drippings into a tall clear container or glass and spoon off most of the fat from the top. Serve the pan drippings as they are or make gravy, following the procedure on page 8).

Poule-au-Pot with Avocado Mayonnaise

I like to mix the foods of different countries; to my mind the eclectic results are purely American. Here, the classic stewed French hen is served with an ethereal avocado mayonnaise—a marriage of Mexico and France. Stewing hens (or fowl) were once commonplace but are now a

MAKES 6 SERVINGS

Pâté Stuffing:
- **1** pound ground pork
- **1/2** cup plain dry bread crumbs
- **2** large eggs
- **2** tablespoons cognac or plain brandy
- **2** tablespoons butter
- **1** medium onion, peeled and coarsely chopped
- **1** large garlic clove, peeled and sliced
- **1/2** cup (about 3 ounces) diced smoked ham
- **1/2** cup chopped parsley
- **3** whole chicken livers
- **3** tablespoons heavy cream
- **1/2** teaspoon sugar

½ teaspoon grated nutmeg
⅛ teaspoon ground allspice
½ teaspoon salt
¼ teaspoon black pepper

Hen and Broth:

6 to 7-pound stewing hen (fowl)
3 quarts homemade Basic Chicken Stock (page 47) or canned broth
1 cup dry white wine
1 pound lean chuck steak, cut in 6 pieces (optional)
1 medium onion, peeled and sliced
1 medium carrot, peeled and sliced
1 medium rib celery, sliced
5 whole cloves
2 bay leaves

Accompaniments:

1 small head green cabbage, cut in six wedges
12 small to medium red-skinned potatoes
6 small white turnips, peeled
6 medium parsnips (optional), peeled and halved lengthwise
6 to 12 medium carrots, peeled
6 medium leeks
6 large sprigs parsley
Avocado Mayonnaise (page 384)
Cornichons (optional)

specialty item. They take a long time to simmer to tenderness, but remain full of flavor. The result is a bird much tastier than a broiler-fryer. With all the accompaniments, this is a complete winter meal, one that will warm the house and the heart. It's a good idea to prepare this through Step 4 a day before you want to serve it.

1. Prepare the pâté stuffing: In a large bowl combine the pork, bread crumbs, eggs, and cognac. In a small skillet melt the butter over moderate heat. Add the onion and garlic; sauté to soften, 3 to 5 minutes.
2. In a food processor, combine the smoked ham, parsley,

chicken livers, cream, and sautéed onion mixture; blend to a purée (or grind in a blender, adding the eggs and Cognac so the mixture is more liquid and easier to purée). Add to the pork along with the sugar, nutmeg, allspice, salt, and pepper. Mix well.

3. Prepare the hen and broth: Rinse the hen under cold water, inside and out, and dry with paper towels. Stuff the main cavity with enough of the pâté stuffing so it is almost full but not packed tightly (this allows room for expansion). With a large needle and a dark color of thread, sew the cavity closed. Put the rest of the stuffing in the neck cavity and sew it closed as well. Put away the needle and thread as soon as you are finished.

4. Pour the stock and wine into a large deep pot or dutch oven with a cover. Add the optional chuck steak, the onion, carrot, celery, cloves, and bay leaves. Bring to a boil. Slide in the stuffed hen and simmer, covered, very slowly over low heat for 3 to 4 hours, until tender but not falling apart. Take out the beef pieces after 2 to 2½ hours and reserve for another use (they add good flavor to the broth; the meat can be used to make tacos or barbecued beef sandwiches). Take the hen out when it is done and put it on a platter. Strain the broth; degrease (this can be done by chilling if making a day ahead). This recipe may be prepared a day or two ahead to this point.

5. Prepare the accompaniments: Put the wedges of cabbage into a large pot and cover with cold water; cover and bring to a boil over moderately high heat. Boil for 10 minutes and then drain. If making ahead, reheat in the broth. Combine the potatoes, turnips, and optional parsnips in a large pot; cover with cold water and bring to a boil, covered, over moderately high heat. Boil until tender, 20 to 30 minutes. Take out with a slotted spoon and drain. If making ahead, reheat in the broth.

6. Bring the degreased chicken stock to a boil. Simmer the chicken to reheat if needed. Add the carrots to the stock and simmer while you prepare the leeks: Slice off the root ends and cut off the medium and dark green stems, leaving just the white and light green portions. Cut lengthwise in half and thoroughly rinse out any dirt or sand. Add to the broth and simmer until tender, 10 to 15 minutes. Add the parsley for the last few minutes.

7. Remove the thread and the skin from the hen. Carve the hen into ½-inch-thick slices and arrange on a hot deep platter. Scoop out the stuffing with a large spoon and mound on the platter. Add the vegetables to the platter and ladle some of the hot broth over everything. Serve the remaining broth, hot, in cups. Accompany with the avocado mayonnaise and optional cornichons.

Simple Broiled Chicken

MAKES 4 SERVINGS

3 to 3½-pound broiler-fryer chicken
1 tablespoon olive oil (or soft butter)
1 teaspoon dried herb, such as basil, oregano, thyme, rosemary, or tarragon
½ teaspoon cayenne pepper (optional, for spicy chicken)
Salt and pepper to taste

1. Preheat the broiler. Using poultry shears or a sharp cleaver, split the chicken down the back along one side of the spine. Cut out and discard the spine (backbone). Open the chicken flat, butterfly-fashion, and pound with your hand or the side of the cleaver to flatten. Rub the olive oil over both sides of the chicken.

To make a delicious broiled chicken with crispy skin, all you have to do is rub it with a little olive oil and cook it under the broiler. You can enhance the flavor further by marinating it (see Orange-Basil Marinade, page 379) or by sprinkling it with herbs as suggested.

2. Place skin side down on a broiler pan and broil 4 to 5 inches from the heat source for 15 minutes. Turn the chicken and sprinkle with the herb and cayenne. Broil 5 to 10 minutes longer, or until the skin is crisp and browned and the juices run clear when the thigh is pierced with a fork. Serve hot.

Pozole

Here is a cross between a hearty soup and a stew, almost a meal by itself, that's suitable for a fiesta or a feast. The colorful, crunchy, and fragrant garnishes are very important to the outcome. In Mexico, a whole pig's head is usually added to this soup but I have eliminated it because I encourage you to sample this authentically delicious version made with chicken. Large dried corn kernels or

MAKES TEN 2-CUP SERVINGS

The Corn:

1 pound whole dried hominy or large dried white corn kernels and 1½ tablespoons slaked lime (calcium hydroxide, or *cal*), *or* 1 pound *mote pelado*, *or* five 16-ounce cans white or yellow hominy, drained

The Chicken and Broth:

2 whole chickens, 3 pounds each
1 pig's foot, split (optional)
2 medium onions, peeled and sliced
1 large carrot, peeled and sliced
1 large rib celery, sliced
3 large parsley sprigs
2 large garlic cloves, peeled and sliced
2 teaspoons whole cumin seeds
2 whole bay leaves
8 whole cloves
8 whole black peppercorns
1 tablespoon salt

Pozole:

2 medium onions, peeled and chopped
4 medium carrots (1/2 pound), peeled and thinly sliced
2 ribs celery, finely diced
3 large garlic cloves, peeled and minced or crushed through a press
2 tablespoons chili powder
1 whole bay leaf
1 teaspoon dried oregano, crumbled
1/2 teaspoon whole cumin seeds, slightly crushed
1 tablespoon salt
1/4 teaspoon black pepper

Topping:

2 cups shredded crisp lettuce, such as romaine heart or iceberg
1 1/4 cups sour cream, at room temperature
1 cup finely chopped white onion
1 cup chopped fresh cilantro leaves
10 medium radishes, halved lengthwise and thinly sliced
Red Chile Sauce (optional; recipe follows)
2 limes, cut into wedges
Salt, if needed

hominy are needed, but in a pinch you can substitute canned hominy and skip the cooking steps for the corn. If you can find *mote pelado* (peeled dried corn) you can eliminate the peeling of the kernels. In the Southwest, frozen hominy is available and can be used instead of dried.

1. Prepare the corn: Soak the dried hominy or corn kernels overnight in plenty of cold water to cover. Rinse and drain. Put the corn in a large heavy pot with enough cold water to cover by 2 inches. Unless using *mote pelado* (which requires no peeling), dissolve the slaked lime in 1 cup cold water and pour in through a sieve. (If using *mote pelado*, simply proceed without the lime and without the peeling; simmer 30 minutes.) Bring to a boil over moderate heat and then simmer until the skins can be easily slipped off, 20 to 30 minutes. Cool for about 1 hour, then drain. Rub off the skins between your fingers, then rinse the kernels. With a paring knife, cut out the "beak" or tip of each kernel and discard.

2. Put the peeled corn kernels in a large heavy pot with 3 quarts of cold water. Bring to a boil over moderate heat; lower the heat and simmer, adding 1 to 2 quarts of boiling water as needed, until tender, 1½ to 2 hours. Place a colander over a bowl and drain the corn, reserving 4 cups of the cooking liquid for the pozole. If starting with canned hominy, simply rinse and drain.

3. Prepare the chicken and stock: Put the whole chickens in a large pot such as an 8-quart dutch oven or kettle; add 4 quarts of cold water along with the pig's foot, onions, carrot, celery, parsley, sliced garlic, cumin, bay leaves, whole cloves, peppercorns, and salt. Cover and bring to a boil over moderate heat. Lower the heat and simmer until the chickens are cooked, about 40 minutes. Take them out with tongs, letting any broth drain back into the pot, and set aside on a platter until cool enough to handle. Pull off and discard the skin. Pull off the breast and thigh meat and reserve for the pozole; return all the rest of the meat and bones to the stock. Simmer the stock, covered, over low heat for 3 to 4 hours longer to intensify the flavor. Let cool slightly and then strain. Discard all of the solids (don't attempt to salvage any of the chicken meat after it has simmered for such a long time because all the flavor will be in the stock, not the meat). Degrease the stock by spooning off the fat, or by blotting it with paper towels, or better yet, if you have the time, cool to room temperature, then chill overnight; the solidified fat can then be lifted or spooned off very easily. You will have about 3 quarts of rich stock. The recipe can be prepared a day ahead to here and refrigerated.

4. Complete the pozole: Put 3 quarts stock in a large heavy soup pot along with the reserved 4 cups cooking broth from the corn. (If using canned hominy skip this, and don't add the canned hominy until the broth has simmered for an hour.) Add the prepared peeled hominy along with the chopped onion, sliced carrots, diced celery, minced garlic, chili powder, bay leaf, oregano, cumin, salt, and pepper; bring to a boil over moderate heat. Simmer over low heat until the corn kernels become very tender and open like flowers, about 1½ hours.

5. Tear the chicken meat into bite-sized pieces (about ½ by 2 inches) and add to the *pozole*. If the broth has cooked down too much add a cup or two of water. Bring to a boil just to heat the chicken. Serve hot.

6. Serving and topping: Ladle about 2 cups of the pozole into each large shallow soup dish; top each with about 3 tablespoons shredded lettuce, 2 tablespoons sour cream, 1 tablespoon chopped onion, 1 sliced radish, and red chile sauce to taste; do not stir. Serve with lime wedges on the side and squeeze over the top before eating. Add salt to taste.

Red Chile Sauce

1. Tear the stems from 4 large dried chiles ancho (2 ounces) and 4 large dried chiles pasilla (1 ounce) and open up the chiles. Scrape off and discard the seeds and pull out and discard any loose veins. Tear each pepper into 3 or 4 pieces and put them in a bowl. Add enough boiling water just to cover, 1 to 1½ cups. Let soak for 1 hour. Drain, reserving the liquid.

2. Put the peppers in a blender with ½ cup of the soaking liquid and blend to a purée.

3. Force through a fine sieve to make a chile purée of medium thickness, adding a bit more of the soaking liquid only if too thin.

Main Dish Chicken Pot Pies

These plump, fragrant pies with their simple flavors are a good example of pure home-style Americana cookery. Although this recipe makes two large pies (single- or double-crusted as you prefer), you can in-stead make 8 small ones if you have enough 5-inch pie pans. If you have 3 cups of leftover cooked chicken and 2½ cups of canned broth you can skip the first part of the recipe entirely and jump right to the filling.

MAKES TWO 9-INCH PIES

Flaky Pastry (page 378)

The Chicken:

3½ pound chicken
1 cup dry white wine
1 medium onion, peeled and sliced
1 large carrot, peeled and sliced
1 large rib celery, sliced
7 whole cloves
1 tablespoon dried basil
1 bay leaf

Filling:

3 medium red-skinned potatoes (¾ pounds total), peeled and cut into ½-inch dice
3 medium carrots (½ pound total), peeled and cut into ¼-inch slices
3 cups cooked chicken in ½-inch dice (from above or other, on hand)
1 10-ounce package frozen peas, thawed slightly
¼ cup chopped fresh parsley
4 tablespoons (½ stick) butter (or 2 tablespoons butter and 2 tablespoons Rendered Chicken Fat, page 337)
1 small onion (2 to 3 ounces), peeled and finely chopped
1 medium garlic clove, peeled and minced or crushed through a press (optional)
½ cup all-purpose flour
2½ cups chicken broth or stock (reserved from above, or canned if using leftover cooked chicken)

1/3 cup dry sherry

1/2 teaspoon dried thyme or tarragon, crumbled

1/4 teaspoon grated nutmeg

2 teaspoons salt (reduce to 1 teaspoon if using canned broth)

1/4 teaspoon black pepper

Glaze:

1 egg yolk

1 teaspoon cold water

1. Prepare the pastry as instructed on page 378 and chill until ready to assemble the pies.

2. Prepare the chicken: Put the chicken in a large pot and add 3 cups of cold water. Add the white wine, onion, carrot, celery, whole cloves, basil, and bay leaf. Cover and bring to a boil over moderate heat. Reduce the heat to low and simmer just until the chicken is cooked through, 30 to 40 minutes. Transfer the chicken to a platter to cool, pouring any broth that accumulates back into the pan. Strain the broth and degrease by blotting with a paper towel or spooning it carefully from the surface. Boil the broth until reduced to 2½ cups.

3. When the chicken is cool enough to handle, pull off and discard the skin. Pull the meat from the bones and cut into ½-inch dice; you should have about 3 cups. Discard the bones.

4. Prepare the filling: Bring a large pot of lightly salted water to a boil over high heat. Drop in the potatoes and carrots. When the boil returns, blanch for 2 minutes. Drain in a colander and put in a large bowl. Add the diced chicken, peas, and parsley; toss.

5. Melt the butter in a large heavy saucepan over moderate heat. Add the chopped onion and garlic and sauté to soften, about 3 minutes. Stir in the flour with a fork or a whisk; cook, stirring, for 2 to 3 minutes to lightly toast the flour. The mixture will be somewhat dry but it is best to use as little fat as possible. Pour in the chicken broth and sherry and, stirring constantly, add the thyme or tarragon, nutmeg, salt, and pepper. Bring to a boil, stirring, and then simmer over low heat until very thick, about 3 minutes. Pour over the chicken and vegetable mixture and toss well. Cool to room temperature.

6. Preheat the oven to 400°. If baking both pies at once, evenly space two shelves; if baking only one, center a shelf.

7. For double-crust pies: On a lightly floured surface, roll one-fourth of the pastry into a 12-inch round. Fold in quarters, pick up carefully, and unfold into a 9-inch pie pan without stretching the dough. Lightly moisten the overhanging pastry with water. Fill with half of the cooled filling (3½ to 4 cups). Roll out another portion of pastry to an 11-inch round; fold in half and carefully unfold over the filling. Pinch the two crusts together and then tuck under all around to form a raised edge. Crimp decoratively with your fingers. Repeat to make a second pie.

8. Glaze the pie: In a cup stir together the egg yolk and water. Paint the top of the pie but not the fluting, using a pastry brush dipped in the egg yolk glaze. Cut 5 steam holes, each about ½ inch long, radiating from the center. Place on a baking sheet and put in the preheated oven. Bake 45 to 55 minutes, until the pastry is crisp and golden brown and the filling inside is bubbly. Cool on a rack for at least 1½ hours before slicing. If baking both pies at once, reverse their shelf positions halfway through the baking so they brown evenly.

9. For single-crust pies you will need only half the amount of pastry and the pies can be served just 15 minutes after baking. Put half the filling into each of two 9-inch pie pans. Cover each with pastry, sealing and crimping as in Step 7. Glaze as in

Step 8. Bake on separate baking sheets for 40 to 50 minutes. Cool on racks for 15 minutes before serving.

10. For individual pot pies, follow Steps 7 and 8, using smaller pastry rounds rolled from a full recipe of pastry. (You will need to reroll the scraps.) Bake for 40 to 45 minutes and cool 15 minutes before serving.

Mom's Chicken and Dumplings

This is a rich and hearty old-fashioned stew like the ones my mother used to make on cold rainy days during my childhood. I can still recall how steamy the windows became when she made it; so steamy that my brothers and I drew designs on them. Chicken and dumplings, to me, is the ultimate comfort food. The 20 minutes that the dumplings take to cook always seems like an eternity, but there is no rushing them. In a pinch you can start with 6 cups canned chicken broth and 1 pound (4 cups) cooked chicken meat, and skip Step 1.

MAKES 6 TO 8 SERVINGS

Chicken and Broth:

- 3½ pound chicken
- 6 cups Basic Chicken Stock (page 47) or canned broth
- 1 medium onion, peeled and sliced
- 1 large rib celery, sliced
- 1 large garlic clove, peeled and sliced
- 1 bay leaf
- 5 whole cloves

Stew:

- 6 tablespoons (¾ stick) butter
- 6 to 8 medium carrots (1 pound), peeled and cut into 1-inch lengths
- 8 small white onions (¾ pound), peeled
- ½ cup all-purpose flour
- 6 cups chicken stock, reserved from above
- 1 cup dry white wine
- 1 bay leaf
- ½ teaspoon dried tarragon, crumbled
- ½ teaspoon dried thyme, crumbled
- 2 teaspoons salt
- ¼ teaspoon black pepper
- 4 medium-large red-skinned potatoes (1½ pounds), peeled and cut into 1-inch chunks
- 3 medium ribs celery, cut in 1-inch lengths
- 1 10-ounce package frozen peas, thawed slightly
- ¼ cup chopped parsley
- 2 tablespoons cornstarch

Dumplings:

1½ cups all-purpose flour
2 teaspoons baking powder
½ teaspoon salt
¾ cup milk

1. Prepare the chicken and broth: Put the chicken, breast side up, in a large pot or flameproof casserole. Add the stock, onion, celery, garlic, bay leaf, and cloves. Bring to a boil over moderate heat. Cover and simmer over low heat, turning twice, just until cooked, 30 to 40 minutes (do not overcook because the chicken will cook longer while the dumplings steam). Remove the chicken and let it cool on a platter. Strain the broth; degrease by blotting with a paper towel. You should have 6 cups. If necessary, add water to make the total. Pull off the chicken skin and discard it. Tear the meat into pieces about 1 by 3 inches; keep covered. Discard the bones.

2. Prepare the chicken stew: Put the butter in a large 4- to 5-quart heavy dutch oven or flameproof casserole and melt over moderate heat. Add the carrots and onions; sauté over moderate to moderately high heat until vegetables are speckled brown all over. Remove them with a slotted spoon and reserve.

3. Add the flour to the butter and stir over moderate heat until lightly browned, 2 to 3 minutes. Pour in the 6 cups chicken stock and the wine; stir in the bay leaf, tarragon, thyme, salt, and pepper. Stirring constantly, bring to a boil over moderate heat to make a thin gravy. Return the carrots and onions to the pot; add the potatoes and celery. Cover and simmer over low heat, stirring occasionally, until the vegetables are tender, 25 to 30 minutes. Add the reserved chicken, the peas, and the parsley; return to a boil. Lower the heat and keep at a steady simmer. In a cup stir the cornstarch with 2 tablespoons cold water and reserve.

4. Prepare the dumplings: In a medium bowl stir together the flour, baking powder, and salt to blend evenly. Make a well in the center and pour in the milk. Quickly stir with a spoon to make a thick, sticky batter. Drop by slightly mounded tablespoonfuls all over the simmering stew, leaving about ½ inch between dumplings. Simmer, uncovered, without disturbing for exactly 10 minutes. Cover tightly and simmer without disturbing for exactly 10 minutes longer.

5. With a slotted spoon, remove the dumplings and put them on a hot platter. Stir the cornstarch mixture and add it to the stew all at once, swirling it in a big circle. Stir over moderately high heat until thickened. Turn off the heat. If not serving right away, return the dumplings to the stew and keep covered. Serve hot.

Cold Ginger Chicken

My cousins, Betty and Anthony, who live in Hawaii, brought me this favorite recipe during a recent trip to New York. It is white-cut chicken, cooked without soy sauce, simmered and then steeped in hot water before being plunged

MAKES 4 SERVINGS

White-cut Chicken:

3½ to 4-pound chicken
  3 large garlic cloves, peeled and sliced or crushed through a press
  1 teaspoon salt

Scallion-Ginger Sauce:

¾ cup finely minced white and green parts of scallions (6 to 8 medium)
½ cup peanut oil
⅓ cup minced peeled fresh ginger

¼ cup chopped fresh cilantro
¾ teaspoon salt
½ teaspoon ground white pepper
1 lime

into ice water to firm the meat. The chicken is served cold, and the sauce at room temperature.

1. Prepare the chicken: Pull out any fat from the chicken and discard it. Put the chicken in a large pot such as an oval dutch oven and add enough cold water to just cover it. Remove the chicken. Add the garlic and salt to the water and bring to a boil over high heat. Return the chicken to the pot, breast side down, and bring back to the boil. Lower the heat, cover, and simmer for 15 minutes. Turn and simmer 12 minutes longer. Turn off the heat and let the chicken steep, without peeking, for 45 minutes.

2. Meanwhile, fill a large bowl or pot with about 8 cups of ice cubes and cold water. Drain the chicken and plunge it into the cold water. Let it soak for 15 minutes; drain. Chill for at least 2 hours.

3. Prepare the scallion-ginger sauce: In a small saucepan combine the scallions, peanut oil, and ginger; let sizzle over low heat, stirring frequently, for 5 minutes. Remove from the heat and stir in the cilantro, salt, and white pepper. Let cool to room temperature before serving.

4. Cut the chicken into small pieces, the Chinese way, with a cleaver: Cut off wings and cut in 3 pieces; cut breast in half, then each half in 8 pieces; cut drumsticks and thighs into 5 pieces. As you work, keep pieces together so you can reassemble them as a whole chicken. Reassemble the chicken on a platter and squeeze the juice of the lime over it. Spoon all of the sauce over the chicken and serve.

3 *Whole Chickens, Cut Up*

Whole birds, precut into serving pieces, are abundantly available in supermarkets and are a boon to busy cooks. They save time both in preparation and in cooking. All you have to do is take the pieces from their package, give them a quick rinse, and pat them dry. The greatest convenience of all: no butchering mess to clean up. Of course you will pay slightly more for the convenience of precut pieces, but to most, it's worth it. (When you buy a whole chicken from a butcher shop the butcher will usually cut up your chicken at no extra charge.)

Prepackaged chicken pieces are always a combination of many birds; you'll get a wing from one bird, a thigh from another, and the breast from yet one or two more. When you cut up your own birds, at least you know that all the pieces come from the same bird. The tenderness and juiciness varies from bird to bird, so in some recipes this could make a difference.

The easiest way for a beginner to cut up a whole chicken at home is by using poultry shears. They are heavy-duty and made for cutting through bones with ease. Of course a heavy cleaver is just as efficient, if not more, for the experienced cook.

Basic Chicken Stock

MAKES 2 QUARTS

4 pounds chicken parts, or a whole chicken
2 medium peeled onions, sliced
2 celery ribs, sliced
2 medium carrots, peeled and sliced
2 medium leeks (optional), cleaned thoroughly and sliced
5 sprigs parsley
1 or 2 bay leaves
1 teaspoon dried thyme
4 whole cloves
4 whole black peppercorns
Salt

1. With a cleaver or large heavy knife, cut a few slashes in the chicken. Put in an 8-quart heavy stockpot and add 4 quarts of cold water. Bring to a boil over moderate heat. Simmer over low heat for 15 minutes, skimming any foam from the surface.
2. Add all of the remaining ingredients (use 1 teaspoon salt) and simmer for 3 to 4 hours, adding more water if necessary to keep the chicken and vegetables barely covered.
3. Scoop out the largest ingredients with a slotted spoon and put them in a colander set over a large bowl. Let drain, then discard the solids. Pour the rest of the stock and solids into the colander and strain. Strain the stock once again, through a fine strainer. Cool to room temperature. You can skim the fat from the top if you want to use the stock right away, but it is easiest to chill it overnight so the fat on top solidifies and can be lifted off.
4. To make a stronger stock, simply boil to reduce it. Salt to taste after reducing.

Simple chicken stock is the base for many sauces, gravies, and stews. This economical version can be made from just backs and necks or wings, or any part of the bird that happens to be a bargain. You can even start with a whole bird and pull off the breast and thigh meat as soon as it is cooked through (to use in other dishes), then return the rest of the meat and bones to the pot.

Superior Chicken Broth

This is a rich, delicious chicken broth that can be served without adornment or enhancement, or it can be used in any soup or sauce. Make some and keep it on hand in the freezer.

MAKES 1½ QUARTS

6 pounds chicken parts, or 2 whole chickens
4 ounce slice smoked country ham or smoked ham hock
1 cup dry white wine
3 ribs celery, sliced
2 medium onions, peeled and sliced
1 carrot, peeled and sliced
1 large sprig parsley
2 large garlic cloves, peeled and sliced
8 whole cloves
2 bay leaves
1 tablespoon dried basil
1 teaspoon dried thyme
1 teaspoon dried tarragon
Salt

1. With a meat cleaver or sharp heavy knife, cut slashes into the chicken; place in a large stockpot or dutch oven and add the ham, 3 quarts cold water, white wine, celery, onions, carrot, parsley, garlic, whole cloves, bay leaves, basil, thyme, tarragon, and 1 teaspoon salt. (If you like, you can make a bouquet garni of the cloves, bay leaves, basil, thyme, and tarragon.) Bring to a simmer over moderate heat. Skim the surface of fat and scum as needed. Reduce the heat to very low and simmer, partially covered, for 10 to 12 hours or overnight.

2. Remove the largest ingredients from the broth with a slotted spoon and place in a colander set over a bowl. Lightly press to extract some of the liquid. Discard the solids and pour the rest of the broth into the colander to strain. Strain again through a fine strainer. Skim any fat from the surface, or cool to room temperature, then chill, and take off fat after it has solidified.

3. Boil the stock over moderately high heat until it has reduced to 1½ quarts. Add salt to taste. Cool to room temperature, then store in the refrigerator. If not using within a day or two, pour into small containers and freeze.

Chinese Chicken Broth

MAKES 2 QUARTS

2 quarts Basic Chicken Stock (page 47) or canned broth
¾ cup dry sherry
8 slices fresh ginger
3 medium scallions, sliced
2 large garlic cloves, peeled and sliced
1 tablespoon soy sauce
2 teaspoons oriental sesame oil

When you don't have time to make a basic chicken stock, use the following procedure to doctor up canned broth.

1. Combine the chicken stock and sherry in a large soup pot and bring to a boil over high heat. Add the ginger, scallions, garlic, and soy sauce. Simmer, uncovered, over moderate heat for 15 minutes. Strain. Discard the solids. Add the sesame oil to the stock and serve hot.

Jewish Chicken Broth

This is perfect to sip as is or to use for Matzo Ball Soup (page 51) or Kreplach Soup (page 324) or for any chicken soup. This is so good because lots of chicken is used to make it and it is simmered for a long time. If you use whole chickens, you can remove the breast meat from the kettle as soon as it is tender and reserve it for a recipe using cooked chicken (see Chapter 9). But don't attempt to eat the rest of the chicken, after it has cooked so long; all the flavor will be in the broth and the meat will be stringy and tasteless.

MAKES 3 QUARTS

5 to 6 pounds chicken parts or 2 whole chickens
2 large onions, peeled and quartered
2 large carrots, peeled and cut in chunks
2 large ribs of celery, cut in chunks
1 small bunch parsley
2 bay leaves
2 to 3 teaspoons kosher salt

1. Put the chicken parts or whole chickens into a large 5- to 6-quart kettle, stockpot, or dutch oven and add 4 quarts of cold water. Add the onions, carrots, celery, parsley, bay leaves, and 1 teaspoon of the salt. Bring to a boil over moderate heat, skimming any foam from the surface as it accumulates. Cover the pot, leaving the lid slightly askew, and simmer over very low heat (so the stock bubbles very gently), stirring once in a while, for about 5 hours.

2. The stock will be very hot, so take care when you strain it. (If you are at all apprehensive it is better to let it cool slightly, but you must strain it while still relatively hot.) As a precaution, perform the procedure in the kitchen sink. Put a large colander in a large bowl or pot and pour the contents of the pot into it. Shake the colander to drain off as much stock as possible. Discard the solids. Strain again, this time through a fine sieve. If you want it even clearer, strain once more through several layers of dampened cheesecloth.

3. Cool the broth to room temperature and then chill until the fat on top solidifies. Take off the fat and discard it. Boil the degreased broth down to 3 quarts to intensify the flavor and add salt to taste.

Matzo Ball Soup

1½ quarts Jewish Chicken Broth (page 50) or canned broth
3 large eggs
3 tablespoons Rendered Chicken Fat (page 337) or vegetable oil
¾ cup matzo meal (see Note)
1 teaspoon salt
⅓ cup seltzer, club soda, or plain water
2 tablespoons finely chopped parsley (optional)

1. Make the broth well ahead of time so it is degreased and clear. Some cooks simmer their matzo balls in boiling chicken broth instead of water; if you want to do that you'll need an extra 1½ quarts.

2. Combine the eggs and chicken fat or oil in a medium bowl and blend with a whisk or a fork. Stir in the matzo meal and salt. Stir in the seltzer and optional parsley to make a batter. Chill in the refrigerator for 1 hour.

3. Fill a large pot with 2 to 3 quarts of water (or 1½ quarts broth plus 2 cups water) and bring to a boil over high heat. Dip your hands into cold water, then take 2 tablespoons of the matzo mixture and roll it into a ball between the palms of your hands; drop it into the boiling water. Working quickly, shape 12 balls and drop them in. Cover the pot, lower the heat slightly, and simmer for 20 to 25 minutes, until cooked through. Scoop balls out with a slotted spoon and put two in each of six soup bowls.

4. Bring the fresh broth to a boil, ladle 1 cup into each bowl, and serve hot.

NOTE: Matzo meal is available in any supermarket with a kosher section.

Matzo balls are dumplings that should be slightly heavy and dense; they're not supposed to be light and fluffy. I know one cook who insists on adding ⅛ teaspoon of baking powder to them, but that's not kosher and that's not the way they're supposed to be. I like chopped parsley in mine, but I have made that ingredient optional because usually they are made without it.

Chicken Noodle Soup

Here is a simple soup, the kind my mother used to make. What you do is pull the thigh and breast meat from the bones as soon as those parts are done and return the bones and the rest of the meat to the stock to simmer longer and intensify the flavor. That way you don't add overcooked chicken to your soup. It is best served as soon as the noodles are cooked, before they become soggy. If you have to hold the soup for any length of time, boil the noodles separately and add some to each serving so they have a good texture.

MAKES 14 CUPS

Broth:

3½ pound chicken, quartered
1 cup dry white wine
2 large carrots, peeled and sliced
2 medium onions, peeled and sliced
2 large ribs celery, sliced
2 large sprigs parsley
2 large garlic cloves, peeled and sliced
5 whole cloves
5 whole peppercorns
2 bay leaves
1 tablespoon dried basil
½ teaspoon dried thyme
2 teaspoons salt

Soup:

3 medium carrots, peeled and cut in ½-inch dice
2 medium ribs celery, cut in ½-inch dice
2 medium onions, peeled and chopped
1 bay leaf
6 ounces medium or wide egg noodles
¼ cup chopped parsley
Salt to taste

1. Prepare the broth: In a large stock pot or dutch oven, combine the chicken with 3 quarts cold water, the wine, carrots, onions, celery, parsley, garlic, whole cloves, peppercorns, bay leaves, basil, thyme, and salt; bring to a boil over moderate heat. Cover and simmer over low heat just until the chicken is cooked through, 25 to 30 minutes. Remove the chicken pieces with tongs and put on a plate until cool enough to handle, about 15 minutes. Pull off the skin and the meat from just the thighs and the breasts (not the drumsticks—some meat is needed to flavor broth) and reserve it, covered, for the soup. Return all the rest of the meat and skin and bones to the broth and keep at a bare simmer, covered, over low heat, stirring occasionally, for 3 hours.

2. Put a colander in a large bowl and strain (I like to do this directly in the sink just in case some spills). Discard the solids. Then strain the broth again through a sieve. Blot the top with paper towels to degrease (or spoon off, or cool to room temperature, then chill, and remove fat solidified on top). You will have 2½ to 3 quarts broth.

3. Prepare the soup: Put the broth in a large soup pot or dutch oven and place over moderate heat. Add the carrots, celery, onions, and bay leaf; simmer until the vegetables are tender, about 15 minutes. Bring to a full boil and add the noodles; lower the heat slightly and cook until they are tender, about 6 to 7 minutes. Cut up the reserved breast and thigh meat into ½-inch dice and add; return to the simmer, remove from the heat, and add the parsley and salt to taste. Serve hot.

Chicken alla Cacciatora with Spaghetti

Every version of this popular Italian dish, chicken hunter's style, is different. That's because it was originally made by hunters who never knew what the catch (or dig or find) of the day might be. They always had wine with them, sometimes tomatoes, and they could almost always find a mushroom in the woods.

MAKES 6 SERVINGS

3½ to 4-pound chicken, cut into serving pieces: 2 thighs, 2 drumsticks, 2 wings, and 6 breast pieces
½ cup all-purpose flour
2 tablespoons vegetable oil
1¼ cups dry white wine
2 tablespoons olive oil
3 medium green bell peppers, cored, seeded, and cut lengthwise into ¼-inch strips
2 medium onions, peeled, halved lengthwise and sliced crosswise ¼-inch thick
1 large rib celery, cut in ¼-inch dice
2 large garlic cloves, peeled and minced or crushed through a press
2 teaspoons dried basil, crumbled
1 teaspoon dried rosemary, crumbled
½ teaspoon dried oregano, crumbled
1 28-ounce can whole Italian tomatoes, cut up (save the juice)
1 tablespoon tomato paste
2 teaspoons sugar
2 teaspoons salt
¼ teaspoon black pepper
2 tablespoons butter
½ pound large fresh mushrooms, thinly sliced
¼ cup chopped parsley
1 pound spaghetti
Grated Parmesan cheese (optional)

1. Put all the chicken pieces in a big bag and shake with the flour to coat. Spoon the vegetable oil into a deep 12-inch-wide noncorrosive skillet or dutch oven and place over moderately high heat. Add all of the chicken and brown well for 8 to 10 minutes. Turn and brown about 5 minutes longer. Pour in 1 cup of the wine and boil, turning the chicken with tongs from time to time, until liquid is reduced to a glaze, 3 to 4 minutes. Transfer the chicken pieces to a plate and pour the glaze over them.

2. Wipe out the pan with a paper towel, add the olive oil, and place over moderate heat. Add the bell peppers, onions and celery; sauté to soften and brown, 7 to 10 minutes. Add the garlic, basil, rosemary, and oregano; cook a minute longer, stirring. Stir in the tomatoes and their juice, tomato paste, sugar, salt, pepper, and remaining 1/4 cup wine; return the chicken and the glaze to the pan and bring to a boil. Cover and simmer over low heat for about 20 minutes, until the chicken is hot and cooked through.

3. Meanwhile, melt the butter in a medium skillet. Add the mushrooms and sauté to brown, 2 to 3 minutes; if they are dry, spoon in a little water and boil it away. Add the mushrooms to the chicken during the last 5 minutes of cooking. Remove from the heat and stir in the parsley.

4. Bring a large pot of lightly salted water to a full boil. Drop in the spaghetti, and, stirring constantly, return to the boil. Cook until tender but firm to the bite, stirring frequently. Drain and arrange on dinner plates or on a large platter and top with the chicken *alla cacciatora*. If boiling the pasta ahead, or if you are not serving all of it at once, toss it with a tablespoon or two of olive oil so the strands do not stick together. Serve with grated Parmesan if desired.

NOTE: This dish reheats very well. Add 1/4 cup each of water and wine and simmer over low heat for 15 to 20 minutes.

Chicken Tetrazzini

This old-fashioned spaghetti casserole, named for the Italian opera singer Luisa Tetrazzini, a star during the early part of this century, is traditionally started by cooking a whole chicken and making broth. However, you can instead start with 3 cups of leftover cooked chicken and 3½ cups canned chicken broth and eliminate Steps 1 and 2 of this recipe. It is a dish best served freshly made. Steamed broccoli and a salad are good accompaniments.

MAKES 6 TO 8 SERVINGS

- **3** to 3½-pound chicken, quartered
- **2** ribs celery, sliced
- **2** medium onions, peeled and sliced
- **1** bay leaf
- **2½** teaspoons salt
- **8** tablespoons (1 stick) butter
- **1** large garlic clove, peeled and minced or crushed through a press
- **½** pound mushrooms, sliced
- **⅓** cup all-purpose flour
- **⅓** cup dry sherry
- **1** cup light cream
- **2** teaspoons dried basil, crumbled
- **1** teaspoon dried oregano, crumbled
- **¼** teaspoon black pepper
- **1** cup grated Parmesan cheese
- **1** pound spaghetti
- **¼** plain dry bread crumbs

1. Put the chicken in a pot just large enough to hold it and add 6 cups of cold water. Add the celery, onions, bay leaf, and 1 teaspoon of the salt. Cover and bring to a boil over moderate heat. Lower the heat and simmer just until the chicken is done, about 30 minutes. Using tongs, pull out the chicken pieces and transfer them to a plate until cool enough to handle. Boil the contents of the pan over high heat for 10 minutes. Strain. Degrease by blotting the top with a paper towel (or cool to room temperature, chill, then degrease if making a day ahead). You will need 3½ cups of degreased broth.

2. Pull off and discard the skin and bones from the chicken and tear or cut the meat into bite-sized pieces (about ½ by 2 inches).

3. Adjust an oven shelf to the top third of the oven and preheat to 450°. Lightly butter a 13-by-9-inch shallow casserole. Put a large pot of lightly salted water on to boil.

4. Melt the butter in a large heavy saucepan over moderate heat. Add the garlic and mushrooms and sauté for about 3 minutes. Stir in the flour with a fork and cook for a minute. Stirring constantly, add the 3½ cups chicken broth and the sherry; bring to a boil, stirring. Add the cream, basil, oregano, remaining 1½ teaspoons salt, and black pepper and return to a boil. Lower the heat and simmer, stirring occasionally, for 5 minutes. The sauce will be thin. Remove from the heat and stir in ½ cup of the Parmesan and all of the chicken.

5. When the pot of water comes to a full boil, drop in the spaghetti; stirring constantly, return to the full boil. Stirring frequently thereafter, cook al dente (tender but firm to the bite), 10 to 12 minutes for regular spaghetti, several minutes less if you have used thin spaghetti. Drain in a colander. Put half the spaghetti in the prepared baking dish and spoon on half of the chicken sauce; repeat. (The dish will be soupy but the sauce will be absorbed during baking.) In a small bowl mix the remaining ½ cup Parmesan with the bread crumbs and sprinkle over the top. Bake in the top of the hot oven until bubbly and lightly browned, 12 to 15 minutes. Serve hot with a chilled white wine.

Coq au Vin

This popular French dish of chicken in red wine is both rich and rustic. There are a million ways to make it, but I like this version where the wine and broth are reduced to intensify the flavor. To be truly authentic, you should blanch the bacon in boiling water for a minute to remove its smoky flavor. But I like the smoky flavor it gives to the finished dish; you'll have to choose for yourself. It is a good recipe to prepare ahead of time and for serving at a casual buffet. Parsleyed potatoes and peas make good accompaniments.

MAKES 4 TO 6 SERVINGS

3½ cups (one 750 ML bottle) full-bodied dry red wine, such as burgundy
2 cups beef stock or canned broth
2 large garlic cloves, peeled and minced or crushed through a press
1 bay leaf
½ teaspoon dried thyme, crumbled
6 slices smoked bacon, cut into ½-inch squares
1 pound (18 to 20) small white onions
1 pound medium carrots, peeled and cut into 1½-inch lengths
4 pound chicken, cut into serving pieces: 2 thighs, 2 drumsticks, 2 wings, and 4 breast pieces
2 tablespoons all-purpose flour
¼ cup Cognac or brandy
1 tablespoon tomato paste
1 teaspoon sugar
2 tablespoons butter
½ pound whole small mushrooms (or large ones, quartered)
Salt, if needed
2 tablespoons chopped parsley

1. In a 3-quart noncorrosive saucepan combine the wine, stock, half the garlic, the bay leaf, and thyme. Bring to a boil over moderate heat (watch carefully, as it will foam up and may boil over); boil gently until reduced to 3 cups, about 20 minutes. Set aside.

2. Put the bacon in a deep 12-inch noncorrosive skillet or dutch oven and brown well over moderate heat. Take out the crisp bacon pieces and reserve.

3. Drop the onions (unpeeled) and carrots into a large pot of boiling water. Boil for 2 minutes after the boil returns and then drain. Peel off the outer layer of each onion and slice off a sliver from each end. Add the onions and carrots to the bacon drippings in the pan and sauté over moderately low heat until caramelized and deep golden brown, stirring occasionally, 20 to 30 minutes. Scoop out with a slotted spoon and reserve.

4. If the chicken pieces are wet, dry them with a paper towel. Add all of the chicken, meaty or skin side down, to the skillet and brown very well over moderate heat, about 10 minutes. Turn and brown the other side about 5 minutes. Pile the chicken in the center. To one side, add the remaining garlic and cook 10 seconds. Stir in the flour and cook for 30 seconds. Standing back and averting the face, pour in the Cognac to the far side of the pan and tilt to ignite (if you have a gas flame) or light with a match and flambé. Pour in the reduced wine-broth and stir in the tomato paste and sugar. Bring to a boil, stirring. Return the carrots, onions, and bacon; cover and simmer over low heat for 20 to 30 minutes, until the chicken is cooked through, turning the chicken several times.

5. Meanwhile, melt the butter in a medium skillet and brown the mushrooms; if they seem dry, pour in ¼ cup water and let it boil away and then continue browning, about 3 minutes. Add the mushrooms to the chicken during the last 5 minutes of cooking. Add a pinch of salt if needed. Sprinkle the chopped parsley over the top before serving. Serve hot, with parsleyed potatoes and peas if desired, and a red burgundy (preferably the same one you cooked with).

Chicken Ranchero with Guacamole and Black Bean Tostadas

This is really simpler than it looks if you are prejudging by the length of the ingredient list; the cooking techniques are simple. It is a festive delicious dinner all by itself, although a salad and charcoal grilled zucchini can be added to the menu too. The chicken, which is grilled outdoors over charcoal, must marinate, so plan accordingly. The special *ranchero* sauce is flavored with bacon, *poblano* peppers, and pumpkin seeds.

MAKES 4 SERVINGS

Marinated Chicken:

3½   pound chicken, quartered
1   cup dry white wine
1   medium onion, peeled and sliced
2   large garlic cloves, peeled and sliced
2   fresh jalapeño chile peppers, sliced
¼   cup chopped fresh cilantro (coriander)
3   tablespoons fresh lime juice
2   tablespoons sugar
½   teaspoon salt

Salsa Ranchero:

3   medium-sized fresh poblano chile peppers (½ pound), or one 4-ounce can mild roasted whole green chiles, drained
4   slices hickory-smoked bacon, cut in small squares
⅓   cup (1¾ ounces) coarsely chopped, roasted, shelled pumpkin seeds
2   teaspoons all-purpose flour
¼   cup plain dry bread crumbs
2   cups chicken stock or canned broth
½   teaspoon salt
2   tablespoons chopped cilantro
2   tablespoons fresh lime juice

Tostadas:

Vegetable oil
6   corn tortillas, quartered

Black beans:

1 slice hickory-smoked bacon, cut in small squares
1 medium garlic clove, peeled and minced or crushed through a press
½ teaspoon ground cumin
¼ teaspoon dried oregano, crumbled
¼ teaspoon salt
1 16-ounce can black beans, drained

Guacamole:

2 fresh jalapeño chile peppers
2 tablespoons finely chopped onion
2 tablespoons chopped cilantro
½ teaspoon salt
8 to 12-ounce perfectly ripe California avocado, such as Haas
1 teaspoon fresh lime juice

Grilling and Assembly:

2 tablespoons olive oil
½ cup sour cream, at room temperature
½ cup finely diced tomato
2 tablespoons grated Romano cheese
4 radishes

1. Marinate the chicken: Rinse the chicken quarters and pat them dry. In a blender or food processor, combine the white wine, onion, garlic, jalapeños, cilantro, lime juice, sugar, and salt; blend to purée. Put the chicken pieces in a large self-seal plastic bag or in a large bowl. Add the marinade; seal or cover, and refrigerate for 2 to 6 hours, turning once in a while. Let come to room temperature for about 30 minutes before grilling.

2. Prepare the salsa ranchero: To roast the fresh poblanos, place them directly on the burners of a gas stove over high heat, or as close to the heat source as possible under an electric broiler; turn with tongs until blistered and black all over. Let them cool for a couple of minutes, then put them in a plastic bag and twist the top. Chill 10 minutes. Rub the skins away with your fingertips (this can also be done over a colander under slow running water but you will lose some of the juices). Cut out the stem and ribs and discard the seeds. If using canned chiles, simply drain them and discard the seeds. Cut the chiles into ¼- to ½-inch squares.

3. Put the bacon in a heavy medium-sized nonaluminum skillet and cook over moderate heat until crisp and golden brown, 3 to 5 minutes. Spoon off all but 1 tablespoon of the fat. Add the pumpkin seeds and sauté about 2 minutes, to lightly toast. Stir in the flour and bread crumbs; cook for 1 minute. Add the *poblanos* and pour in the broth. Stirring constantly, bring to a boil and simmer until thickened, a minute or two. Remove from the heat and stir in the salt, cilantro, and lime juice.

4. Prepare the tostadas: Pour ¼ inch of vegetable oil into a heavy medium skillet and place over moderately high heat. Keep the temperature at just below the smoking point as you fry the tortillas. Working in batches, add enough tortilla wedges to fill the pan in a single layer; fry until golden brown, about 2 minutes; turn with tongs and fry until crisp; take out with a slotted spoon and drain on paper towels. Fry remaining tortillas.

5. Prepare the black beans: Put the bacon in a heavy medium skillet and cook over moderate heat until crisp and golden brown, 3 to 5 minutes. Add the garlic, cumin, oregano, and salt; cook for 30 seconds. Add the drained beans and fry without stirring for about 2 minutes. Stir and cook a minute longer. Stir in ½ cup of water and mash the beans slightly with a fork or a potato masher. Reserve. The recipe to this point can be prepared a day ahead.

6. Prepare a charcoal fire: Fill a barbecue or hibachi with charcoal briquettes and ignite them. When ready for grilling, the coals will be covered with gray ash.

7. Prepare the guacamole: Cut the jalapeños lengthwise in quarters. Cut off the stems and slice off the seeds and ribs flush with the chiles. Reserve ½ teaspoon of the seeds and ribs; discard the rest (they contain the volatile oils and you don't want this guacamole too hot). Finely chop the jalapeños and put in a heavy medium ceramic bowl or mortar. Add the seeds and ribs, onion, cilantro, and salt; pound with a pestle or spoon until watery. Cut the avocado in half lengthwise and take out the pit. Spoon the avocado into the bowl and mash coarsely with a fork (leave it a little lumpy). Stir in the lime juice.

8. Grilling and assembly: Take the chicken from the marinade and discard the marinade. Brush the chicken lightly with a little of the olive oil and put it on the hot charcoal. Grill, turning every 5 minutes and brushing with a little oil, until cooked through, 30 to 40 minutes.

9. Heat the salsa ranchero and the black beans in separate pans over low heat, adding a little water if necessary. To assemble the tostadas: Spread each tortilla triangle with 1 tablespoon beans and top with 2 teaspoons guacamole, 1 teaspoon sour cream, 1 teaspoon diced tomato, and ¼ teaspoon grated Romano. Put one chicken quarter in the center of each large dinner plate and top with about ¼ cup of the salsa ranchero. Ring each plate with 6 tostadas, points outward, and garnish with a radish. Serve the remaining salsa ranchero in a bowl.

Chicken Tamales

Perfect for a fiesta or a party, Mexican tamales are a true labor of love. They require a lot of preparation so you should cook the chickens for the filling a day ahead. You will also need to locate dried corn husks (in a Latin American grocery store) before you start cooking. It is not practical to make a small batch. Tamales are usually not spicy hot, nor are they generally served with a sauce in Mexico. If you want to spice them up, serve the Salsa Verde (page 380) in a bowl at the table so guests can spoon up their own. These tamales get their deep sweet corn

MAKES 3 DOZEN

Chicken Filling:

- **2** whole chickens, 3½ pounds each
- **2** large onions, peeled
- **5** large garlic cloves, peeled
- **2** bay leaves
- **8** whole cloves
- **3** tablespoons chili powder
- **½** teaspoon cayenne pepper
- **1** teaspoon dried oregano, crumbled
- **1** teaspoon ground cumin
- **1** tablespoon salt
- **½** teaspoon black pepper

For Wrapping:

- **½** pound package dried corn husks

Tamale Dough:

- **1½** cups quick-cooking (not instant) grits, see Note
- **6** medium ears fresh corn, or 3 cups frozen corn kernels, defrosted

About 3½ cups masa harina (fine corn flour), see Note
- **1** tablespoon salt
- **4** teaspoons baking powder
- **1½** cups (¾ pound), lard, at cool room temperature
- **½** cup (1 stick) butter, at cool room temperature

1. Prepare the chicken filling: Pull out any fat from the main cavity of the chickens and reserve. Reserve the giblets for another use. Halve the chickens and place them in a large 5-quart pot or dutch oven and pour in about 1½ quarts of cold water. Slice one of the onions and 3 of the garlic cloves and add them to the pot along with the bay leaves and whole cloves. Cover, place over moderate heat, and bring to a boil. Lower the heat and simmer just until cooked through, 30 to 40 minutes. With tongs, remove the chickens, letting any broth run back into the pan, and transfer them to a platter. Degrease the broth by skimming or blotting with paper towels. Boil it over high heat until reduced to about 3 cups, 10 to 15 minutes. Strain the broth and discard solids.

2. Pull the skin from the chickens and discard it. Pull off the meat and discard the bones. Tear the meat into irregular shreds, about ½ by 1½ inches.

3. Cut up the reserved chicken fat and put it in a small heavy saucepan with 1 tablespoon water; place over moderate heat until 3 tablespoons of the fat has melted. Spoon the melted chicken fat into a large heavy skillet. Chop the remaining onion and add it to the pan; sauté to soften, 3 to 5 minutes over moderate heat. Mince the remaining 2 garlic cloves (or crush through a press) and add to the pan; cook a minute longer. Stir in the chili powder, cayenne pepper, oregano, cumin, salt, and pepper; cook 30 seconds longer. Pour in 1 cup of the reduced broth and bring to a boil. Remove from the heat and stir in the shredded chicken to make a moist filling.

4. Prepare the corn husk wrappers: Put all of the dried corn husks into a large pot and cover generously with hot tap water. Weight down with a plate or a heavy object to submerge and bring to a boil over high heat. Turn off the heat and let soak for 1 hour or up to 2 or 3 hours.

5. Prepare the steamer: Mexicans use a big deep steamer with a tight-fitting lid to steam their tamales. You can improvise with a roasting pan about 10 by 15 inches or a tall 12- to 18-inch kettle. Either way you must choose a rack or grill that fits inside and prop it up on 3 or 4 custard cups or cans (tomato sauce or tuna are good sizes) that are open at both

flavor from four forms of corn (masa harina, grits, fresh corn kernels, and dried corn husks). While the tamales are steaming, don't let the water boil away or go off the boil or the tamales will be heavy.

ends. Pour enough water in the pan to come within 1 inch of the rack. Add 3 or 4 coins to the water (later these will warn you when the water boils dangerously low) and place the rack in position. Cover with a layer of soaked corn husks. Assemble *all* of the tamales *before* putting them in the steamer.

6. Prepare the tamale dough: Put the grits in a large bowl and pour in 2 cups of boiling water. Let stand, stirring once in a while, for about 30 minutes.

7. Strip the husks and silk from the ears of corn. Working in a large bowl with one ear on end, slice off the kernels close to the cob; repeat with the remaining ears. You should have about 3 cups of kernels. Coarsely grind them in a food processor or blender.

8. After the grits have soaked for 30 minutes, stir in 1 cup of the masa harina along with the chopped corn kernels and salt. Stir the baking powder into the remaining 2½ cups masa harina.

9. A heavy-duty upright electric mixer is the best choice for making tamale dough or you can make it in smaller batches in a food processor (I have seen people do it with a big wooden spoon, but they have big strong arms from making tamales for years). Combine the lard and butter in a large mixer bowl. (If you are using a KitchenAid mixer, choose the paddle attachment, not the whisk.) Beat at high speed until fluffy, about 3 minutes. Spoon in about ¼ of the corn-grits mixture and beat for a minute. Add the rest a spoonful at a time, alternating with spoonfuls of the masa harina mixture and small spoonfuls of the reserved broth (you will have about 2 cups of broth reserved but may need only 1 cup); beat well after each addition and add only enough of the broth to make a fluffy batter the consistency of muffin or corn bread batter. Continue beating to make as fluffy as possible, 2 to 3 minutes. When it's ready, ½ teaspoon slid off a spoon onto cold water will float.

10. Assemble the tamales: Drain the corn husks and separate them so you have stacks of small, medium, and large. You will use mostly the medium and large ones for tamales but small ones can be combined. Place 1 large husk, wide end toward you, on a flat surface. Spread about 2 teaspoons tamale dough near the wide end (illustration A) and slap a second husk over it (illustration B), overlapping the first by 3 or 4 inches and running in the opposite direction (wide ends overlap and small ends extend to top and bottom). With a small spatula, spread about ¼ cup of the tamale dough in the center of the double layer so it is about 3 by 5 inches slightly off-center to the right (illustration C). Spoon about 2½ tablespoons of the chicken filling in the center (illustration D) of the 3-by-5-inch area. Fold the right edge of the double husk up over the filling, toward the center (illustration E); then roll the tamale to the left to enclose the filling (the seam is now on the bottom). Fold the two small ends inward toward the center to make a neat package (illustration F); place, flaps down, on a large tray. Repeat with all the ingredients, stacking the tamales as they are shaped. Reserve remaining husks for the steamer.

A.
B.
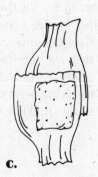
C.
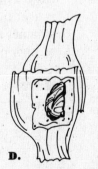
D.

E.

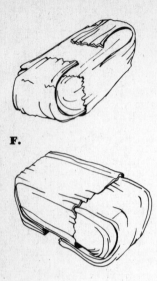

F.

11. Fill the steamer: Place the steamer over high heat and bring the water to a boil before adding tamales (if you have used a large rectangular roasting pan you may have to place it over two burners). Lower the heat while you fill the steamer with tamales. Put a layer of husks on the rack and up the sides of the steamer and fill with tamales, standing them on end and taking care that they do not unwrap. Leave a spot near the front where you can add boiling water to the pan as needed. Cover the tamales with a layer of corn husks and a folded cotton or linen towel (this keeps water from dripping into the tamales). Put a tight-fitting lid on the pan (you can weight it down with a brick or something heavy) and bring to a boil over high heat. Reduce the heat to moderate and keep at a steady boil for about 1½ hours. Listen to the sound that the coins make; as the water boils dangerously low the sound will change to a rattle or jiggle. Keep a kettle of simmering water nearby and replenish as needed. To test for doneness: With tongs, carefully remove a tamale from the center after 1 hour and 15 minutes. Take off the husk; if it easily pulls away from the tamale dough, it is done; if not, steam at least 15 minutes longer and test again. Serve hot, accompanied by Salsa Verde (page 380) and a pot of Pinto Beans with Bacon (page 375), if desired. The tamales are perfectly delightful without any accompaniment and they will remain hot in the steamer for a couple of hours. To reheat tamales, steam a few at a time in a collapsible vegetable steamer for 6 or 8 minutes, or place on a plate in the microwave at high power for a minute or two.

NOTE: This recipe was tested with Quaker brand quick-cooking grits and Quaker masa harina.

Fried Chicken

MAKES 4 SERVINGS

3½ to 4-pound chicken, cut into 8 serving pieces
 1 cup plain low-fat yogurt
 ½ cup milk
 1 tablespoon salt
1⅓ cups all-purpose flour
 ½ teaspoon black pepper
 3 cups (one 24-ounce bottle) vegetable oil
 3 tablespoons bacon fat (optional)

1. If desired, cut the breast halves in half again.

2. In a large bowl stir together the yogurt and milk with 1 teaspoon of the salt. Add the chicken pieces and marinate in the refrigerator for 1 hour and then at room temperature 1 hour longer.

3. In a large sturdy brown paper bag, combine the flour with the remaining 2 teaspoons salt and the pepper.

4. Pour the vegetable oil into a deep 10- to 12-inch chicken fryer or dutch oven and place over moderately high heat. At the first wisp of smoke, add the bacon fat if you're using it and lower the heat slightly so the oil remains at 370°. Take the thighs from the marinade, letting any excess drip back in (but don't wipe off the marinade) and put them in the bag; shake vigorously to coat evenly. Put them in the hot oil, skin side down. Coat all the pieces in the same manner, adding the breast pieces last. Cover the pot and fry over moderate heat for 15 minutes.

5. Uncover, turn the pieces with tongs, and fry, uncovered, until crisp and deep golden brown and cooked through (to

My mother always soaked pieces of chicken in buttermilk before shaking them in a brown paper bag with flour and seasonings when she made fried chicken. The buttermilk tenderized the meat and gave it a tiny tang. But buttermilk is different nowadays. I have found that combining plain yogurt and milk gives a result closer to old-fashioned buttermilk. Although Southern fried chicken is traditionally done in a big cast-iron chicken fryer, I am also giving instructions for deep-frying because it produces consistently good results. I like

check, cut into the center of one thigh), 14 to 17 minutes longer (breasts take about 3 minutes less than thighs). Drain on paper towels. Serve hot, at room temperature, or cold.

NOTE: If you want to deep-fry the pieces, pour in enough vegetable oil to fill an electric deep-fryer to the suggested line (about 1½ inches deep) and heat to 370°. Depending on the size of the fryer, fry without crowding (you can do half at a time in a 6½-inch-diameter fryer). Fry breast pieces about 10 minutes and the remaining pieces about 15 minutes. The deep fat cooks the pieces quicker and, some might argue, crustier.

McGlade's Bar Baby Fried Chicken

Cornish hens are just baby chickens, five weeks old; when they mature they become roasting chickens. I like to cut up Cornish hens into individual serving pieces, soak them in tangy yogurt and spices, and then

MAKES 4 SERVINGS

1	cup plain yogurt
½	cup milk
2	teaspoons salt
1½	teaspoons cayenne pepper
2	1½-pound Cornish hens, each cut into 8 serving pieces
1¼	cups all-purpose flour
1	tablespoon curry powder
½	teaspoon black pepper
	Vegetable oil for deep-frying
2	tablespoons bacon fat (optional)

1. In a large bowl whisk together the yogurt, milk, 1 teaspoon salt, and 1 teaspoon of the cayenne pepper. Add the pieces of hen. Refrigerate for 1 hour and then marinate at room temperature 1 hour longer.

2. In a sturdy heavy brown paper bag, shake together the flour, curry powder, pepper, remaining 1 teaspoon salt, and remaining ½ teaspoon cayenne pepper.

3. Pour 1½ inches vegetable oil into a deep-fat fryer (preferably an electric one with a temperature control) and heat to 370°. When it reaches that temperature, add the optional bacon fat. Two at a time, take the pieces of hen from the yogurt mixture with just the yogurt clinging to them and shake them well in the bag of seasoned flour; lower into the oil. Repeat and add enough pieces so the fryer is full but not crowded. Fry 9 to 10 minutes, until deep golden brown and cooked through. Drain on paper towels. Reheat the oil for each batch and repeat. Serve hot, at room temperature, or cold.

coat them with spicy flour and deep-fry them until crunchy and golden brown. The pieces are small and make good finger food so I bring them to my favorite bar, McGlade's Snug, which is tiny, too.

Sticky-Lick-It Barbecued Chicken

The sherry marinade adds deep flavor to chicken before it is barbecued over charcoal, and becomes a lickity barbecue sauce that glazes and adds even more flavor.

MAKES 4 SERVINGS

- **2** cups dry sherry
- **¼** cup fresh lemon juice
- **2** bay leaves
- **2** large garlic cloves, peeled and crushed through a press
- **1** small onion, peeled and finely chopped
- **3½** to 4-pound chicken, cut into 8 or 10 serving pieces
- **1** 15-ounce can tomato purée
- **¼** cup honey
- **3** tablespoons light molasses
- **1** teaspoon salt
- **½** teaspoon cayenne pepper
- **½** teaspoon dried thyme, crumbled
- **¼** teaspoon black pepper
- **2** tablespoons cider vinegar

1. In a large bowl combine the sherry, lemon juice, bay leaves, garlic, and onion. Add the chicken and toss well. Cover and marinate in the refrigerator 6 hours or overnight.

2. Drain the chicken, reserving the marinade. In a heavy medium nonaluminum saucepan combine the reserved marinade with the tomato purée, honey, molasses, salt, cayenne, thyme, and black pepper. Bring to a boil over moderate heat. Reduce the heat to moderately low and cook, stirring occasionally, until the sauce is thick and rich and reduced to 2 cups, 35 to 45 minutes. Remove from the heat and stir in the vinegar. Remove the bay leaves.

3. Light a charcoal fire. Grill the chicken over glowing coals for 10 minutes, turning 3 or 4 times. Spoon some of the sauce over the pieces and continue grilling, basting liberally with the sauce and turning every 5 minutes, until cooked through, 20 to 30 minutes longer.

Teriyaki Cornish Hens

MAKES 4 SERVINGS

- **4** Cornish hens, 1½ pounds each, thawed if frozen
- **¾** cup (about 4 ounces) chopped peeled fresh ginger
- **2** tablespoons minced garlic
- **½** cup sugar
- **1** cup sake (Japanese rice wine)
- **½** cup soy sauce

1. The day before you want to grill the Cornish hens, rinse them under cool water and pat them dry with paper towels. With poultry shears or a cleaver, cut along each side of the spine to free the backbones, and discard them. Flatten the birds slightly with a mallet or the side of a cleaver, or with the bottom of a cast-iron skillet.

2. In a blender or food processor, combine the ginger, garlic, sugar, sake, and soy sauce. Purée until smooth. Pour the marinade into a large nonaluminum baking dish. Add the hens and turn. Marinate, covered, in the refrigerator for at least 24 hours, turning occasionally.

3. Light a charcoal fire. When the coals are glowing but covered in gray ash, drain the hens and put them bone side down on the grill, about 5 inches from the heat. Grill, turning every 5 minutes or so, until the thigh juice runs clear when the meat is pierced with a fork and the skin is well browned, 18 to 25 minutes.

I love the big taste of these little birds, especially when they are marinated for a day. Don't be alarmed by the large quantity of fresh ginger; it contributes great taste.

Broiled Chutney-glazed Chicken

No chicken dish could be simpler than this recipe from my friend, author Jonathan Moor. All you do is broil chicken halves and spread chutney over them and broil them again until they are bubbly and brown. I like a Caesar salad and mashed potatoes with this dish. Pasta goes well, too.

MAKES 2 SERVINGS

1 small 2½-pound chicken, split lengthwise
1 tablespoon vegetable oil
⅓ cup Major Grey's chutney or other mango chutney, chopped
Salt and pepper

1. Adjust the broiler rack so it is 3 to 4 inches from the heat source and preheat the broiler.
2. If you are splitting the chicken yourself, cut out the backbone along both sides and discard. Place the halves on a broiler pan and brush lightly all over with the vegetable oil.
3. Place skin side down on the pan and broil for 15 minutes. Turn (pour off any fat from the pan) and broil 5 to 10 minutes longer, until speckled brown all over and cooked to the bone (when the thigh is pierced the juices will run clear). Spread the chutney over the chicken and broil until glazed and bubbly, 2 to 3 minutes. Let stand 5 minutes before serving. Sprinkle with salt and pepper to taste.

Vietnamese Chicken with Marinated Onions, Mint, and Rice Noodles

MAKES 4 SERVINGS

3½ pound chicken, cut into serving pieces
2 large garlic cloves, peeled and sliced
½ cup white vinegar
2 tablespoons sugar
1 medium onion, peeled and sliced paper-thin
⅓ cup finely chopped fresh mint, plus 4 sprigs for garnish
¼ cup chopped fresh cilantro
3 tablespoons peanut oil
1 tablespoon fresh lime juice
1½ teaspoons salt
¼ teaspoon black pepper
¼ teaspoon dried hot red pepper flakes
½ pound dried thin rice noodles, or Japanese udon, or thin spaghetti

Fragrant and spicy, this rice noodle dish can also be made with Japanese udon noodles or thin spaghetti. Sliced cucumbers and sliced tomatoes are good around the edge of the platter.

1. Put the chicken in a large heavy pot with 2 cups cold water and the garlic. Bring to a boil over moderate heat. Cover and simmer over low heat until cooked to the bone, 25 to 30 minutes. Take the chicken out and reserve on a plate until cool enough to handle. Strain the broth and reserve it for another use.

2. In a medium bowl stir together the vinegar and sugar; add the sliced onion and let marinate for 30 minutes. Drain, discarding the liquid.

3. In a large bowl, stir together the mint, cilantro, peanut oil, lime juice, salt, black pepper, and red pepper flakes.

4. Pull the skin from the chicken and pull the meat from the bones. Discard the skin and bones. Tear the meat into shreds about ½ inch wide and 2 inches long. Add to the mint dressing; toss to coat. Cover and chill for an hour.

5. Soak the rice noodles in plenty of hot tap water to cover for 20 to 30 minutes. Rinse under cold water; drain and arrange on a large platter. If using Japanese udon noodles, drop them into a large pot of lightly salted boiling water. When a full boil returns, add ¾ cup cold water and return to the boil. Again add ¾ cup cold water and then boil until tender but firm to the bite. Drain; rinse under cold water. Drain and arrange on the platter. If using thin spaghetti, cook as usual, tender but firm to the bite; rinse under cold water, drain and arrange on the platter. Arrange all the marinated chicken and dressing over the noodles. Top with the sliced onions and mint sprigs. Serve cool.

Chicken and Bean Burritos

This burrito recipe takes more effort than the one on page 275 because here you start with a whole chicken that must be simmered before making the filling. The

MAKES 12

3½ pound chicken, cut into serving parts

2 8-ounce cans tomato sauce

2 tablespoons chili powder

2 garlic cloves, peeled and minced or crushed through a press

1 teaspoon dried oregano, crumbled

1 teaspoon ground cumin

    1 bay leaf
    1 teaspoon salt
 1/4 teaspoon black pepper
    4 cups mashed Pinto Beans with Bacon (page 375), or
          canned refried beans
 12 8- to 10-inch flour tortillas
    3 cups (12 ounces) shredded mild Cheddar cheese
    1 to 2 tablespoons hot taco sauce

1. Put the chicken in a large heavy pot and add 1½ cups of
cold water. Add ½ cup of the tomato sauce, the chili powder,
garlic, oregano, cumin, bay leaf, salt, and pepper; bring to a
boil over moderate heat. Cover and simmer over low heat until
cooked through, 25 to 30 minutes. Take out the pieces with
tongs and put them on a plate until cool enough to handle.
2. Boil the cooking liquid over high heat for 10 minutes; remove the bay leaf and pour broth into a 2-cup glass measure.
Pour off the fat from the top. You will need 1½ cups of the
broth.
3. Pull the skin from the chicken and pull the meat from the
bones. Discard the skin and bones. Tear the meat into shreds
about ½ inch wide and 2 inches long. Combine in a medium
saucepan with 1½ cups broth.
4. Heat the beans in a medium saucepan, adding a little water
if needed to make them a good spreading consistency.
5. Heat a skillet or griddle over moderate heat. Warm one tortilla, turning it several times, until soft and pliable, 10 to 20
seconds; do not overheat or the tortilla will dry out. Spread the
tortilla with ⅓ cup of beans. Arrange ¼ cup of filling in line
across a third of the tortilla. Top the filling with ¼ cup cheese,
2 tablespoons of tomato sauce, and ¼ to ½ teaspoon of the hot
taco sauce. Fold one edge of the tortilla up over the filling. Fold
the two ends in over the filling, then roll up and place seam
side down on a platter. Repeat. Serve hot.

key to the special
flavor in these is
the combination of
sauces. They are best
made with homemade
beans, but in a pinch
canned refried beans
can be substituted.
The filling and beans
can be prepared
ahead of time, but as-
semble the burritos
just before serving.

Dijon Mustard Chicken

This is a simple dish to put together. All the cooking is done in the oven and the spicy crumb coating clings to a zesty Dijon mustard layer and turns out crisp and golden brown. For a variation, you can use all chicken thighs, or wings, or whatever combination you like. Good for a lazy supper or picnic.

MAKES 4 SERVINGS

3½ pound chicken, cut into serving parts
⅔ cup Dijon mustard
3 cups coarse fresh bread crumbs (see Note)
1 tablespoon paprika
½ teaspoon dried tarragon, crumbled
½ teaspoon salt
½ teaspoon black pepper
2 large eggs
3 tablespoons butter
3 tablespoons fresh lemon juice

1. Pull the skin from all the chicken parts except the wings and discard. Spoon the mustard into a large bowl and add the chicken pieces, turning to coat. Let marinate at room temperature for 30 minutes.

2. Preheat the oven to 375°. Coat a 13-by-9-inch shallow baking pan with vegetable oil.

3. In a large bowl combine the fresh bread crumbs with the paprika, tarragon, salt, and pepper. Whisk the eggs in a shallow medium bowl with 1 teaspoon water. Melt the butter in a small saucepan over low heat; remove from the heat and stir in the lemon juice.

4. Pick up one piece of chicken, turning it so it is evenly coated with mustard. Dip it first into the egg to coat and then plop it flatter side down into the crumbs. Tap so they adhere and turn once to coat the other side. Place best side up (the first side you coated) in the pan. Repeat to coat all pieces. Spoon the lemon butter evenly over them and bake 50 to 60 minutes, until the tops are golden brown and the meat is cooked to the bone. Let stand at least 10 minutes before serving. Scrape out with a spatula so the crumb coating on the bottom is not left behind in the pan. Serve hot, warm, or cold.

NOTE: To make fresh bread crumbs, tear up several slices of firm homemade-style white bread and grind to coarse soft crumbs in a food processor.

Tea-smoked Chicken with Hoisin Mayonnaise

MAKES 4 SERVINGS

Marinated Chicken:

3½ pound chicken, cut into 8 or 10 serving pieces
½ cup dry sherry
¼ cup grated fresh ginger
6 scallions, sliced (including green part)
2 large garlic cloves, peeled and minced or crushed through a press
1 tablespoon sugar
1 teaspoon salt
1 teaspoon black pepper

Smoking poultry over tea in a wok is a classic Chinese cooking technique. To give a tasty but eclectic twist, I like to serve the deeply flavored mahogany-colored chicken with mayonnaise blended with bottled hoisin sauce (available in Chinese markets and most supermarkets). You will need an old wok or dutch oven because the pot is placed over a flame for 20 minutes while the tea, sugar, rice, and cinnamon smolder. To my nose, a pleasant smoky scent is left in the kitchen for the day, but if you have good ventilation that won't happen. The chicken is also good cold and is an excellent choice for picnics. You might serve cold noodles with asparagus or sesame green beans alongside. The chicken must marinate at least 6 hours before cooking.

Tea Smoking:

- ½ cup black tea leaves, such as lichee or rose black
- ½ cup packed brown sugar
- ½ cup raw white rice
- 2 3-inch cinnamon sticks, crushed with a hammer

Hoisin Mayonnaise:

- ⅔ cup Mayonnaise (page 383)
- 3 tablespoons hoisin sauce
- 2 teaspoons lemon juice

1. Marinate the chicken: Pull off and discard any loose pieces of fat from the chicken. In a large bowl stir together the sherry, ginger, scallions, garlic, sugar, salt, and pepper. Add the chicken, turning to coat; cover and chill for 6 to 12 hours. Brush off the marinade.

2. Put the pieces of chicken on a heatproof plate with a raised rim (to hold the juices) or in a pie pan. Place in a large steamer (or wok on a rack or over double-crossed chopsticks) over 1½ inches of boiling water. Cover and steam over moderately high heat until the juice from a thigh runs clear when pierced, 18 to 20 minutes. Reserve the juices for another use.

3. Smoke the chicken: Using heavy-duty aluminum foil, line the inside of a large heavy wok or dutch oven, using two sheets, one in each direction, so the foil extends by 4 inches. Add the tea, brown sugar, rice, and cinnamon sticks; mix together. Position a rack or double-crossed chopsticks in the wok above the mixture. Place the chicken on a heatproof plate or in a pie pan and balance in the center. Line the inside of the lid with foil in two directions as before so there is a 4-inch overhang. Invert over the wok. Tightly roll up the foil from the lid and the bottom of the wok all around to seal. Place on a wok ring over moderate heat and let smoke for 20 minutes without disturbing. Turn off the heat and leave undisturbed for 30 minutes longer. Serve hot or cold.

4. Prepare the hoisin mayonnaise: In a small bowl stir together the mayonnaise and hoisin sauce to blend. Stir in the lemon juice. If making ahead, cover and refrigerate. Serve cold.

Filipino Chicken Adobo

MAKES 4 SERVINGS

- **3** to 3½-pound chicken, cut into 8 serving pieces
- **2** tablespoons minced garlic
- **1** teaspoon black pepper
- **1** bay leaf, cut into ½-inch strips
- **¾** cup white vinegar
- **¼** cup soy sauce
- **3** tablespoons vegetable oil

1. Pat the chicken dry with paper towels.

2. In a large deep bowl combine the garlic, pepper, bay leaf, vinegar, and soy sauce; stir together and add the chicken, turning to coat both sides. Cover and marinate in the refrigerator for 2 hours.

3. Combine the chicken and marinade in a 9- to 10-inch heavy nonaluminum skillet. Place over moderate heat and bring to a boil, turning the chicken several times with tongs. Lower the

The big flavors of vinegar and garlic permeate pieces of delicate chicken in the marinade, braising liquid, and glaze. This dish gets even better when made ahead. Serve with rice noodles or vermicelli and sliced tomatoes. You can tear the meat into shreds and make a salad over the noodles if desired, adding

diced tomatoes, sliced scallions, and parsley or cilantro.

heat and simmer over moderately low heat, turning with tongs several times, for 15 minutes. Take out and reserve on a platter. Boil marinade until reduced to ⅔ cup, about 5 minutes. Pour the sauce into a cup, spoon off most of the fat from the top, and fish out the pieces of bay leaf.

4. Spoon the vegetable oil into a large heavy nonaluminum skillet and place over moderately high heat. Add the chicken, skin side down, and brown well, 3 to 5 minutes (a spatter screen is good to use here). Turn and brown over very low heat until cooked through, 3 to 5 minutes longer. Arrange the chicken on a platter and spoon the sauce over it. Serve hot, at room temperature, or cool.

Chicken with Brown Rice and Wild Rice

Here is a fine excuse to cook brown rice; the chicken is almost secondary. The dish is good and grainy; also chewy and full of flavor. You might consider serving buttered broccoli alongside, or perhaps roasted and

MAKES 6 SERVINGS

½	cup wild rice
1	tablespoon vegetable oil
3½	to 4-pound chicken, cut into serving pieces
1½	cups brown rice
2	medium onions, peeled and chopped
2	large garlic cloves, peeled and minced or crushed through a press
1	14- to 16-ounce can whole tomatoes
3	cups Basic Chicken Stock (page 47) or canned broth
½	cup dry white wine

1 bay leaf
2 teaspoons dried basil, crumbled
1 teaspoon ground cumin
1 teaspoon celery salt
½ teaspoon dried thyme, crumbled
2 teaspoons salt
¼ teaspoon black pepper
2 tablespoons olive oil
¼ cup chopped parsley (optional)

peeled red and green bell peppers, spritzed with balsamic vinegar and drizzled with olive oil. Soak the wild rice well ahead of time.

1. In a medium bowl combine the wild rice with 2 cups of cold water and soak for 8 hours or overnight. Drain.

2. Spoon the vegetable oil into a large heavy flameproof casserole or dutch oven and place over moderately high heat. If desired, cut the breast halves in half again. Brown the chicken pieces well, about 5 minutes. Turn with tongs and brown about 3 minutes longer. Take out and reserve.

3. Add the brown rice to the pan drippings and sauté over moderate heat, stirring, until lightly toasted, 3 to 4 minutes. Add the onions; sauté 3 to 4 minutes to soften. Add the garlic and cook a minute longer.

4. Drain the tomatoes, reserving the juice for another purpose. Cut them in half and gently squeeze out the seeds. Drain the pieces and then coarsely chop. Add the tomato pieces to the pan along with the chicken stock, white wine, wild rice, bay leaf, basil, cumin, celery salt, thyme, salt, and pepper. Bring to a boil over moderately high heat.

5. Add all the chicken except the breast pieces. Add the olive oil. Cover and simmer over low heat for 30 minutes. Stir gently. Add the breast pieces, cover, and simmer until the rice is tender but slightly chewy and the liquid absorbed, 20 to 30 minutes longer. Sprinkle with the parsley and serve hot or warm.

Arroz con Pollo

Chicken and rice is a robust paellalike casserole (without seafood) that is favored by all Spanish-speaking countries. It is more than just chicken and rice and there are a hundred different ways to make it. Here is my favorite version, always a hit with my Latino friends. There are two ways to achieve the characteristic flavor and yellow tint: by using achiote seeds (favored in Puerto Rico and Cuba) or with saffron (preferred in Spain). I like it made with both. A little of the costly saffron goes a long way, but adds great flavor.

MAKES 6 SERVINGS

- **4** pound chicken, cut into serving pieces
- **3** tablespoons cider vinegar or wine vinegar
- **2** large garlic cloves, peeled and minced or crushed through a press
- **1** teaspoon dried oregano, crumbled
- **1½** teaspoons salt
- **½** teaspoon black pepper
- **2** large red bell peppers, or one 4-ounce jar pimientos, drained
- **3** tablespoons *achiote* oil (see Note) or 2 tablespoons vegetable oil
- **2** medium onions, peeled and chopped
- **2** large green bell peppers, cut into ½-inch squares
- **2½** cups long-grain white rice
- **¼** pound smoked ham, cut into ¼-by-2-inch sticks
- **1** 14- to 16-ounce can whole tomatoes, drained, seeded, and quartered
- **3** cups homemade Basic Chicken Stock (page 47) or canned broth
- **½** cup dry sherry or white wine
- **1** bay leaf
- **¼** teaspoon saffron strands (optional)
- **½** cup sliced pimiento-stuffed green olives
- **¼** cup chopped fresh parsley
- **1** tablespoon capers (optional)
- **1** 10-ounce package frozen peas, thawed

1. Cut the chicken into the following serving pieces: 2 thighs, 2 drumsticks, 2 wings, and 6 breast pieces.

2. In a large bowl, stir together the vinegar, garlic, oregano, 1 teaspoon of the salt, and the pepper. Add the chicken, tossing the pieces to coat. Cover and let marinate at room temperature for 1 hour (or as long as overnight in the refrigerator).

3. To roast the red peppers, place them directly on the burners of a gas flame or as close to the heat as possible if using an electric broiler; turn several times with tongs until the peppers are blistered and black all over. Let them cool for a minute and then put them in a plastic bag. Twist the top and chill for at least 10 minutes. Rub the skins away with your fingers and cut out the stems; pull out and discard the seeds and ribs (this step can be done over a colander under slowly running water, but some of the juices will be lost). Cut the peppers into strips about ½ inch wide and 2 inches long. If using pimientos, cut them into strips. Set aside.

4. Drain the chicken and reserve the marinade. Spoon 2 tablespoons achiote oil or vegetable oil into a heavy 12-inch flameproof casserole or dutch oven and place over moderately high heat. Arrange half the chicken pieces in the hot oil and brown well, about 5 minutes. (Use a spatter screen if available, otherwise brown uncovered.) Turn with tongs and brown 3 to 5 minutes longer. Transfer the pieces to a plate and brown the remaining chicken in the oil remaining in the pan. Remove and hold all breast pieces separately. Preheat oven to 325°.

5. Add the onions and green peppers to the pan and sauté over moderate heat to soften, about 5 minutes. Add the rice and optional remaining 1 tablespoon *achiote* oil; sauté until the rice grains are chalky and lightly browned, 2 to 3 minutes, stirring. Stir in the ham and cook a minute longer. Add the drained tomatoes, chicken stock, sherry, reserved marinade, bay leaf, optional saffron, and remaining ½ teaspoon salt. Bring quickly to a boil over high heat. Return all but the breast pieces of the chicken to the pan; lower the heat and simmer, turning the chicken occasionally, until the sauce is no longer soupy, about 15 minutes uncovered. Remove from the heat. Add the red pepper or pimiento strips, green olives, parsley, and capers. Return the breast pieces and toss gently with a large spoon. Place the pan in the oven and bake uncovered for 15 minutes. Top with the peas, cover, and bake 10 to 15 minutes longer. Remove from the oven and let stand at least 10 minutes before serving.

NOTE: To make *achiote* oil, combine 2 tablespoons whole *achiote* seeds (annatto) with 3 to 4 tablespoons vegetable oil in a small saucepan. Place over low heat and sauté until bright orange, 1 to 3 minutes. Let cool, then strain.

Chicken Breasts

4

Delicate white chicken breast, everyone's favorite, is rich and tempting, light and delicious. It has a good flavor and tender juicy texture when properly cooked, so it's at home in almost any dish from dainty little tea sandwiches to hearty pizza rustica.

Chicken breasts are popular from the Mideast to the Far East and from South America to Northern India. The versatile white meat seems to be first choice when carved from a golden roast chicken dinner with all the trimmings, and the first to be grabbed from any pile of fried chicken at a picnic.

When poached in broth the way it's done in Mexico, the fine meat can be pulled from the bones in delicate shreds and turned into tacos, tortas, and crepas. Italy and France have given us inspired chicken breast preparations, and we can claim some dandy ones for the United States, too. Asian cooks are unsurpassed when it comes to utilizing small amounts of breast meat to produce large, tasty dishes.

Layered between slices of bread, diced into soups and stews, or split and charred on the grill, chicken breasts can be transformed magically into a multitude of personalities.

Simple Poached Chicken Breast

Use this easy technique to cook a chicken breast when you need cooked chicken for a recipe, or just want to make a sandwich and have no leftover chicken.

MAKES 12 OUNCES OF MEAT AND 2 CUPS BROTH

1½   pound whole chicken breast (with skin and bones), split
1   large garlic clove, peeled and sliced
1   bay leaf

In a heavy medium saucepan combine the chicken breast, garlic, bay leaf, and 2 cups cold water. Cover and bring to a boil over moderate heat. Lower the heat and simmer gently, partially covered, until cooked through, 15 to 20 minutes. To test for doneness, cut into the thickest part with a knife to see if it is no longer pink. The trick to juicy cooked chicken is to stop cooking it the moment that this happens. A few minutes longer can dry out the meat. Remove from the broth and set aside until cool enough to handle. Pull the meat from the skin and bones. Slice or dice as needed.

Creamy-Chunky Chicken Soup

This is a soup of contradictions: light yet hearty; elegant, yet at the same time homey; with simple but complicated flavors! It's my choice when I want to feel pampered on an icy cold day. The

MAKES 12 CUPS

1   pound chicken breast, with skin and bones
1   cup dry sherry
4   tablespoons (½ stick) butter
2   medium carrots, peeled and cut into ¼-inch dice
2   medium celery ribs, cut in ¼-inch dice
1   medium onion, peeled and chopped
1   small garlic clove, peeled and minced or crushed
    through a press

½ teaspoon dried basil, crumbled
1 bay leaf
¼ teaspoon grated nutmeg
½ cup all-purpose flour
6 cups Basic Chicken Stock (page 47)
3 medium-large baking potatoes (1½ pounds), peeled and cut into ½-inch dice
1 cup heavy cream
2 teaspoons salt
¼ teaspoon black pepper
2 tablespoons finely chopped fresh parsley
Tiny parsley sprigs for garnish

soup is best when made from homemade chicken stock, but you can use 6 cups canned broth when time is against you. When making home-made broth, make it well ahead of time or keep some in the freezer for emergencies.

1. Put the whole chicken breast in a heavy medium pot with the sherry and 1 cup cold water; bring to a boil over moderate heat. Cover and lower the heat; simmer just until the chicken is cooked through, 15 to 20 minutes. Transfer to a plate until cool enough to handle. Reserve the broth.

2. Melt the butter in a large 4-quart soup pot or saucepan over moderate heat. Add the carrots, celery, and onion; sauté to soften and color lightly, 5 to 7 minutes. Add the garlic, basil, bay leaf, and nutmeg; cook 1 minute. Stir in the flour and toast for a minute over moderate heat. Stir in the 6 cups broth and the reserved broth (about 2 cups) from the breast; stirring constantly, bring to a boil. Add the potatoes and cream; when simmer returns, lower the heat and simmer, stirring frequently, until the potatoes are very tender, about 30 minutes.

3. Pull off the skin and bones from the chicken and discard them. Cut the meat onto fine ¼- to ⅓-inch dice and add to the soup. Stir in the salt and pepper and simmer for about 5 minutes. Remove from the heat and stir in the chopped parsley. If necessary, add a little more salt to taste. You can also add an extra pinch of grated nutmeg if desired. Serve hot in large shallow soup plates. Garnish with parsley sprigs.

Crunchy Chicken-Macaroni Salad

Here is a great variation on a favorite American picnic and barbecue salad. You can follow the instructions below for cooking the chicken, or use 2 cups diced leftover cooked chicken if you have it.

MAKES 8 TO 12 SERVINGS (10 CUPS)

1½ pound whole chicken breast with skin and bones, split lengthwise, or 2 cups cooked diced chicken breast

1 bay leaf

1 large garlic clove, peeled and sliced

4 large eggs

½ pound small elbow macaroni

2 tablespoons olive oil

1 medium red bell pepper, trimmed and finely chopped

1 medium green bell pepper, trimmed and finely chopped

1 cup finely diced celery

½ cup finely chopped carrot

½ cup thinly sliced scallions, including green parts (8 medium)

¼ cup chopped parsley, plus 1 sprig

1 6-ounce can pitted black olives

1 cup Mayonnaise (page 383)

2 to 3 tablespoons cider vinegar

1 tablespoon brown mustard

½ teaspoon dried basil, crumbled

½ teaspoon dried oregano, crumbled

½ teaspoon dried tarragon, crumbled (optional)

1 teaspoon salt

½ teaspoon black pepper

1. Put the chicken breast in a heavy medium pot along with the bay leaf, garlic, and 1½ cups cold water; cover and bring to a boil over moderate heat. Lower the heat and simmer just until cooked through, 15 to 20 minutes (the flesh will no longer be pink when the thickest part is cut). Transfer to a plate and cool to room temperature. Reserve the broth for another use.

2. Place the eggs in a small heavy pan and cover generously with cold water. Place over moderate heat and bring to a boil. Lower the heat and keep at a bare simmer for precisely 10 minutes from the time the boil began. Rinse under cold water and cool to room temperature.

3. Bring a large pot of lightly salted water to a boil over high heat. Drop in the macaroni and begin stirring immediately; continue stirring until a full boil has returned. Stir frequently thereafter and cook to the al dente stage (tender but firm to the bite), 8 to 10 minutes. Drain in a colander and rinse under cold water. Toss in a large bowl with the olive oil.

4. Add to the macaroni the red and green peppers, the celery, carrot, scallions, and chopped parsley. Reserve 3 whole olives for garnish and slice the rest. Reserve 1 egg for garnish and chop the rest. Add the sliced olives and chopped eggs to the salad.

5. Pull off the skin and bones from the chicken and discard them. Cut the meat into 1/2-inch dice and add to the salad.

6. In a medium bowl stir the mayonnaise with 2 tablespoons of the vinegar and the mustard. Stir in the basil, oregano, optional tarragon, salt, and pepper. Pour over the salad and toss well. Cover and chill for 1 hour. Taste and add the remaining tablespoon vinegar if desired. Mound the salad on a large platter. Slice the remaining hard-cooked egg and garnish salad with it and the 3 whole olives and sprig of parsley. Serve cold.

Chicken Salad with Basil and Wine Mushrooms

Instead of using diced poached chicken in this salad, raw chicken breast cubes are browned well in olive oil to contribute a good toasted flavor. You will need fresh basil for this recipe.

MAKES 6 SERVINGS (6 CUPS)

- **3** tablespoons olive oil
- **2** pounds skinless boned chicken breasts, cut into $3/4$- to 1-inch cubes
- **4** medium carrots ($1/2$ pound), peeled and cut into $1/4$-by-2-inch julienne
- **3/4** cup sour cream
- **1/2** cup Mayonnaise (page 383)
- **2** tablespoons lemon juice
- **2** teaspoons Dijon mustard
- **1** teaspoon salt
- **1/2** teaspoon black pepper
- **1** cup finely shredded (chiffonade) fresh basil leaves, plus fresh basil sprigs, for garnish
- **1/2** cup grated Parmesan cheese
- **1** pound (about 36) whole small fresh mushrooms
- **1** cup dry white wine

1. Spoon $1^{1}/_{2}$ tablespoons of the olive oil into a large heavy skillet and place over moderately high heat. Add half the chicken cubes, stir once to lightly coat them with oil, and let brown well without stirring, 3 to 4 minutes. Turn and cook a couple minutes longer, just until cooked through. Remove with a slotted spoon and transfer to a plate. Repeat with the remaining olive oil and chicken; cool to room temperature.

2. Pour about 2 quarts of water into a large saucepan and bring to a boil over high heat. Add a pinch of salt and the carrots; when the boil returns, boil for 2 minutes. Rinse under cold water and drain.

3. In a large bowl stir together the sour cream, mayonnaise, lemon juice, mustard, salt, pepper, shredded basil, and Parmesan cheese. Add the chicken and all but ¼ cup of the carrots and toss well. Cover and chill at least 3 hours.

4. Combine the whole mushrooms and wine in a medium-sized nonaluminum pan; bring to a boil over moderately high heat and cook until tender, 3 to 4 minutes. Transfer to a bowl and cool completely. Drain, reserving the liquid for a soup or a sauce.

5. Mound the salad on a large serving platter; ring the edge with the wine mushrooms and garnish the top with the reserved carrots. Add a basil sprig or two to one side and serve cold.

Chicken Divan

I don't care about fashion when it comes to food. I love chicken divan and I always will. My mother made it frequently back in the 1950s but no one dares to do it today. Call it retro if you will, but try it.

MAKES 4 SERVINGS

- **2** whole chicken breasts, 1 pound each, split, or 1 pound cooked chicken breast
- **1½** pound head broccoli
- **3** tablespoons butter
- **1** small garlic clove, peeled and minced or crushed through a press
- **¼** cup all-purpose flour
- **1¾** cups hot chicken stock (reserved from cooking the breasts, or canned or other homemade if using leftover cooked chicken)
- **¼** teaspoon grated nutmeg
- **1½** teaspoons salt
- **⅛** teaspoon black pepper
- **½** cup heavy cream
- **2** tablespoons dry sherry
- **½** cup grated Parmesan cheese

1. Put the chicken breasts in a heavy medium-large pot with 2 cups of water. Cover and bring to a boil over moderate heat. Turn the heat to low and simmer just until cooked through, about 20 minutes. Transfer to a plate to cool, and reserve the broth. If starting with leftover cooked chicken, simply cut into slices about ¼ inch thick and reserve.

2. Cut off all but about 2 inches of the stem portions from the broccoli (discard or reserve for another use). Cut the broccoli florets downward through the stems into slices about ¼ inch thick. (It's okay if some of them fall apart.) Steam on a rack over boiling water, covered, just until tender, about 5 minutes. Keep warm. When the chicken is cool enough to handle, pull off and discard the skin and bones and cut the chicken into slices about ¼ inch thick.

3. Preheat the broiler. Lightly butter four individual gratin dishes or one large one.

4. Make the sauce: Melt the butter in a heavy medium saucepan over moderate heat. Add the garlic and sauté for 30 seconds. Stir in the flour with a fork or a whisk and cook, stirring frequently, until toasted light brown, a minute or two. Pour in the hot chicken stock and, whisking constantly, bring to a boil. Stir in the nutmeg, salt, and pepper. Lower the heat and simmer, stirring frequently, for about 5 minutes to thicken. Remove from the heat.

5. Pour the heavy cream into a small deep bowl and beat with a hand-held electric mixer until stiff. Fold the whipped cream into the hot chicken sauce and then fold in the sherry.

6. Arrange ¼ of the broccoli in each individual gratin dish or all of it in a large one. Spoon half of the sauce over the broccoli to coat. Arrange the chicken slices over the broccoli. Remove 2 tablespoons of the Parmesan and reserve for topping and fold the rest into the remaining sauce. Top the chicken slices with the cheese sauce and sprinkle with the reserved 2 tablespoons Parmesan. Working in batches if necessary, broil until browned and bubbly, 2 to 4 minutes, depending on your broiler. Serve hot.

Chicken Schizophrenia

Here is an easy micro-waved dish with a built-in sauce that tastes as if it took hours to prepare! By changing just one in-gredient, it can take on any number of per-sonalities. Instead of the pepperoni or sau-sage listed below, try crisp crumbled bacon or smoked ham, or roasted red bell pep-per, sliced black ol-ives, or scallions. Just 10 minutes in the mi-crowave does the trick! The recipe was tested in a large (700-watt) microwave with a turntable. If yours is different, turn the dish once in a while and if the chicken is not cooked through after the specified

MAKES 4 SERVINGS

2 tablespoons all-purpose flour
1/2 cup sour cream
1/4 cup heavy cream
2 tablespoons mayonnaise
1 tablespoon lemon or lime juice
1 teaspoon mustard (any kind)
1 medium garlic clove, peeled and minced or crushed through a press
1/2 teaspoon dried basil, oregano, thyme, or rosemary, crumbled
1/2 teaspoon salt
1/4 teaspoon black pepper
20 thin pepperoni slices (1½ ounces), slivered, or 1 Italian sausage (3 to 4 ounces; see Note below)
4 ounces (4 large) fresh mushrooms, sliced
4 skinless boned chicken breast halves, 4 to 6 ounces each
2 tablespoons grated Parmesan cheese
1 tablespoon chopped parsley (optional)

1. Spoon the flour into a 9-inch round shallow microwave dish or glass pie pan. Stir in the sour cream to blend. Add the heavy cream, mayonnaise, lemon juice, mustard, garlic, basil, salt, and pepper; stir to blend. Stir in the pepperoni (if using sausage, it was already cooked in this dish). Cover with waxed paper and zap at full power for 1 minute.

2. Add the mushrooms, re-cover, and zap at full power for 1 minute. Uncover and stir.

3. Arrange the chicken breasts, wide sides outward, radiating from the center on top of the sauce. Cover with waxed paper and zap at full power for 3 minutes. Turn the breasts, cover again, and zap for 3 minutes more. Uncover, and stir the sauce so it coats the chicken. Sprinkle with the Parmesan and zap 2 minutes longer. Test for doneness. If desired, sprinkle with parsley. Serve hot.

NOTE: Slit the sausage and take the meat from the casing; crumble it into a 9-inch round shallow microwave dish or glass pie pan. Zap at full power for 1 minute; drain off fat if present. Leave the sausage in the dish.

time, continue cooking at 1-minute increments until done. The dish is good served with pasta, potatoes, or rice and your favorite vegetable.

Monterey California Casserole

Here is a great and hearty casserole that can be eaten shortly after baking or made hours or even a day ahead of time and reheated in a microwave or a conventional oven. It is best when made from freshly roasted and peeled poblano peppers but you can substitute a canned version. Many variations of this layered rice, cheese, chile, and sour cream casserole are around, but this one with chicken is my favorite.

MAKES 8 SERVINGS

- **1** pound (6 to 8 medium) fresh poblano chile peppers, or two 4-ounce cans mild roasted peeled green chiles
- **1** tablespoon butter, softened
- **1** pound (3 medium) zucchini, sliced on the diagonal ½ inch thick
- **1½** cups long-grain white rice
- **1** tablespoon olive oil
- **1½** teaspoons salt
- **¼** cup chopped fresh cilantro (optional)
- **1** pound (4 medium) skinless boned chicken breast halves
- **1** 8- to 12-ounce tomato, sliced ¼ inch thick
- **¼** teaspoon black pepper
- **3** cups (12 ounces) shredded Monterey Jack cheese
- **2** cups sour cream
- **1** teaspoon dried basil, crumbled
- **1** teaspoon dried oregano, crumbled
- **1** teaspoon celery salt
- **¼** cup sliced scallions, including green parts
- **¼** cup chopped fresh parsley leaves
- **½** teaspoon paprika

1. Roast the fresh poblanos by placing them directly on the burners of gas flames or as close to the heat source as possible under the broiler; turn them frequently with tongs until they are black and blistered all over. Let them cool for a minute or two and then enclose them in a plastic bag and chill them for at least 10 minutes (this can be done a day ahead). Rub the skins away and cut out the stems and seeds (this can be done in a colander under gently running water if desired, but some of the juices will wash away as well). If using canned chiles, simply drain and remove the seeds. Cut the chiles lengthwise into ½-inch strips.

2. Preheat the oven to 350°. Coat a 13-by-9-by-2-inch baking dish with the softened butter. Fill a large heavy saucepan with 2 to 3 quarts of water and bring to a boil over high heat.

3. Drop the zucchini slices into the boiling water and when the boil resumes, cook for 30 seconds. Scoop out with a slotted spoon and reserve. Gradually add the rice to the boiling water (still over high heat) so the boiling does not stop. Stir once or twice and boil for 7 minutes. Add 1 cup of cold water to stop the boiling and drain in a strainer. Turn into a bowl and stir in the olive oil, ½ teaspoon of the salt, and the optional cilantro. Let cool slightly.

4. Spread the rice in the buttered pan. Cut the chicken across the grain into slices about ¼ inch thick and arrange over the rice. Add the poblanos, zucchini, and tomato slices and sprinkle with ½ teaspoon of the remaining salt and the pepper. Scatter 2 cups of the cheese shreds over the top. In a medium bowl, stir together the sour cream, basil, oregano, celery salt, scallions, parsley, and remaining ½ teaspoon salt. With a spoon handle or your finger poke holes through the layers in the casserole (about 12 in all) and spread the sour cream mixture over the top. Sprinkle with the remaining 1 cup cheese and the paprika. The casserole will be full. Bake in the center of the oven until hot, bubbly, and golden brown, 50 to 60 minutes. Cool in the pan for at least 10 minutes. Cut into rectangles and scoop out with a spatula. Serve hot.

Chicken Marsala Cordon Bleu

Here is a surprise and delight of a dish that I created by combining two classic veal treatments with chicken breasts. I have also used ham in place of prosciutto to make it more accessible. This dish is especially good with roasted new potatoes and green peas, asparagus, or broccoli. You can stack pounded chicken cutlets between sheets of plastic wrap and freeze so they are ready at a moment's notice.

MAKES 4 SERVINGS

- **4** skinless boned chicken breast halves, 4 to 6 ounces each
- **2** tablespoons butter
- **1½** tablespoons olive oil
- **¼** cup all-purpose flour
- **1** medium garlic clove, peeled and minced or crushed through a press
- **½** teaspoon dried rosemary, crumbled
- **½** pound fresh mushrooms, thinly sliced
- **½** cup dry marsala wine
- **½** teaspoon salt
- **⅛** teaspoon pepper
- **4** thin slices (4 ounces) ham, each about 4 by 6 inches
- **4** thin slices (4 ounces) provolone cheese, each a 4-inch round
- **1** tablespoon chopped fresh parsley

1. Splash a little cold water over both sides of each chicken breast half and place, smooth side down, on separate sheets of waxed paper or heavy plastic wrap; fold out the flap of flesh (the fillet) to one side and top with additional sheets of waxed paper or plastic wrap. Working gently and starting in the center, pound the cutlets so they are between ⅛ and ¼ inch thick. Immediately peel off the top sheets of paper and discard them; pick up each cutlet to prevent it from sticking to the paper and then return to the paper.

2. Put 1 tablespoon each of the butter and olive oil in a large heavy noncorrosive skillet over moderately high heat. Spread the flour on a sheet of waxed paper or on a plate; dip one cutlet into the flour, turning to lightly coat, and put into the hot pan; repeat with a second cutlet. Brown well, 1 to 2 minutes; turn and cook on the other side about 1 minute longer, until almost cooked through. Take out and transfer to a plate; cover with aluminum foil. Add ½ tablespoon each of the butter and olive oil to the pan; dredge the remaining two cutlets and cook in the same manner. Hold with the others until needed.

3. Add the remaining ½ tablespoon butter to the pan, along with the garlic and rosemary; sauté for 30 seconds and then add the mushrooms; brown well, 1 to 2 minutes, adding 1 or 2 tablespoons of water if the pan seems dry. Pour in the marsala and add the salt and pepper; boil for about 1 minute. Return all the cutlets in a single layer (slightly overlapping is okay) to the pan. Top each with a slice of ham, trimmed around the corners if necessary to fit, and a slice of provolone, halving each slice and arranging two halves over each cutlet if necessary to fit. Cover the pan and bring to a boil over moderate heat. Lower the heat and simmer until the cheese melts, 1 to 2 minutes. Take the cutlets out with a spatula and transfer to hot dinner plates. Spoon the mushrooms and sauce over them and sprinkle with chopped parsley. Serve hot.

Potted Chicken Spread

Perfect atop crackers
or croutons with cock-
tails, this tasty herb-
scented spread can be
made a day or two
ahead.

MAKES ABOUT 2 1/2 CUPS

1 1/4 to 1 1/2-pound whole chicken breast, split
1 cup dry white wine
1 large garlic clove, peeled and minced or crushed through a press
1 bay leaf
1 teaspoon dried tarragon, crumbled
2 hard-cooked eggs (see page 352), finely chopped
1/4 cup Mayonnaise (page 383)
3 tablespoons butter, softened
3 medium scallions, 2 minced and 1 sliced
2 teaspoons mustard (any kind)
1 teaspoon salt
1/4 teaspoon black pepper

1. In a medium nonaluminum saucepan combine the chicken, wine, garlic, bay leaf, and tarragon; bring to a boil over moderate heat. Cover and simmer over low heat until cooked through, 20 to 25 minutes. Transfer the chicken to a plate and let stand until cool enough to handle.

2. Strain the broth and return it to the pan; boil over high heat until reduced to 1/4 cup, about 5 minutes (watch carefully during last minutes to avoid boiling away completely).

3. When the chicken is cool enough to handle, pull off and discard the skin and bones. Cut the meat into fine (1/4- to 1/2-inch) dice. Put in a bowl, add the reduced broth, and toss.

4. Stir in the eggs, mayonnaise, butter, minced scallions, mustard, salt, and pepper. Pack into a small crock. Cover and chill at least 4 hours. Garnish the top with the sliced scallion and serve cold with crackers.

Shredded Chicken Filling

MAKES ABOUT 2 CUPS

1½ pound whole chicken breast with skin and bones, split lengthwise
1 tablespoon vegetable oil
2 large garlic cloves, peeled and minced or crushed through a press
½ teaspoon salt
¼ teaspoon black pepper

1. Put the chicken breast in a heavy medium pot. Add 1½ cups cold water, cover, and bring to a boil over moderate heat. Reduce the heat to low and simmer just until cooked through, 15 to 20 minutes (cut into the thickest part to see if it is done). Cool in the broth to room temperature. Take the chicken out and boil the broth over moderate heat until reduced to ¼ cup.
2. Pull off the skin and discard it. Pull the meat from the bones. Discard the bones and tear the meat, in the direction of the grain, into shreds ¼ to ½ inch wide and about 1 to 2 inches long.
3. Spoon the oil into a heavy medium-large skillet and place over moderate heat. Add the garlic and sauté to soften but not brown, about 30 seconds. Add the chicken and toss; stir in the reserved broth along with the salt and pepper.

Use this simple moist chicken filling for tacos, taquitos, and tortas, and to top tostadas.

Singapore Noodles (Singapore Mai Fun)

Mai fun are rice noodles or rice sticks. The fine ones are generally used to make this delectable curry-flavored noodle dish. (Curry is usually present in dishes labeled "Singapore.") This dish requires a multitude of ingredients; that's why it tastes so good and complex. It doesn't double well, but it is most convenient to buy twice as many ingredients as you need for a single batch, so consider making it twice in a row. You'll find it so delicious that you'll probably take my advice. Do not substitute the thin clear dried

MAKES 4 SERVINGS

- ½ pound fine (1/16-inch) dried rice noodles or rice sticks *(mai fun)*
- ½ pound skinless boned chicken breast, cut into strips about ¼ by 2 inches
- 2 tablespoons light soy sauce
- 1 tablespoon dry sherry or Chinese rice wine
- 1 teaspoon ginger juice (see Note)
- 1 teaspoon cornstarch
- 1 teaspoon sugar
- 1 tablespoon oriental sesame oil
- 2 large eggs
- ¼ cup peanut oil or other vegetable oil
- ¼ pound small shelled raw shrimp
- ½ cup raw pork loin, cut in ¼- by 2-inch shreds
- 1 large garlic clove, peeled and minced or crushed through a press
- 1½ tablespoons curry powder
- 12 medium scallions, cut into 2-inch lengths, including stems
- ½ medium red bell pepper, cut in ⅛-by-2-inch shreds
- ½ medium green bell pepper, cut in ⅛-by-2-inch shreds
- ½ cup smoked ham cut into shreds ¼ by 1½ inches
- 1½ cups fresh bean sprouts or shredded Napa cabbage
- 1 cup chicken stock or canned broth

1. Drop the rice noodles into a large pot of boiling water; stir and return to the boil. Boil for about 1 minute, until barely tender. Drain in a colander and rinse under cold water. Let dry for 30 minutes, shaking once in a while. This firms up the noodles. If drying longer, cover with plastic.

2. In a medium bowl combine the chicken, soy sauce, sherry, ginger juice, cornstarch, sugar, and 1 teaspoon sesame oil. Let marinate at room temperature for 30 minutes while you prepare the rest of the ingredients.

3. In a small bowl whisk the eggs with the remaining 2 teaspoons sesame oil.

4. Place a large heavy wok or dutch oven over high heat. Add 1 tablespoon of the peanut oil. When hot, add the shrimp and stir-fry 30 to 40 seconds, just until cooked. Scoop out and transfer to a plate and reserve. Add ½ tablespoon more oil and stir-fry the pork for 30 seconds. Transfer to a plate. Add ½ tablespoon more oil to the pan; add the eggs and scramble for 10 seconds. Take out and reserve with the pork. Wipe the wok clean with paper towels.

5. Put the remaining 2 tablespoons oil in the wok and add the garlic and curry powder; stir-fry for 10 seconds. Add the scallions and stir-fry 15 seconds. Add the red and green pepper, ham, and bean sprouts; stir-fry for about 30 seconds over high heat. Add the chicken with any marinade in the bowl, and stir-fry 30 seconds longer. Pour in the chicken stock and bring to a boil.

6. Add the noodles, pork, and eggs; toss gently and cook for 1 minute. Toss in the shrimp and serve hot.

N O T E : Grate about ¼ cup fresh ginger onto a damp square of cheesecloth; roll up tightly and wring out juice over a small bowl, or squeeze it in a garlic press a little at a time.

noodles labeled bean threads; although they have a similar appearance when dry, they are completely different when cooked. Prepare all the ingredients before starting to cook.

Chicken Fried Rice

This is a dish that you make when you have a carton of plain white rice left over from a Chinese take-out meal. In China fried rice is rarely eaten with other dishes because it would interfere with their flavors (plain steamed white rice is the classic accompaniment). Instead, fried rice is usually served as a snack or light meal all by itself, a way to use up leftovers. This version is packed with Chinese flavors and textures. Be flexible when you make it; for example, you can leave out the mushrooms and red peppers entirely and use extra celery, even

MAKES 6 SERVINGS

- **4** to 5 large eggs
- **1** tablespoon plus 1 teaspoon oriental sesame oil
- **1** teaspoon salt
- **¼** cup vegetable oil
- **½** to ¾ pound skinless boned chicken breast, thinly sliced across the grain, or 1 to 1½ cups diced cooked chicken
- **1** tablespoon minced fresh ginger (optional)
- **1** large garlic clove, peeled and minced or crushed through a press
- **1** large onion, peeled and slivered lengthwise
- **1** medium red bell pepper, cut in ¼-by-2-inch julienne
- **1** large rib celery, thinly sliced on a severe angle
- **½** pound fresh mushrooms, sliced
- **1** cup frozen peas, thawed (half of a 10-ounce package)
- **4** cups cold leftover cooked rice
- **3** tablespoons soy sauce
- **3** medium scallions, thinly sliced, including green parts

1. Place a large heavy well-seasoned wok or dutch oven over high heat. In a medium bowl, use a fork or a whisk to stir together the eggs with 1 tablespoon of the sesame oil and ½ teaspoon of the salt. Spoon 1 tablespoon of the vegetable oil into the wok and rotate to coat. Add the eggs and lightly scramble, just until set. Scrape out onto a plate and break up with a spoon.
2. Wipe out the wok with a paper towel and spoon in 1 more tablespoon of vegetable oil. Add the chicken and stir-fry over high heat just until cooked through, 1 to 2 minutes; turn out onto the plate with the eggs.
3. Add the remaining 2 tablespoons vegetable oil to the wok; when very hot, add the ginger and garlic and cook for 10 sec-

onds. Add the onion, bell pepper, celery, and remaining ½ teaspoon salt; stir-fry for 1 to 2 minutes, until tender-crunchy. Add the mushrooms and cook a minute longer. Add the peas and cook about 30 seconds longer, until hot. Add the rice, rubbing the grains to separate them. Stir-fry for 1 minute. Return the chicken and the eggs to the wok and stir-fry to heat through, about 30 seconds. Stir in the soy sauce, scallions, and remaining 1 teaspoon sesame oil. Serve hot.

fried cabbage, instead, and you can always throw in a sliced zucchini, a slivered carrot, or an extra onion. You can also substitute leftover cooked chicken for the raw, and you can add a bit of ham if you have some.

Stir-fried Chicken with Pineapple and Pecans

Although most Chinese recipes calling for velvetized chicken breast (which makes the meat very tender and tasty) require a huge amount of oil, this version shows you how to achieve the results in no-calorie water. The dish is best made from fresh pineapple, but canned will suffice in a pinch. Be sure to have all of the ingredients ready before you start to cook.

MAKES 4 SERVINGS (6 CUPS)

Velvetized Chicken:

- **1** tablespoon cornstarch
- **2** tablespoons dry sherry or Chinese rice wine
- **1** large egg white
- **5** thin slices ginger
- **1/2** teaspoon salt
- **1** pound skinless boned chicken breast halves, thinly sliced in 1/8-inch slices across the grain
- **1** tablespoon peanut oil

Sauce:

- **1** tablespoon cornstarch
- **1/4** cup granulated sugar
- **1/4** cup rice vinegar or 3 tablespoons white vinegar
- **1/4** cup pineapple juice
- **2** tablespoons light soy sauce
- **2** tablespoons dry sherry or Chinese rice wine
- **1** tablespoon oriental sesame oil

Stir-fry:

- **2 1/2** tablespoons peanut oil
- **1/2** cup small pecan halves
- **1/4** cup (2 to 3 medium) minced scallions, including green parts
- **2** teaspoons minced fresh ginger
- **1** medium garlic clove, peeled and minced or crushed through a press

1 large red bell pepper, trimmed and cut in 1-inch squares
1 large green bell pepper, trimmed and cut in 1-inch squares
1½ cups fresh or canned pineapple chunks about 1 inch square and ⅓ inch thick

1. Velvetize the chicken: In a medium bowl stir together the cornstarch and sherry to dissolve. Stir in the egg white, ginger, and salt. Press the ginger slices with a spoon to release flavor. Add the chicken, stirring once or twice, and let marinate in the refrigerator for 1 hour.

2. Pour 4 cups of hot water into a heavy saucepan; add the peanut oil and bring to a full rolling boil over high heat. Turn off the heat. Slide the chicken in and stir for exactly 10 seconds. Drain in a strainer, shaking out the water. Put on a plate, stir once, and cool slightly. Discard ginger slices.

3. Make the sauce: In a medium bowl stir the cornstarch with ¼ cup cold water to dissolve. Stir in the sugar, vinegar, pineapple juice, soy sauce, sherry, and sesame oil.

4. Stir-fry: Place a large heavy wok or dutch oven over high heat. When it is very hot add ½ tablespoon of the peanut oil and the pecans. Stir-fry until deep brown, about 1 minute. (Watch very carefully; the nuts can turn from toasted brown to burnt in seconds.) Scoop out and reserve for garnish. Wipe out the wok with paper towels and return to high heat.

5. Spoon in the remaining 2 tablespoons peanut oil. When very hot, add the scallions, ginger, and garlic; cook for 5 seconds and then add the red and green peppers; stir-fry for 30 seconds. Add the pineapple and velvetized chicken; stir-fry 10 seconds. Give the sauce a good stir and add it. Stirring constantly, bring to a boil; the sauce will thicken. Turn out onto a large platter and scatter the toasted pecans over the top. Serve hot.

Chicken Latkes

When made with chicken, the popular Jewish potato pancakes called latkes are perhaps even better. They are crisp on the outside and around the edges while moist and tasty within. You can use leftover cooked chicken and canned broth instead of cooking a breast as described below.

MAKES 1 DOZEN 3-INCH PANCAKES

1 pound chicken breast, split, or 1½ cups finely chopped cooked chicken plus ½ cup canned broth
1 large garlic clove, peeled and sliced
¼ cup Rendered Chicken Fat (page 337), or vegetable oil
1 medium onion, peeled and finely chopped
3 large eggs
½ cup matzo meal
1 teaspoon salt
⅛ teaspoon black pepper
1½ cups applesauce (optional)
1 cup sour cream (optional)

1. Put the chicken breast in a heavy medium saucepan and pour in about 1 cup cold water. Add the garlic and bring to a boil over moderate heat; cover, lower the heat, and simmer just until cooked through, 15 to 18 minutes. Transfer to a plate until cool enough to handle. Strain the broth and reserve ½ cup for this recipe. Pull off and discard the skin and bones. Finely chop the chicken.

2. Spoon 2 tablespoons of the chicken fat or vegetable oil into a small heavy skillet. Place over moderate heat, add the onion, and sauté until soft and lightly colored, about 5 minutes.

3. Crack the eggs into a large bowl and blend with a whisk or a fork. Stir in the matzo meal, salt, pepper, onions, chicken, and ½ cup broth; stir and let stand for 30 minutes.

4. Coat a large heavy skillet or griddle with 1 tablespoon of the remaining chicken fat or oil and place over moderate heat. When very hot, ladle on the pancakes, using a scant ¼ cup for each and spreading them into 3-inch rounds as you work. Brown well, turning once, 2 to 3 minutes per side. When done they should be deep golden brown and crisp. Repeat with the remaining chicken fat and batter. Serve hot, with the optional applesauce and sour cream if you like.

Chicken Hash

MAKES 4 SERVINGS

1½ pound chicken breast, split, or 2 cups diced cooked chicken (½-inch dice)
 2 large (½ pound) baking potatoes, or 2 cups diced (½-inch) cooked potatoes
 ¼ cup vegetable oil
 1 large onion, peeled and chopped
 ¼ cup chopped fresh parsley
 2 teaspoons all-purpose flour
 1 teaspoon salt
 ¼ teaspoon black pepper
 ½ cup heavy cream

1. Put the chicken breast in a medium pot and add about 1½ cups of cold water; bring to a boil over moderate heat. Lower the heat, cover, and simmer just until cooked through, 15 to 18 minutes. Take out and transfer to a plate until cool enough to handle. Reserve the broth. Pull off the skin and bones and cut the chicken into ½-inch dice.

2. The potatoes can be cooked in a microwave or conventional oven. Prick them 6 or 8 times. Cook in a microwave for 6 min-

Creamy, rich, and moist inside while crusty-crunchy deep golden brown on the outside, this hash is sure to be a hit for breakfast, brunch, dinner, or camping trips. Of course you can serve fried eggs atop, but it is also excellent with sautéed mushrooms. Apricots are a good accompaniment, and so are oranges.

utes at high power; remove and wrap tightly in aluminum foil for at least 10 minutes. Unwrap and let cool. In a conventional oven, bake at 350° for 45 minutes to 1 hour, until tender when pierced with a fork. Let cool. Peel the potatoes and cut them into ½-inch dice.

3. Spoon 1 tablespoon of the vegetable oil into a 10- to 12-inch heavy skillet, preferably one with a nonstick surface or a well-seasoned one with gently sloping sides. Add the onion and sauté to soften and lightly brown, about 5 minutes. Scoop out into a large bowl and wipe out the skillet with a paper towel. Add 2 tablespoons of the remaining oil to the pan and place over moderate heat. Keep the pan hot until needed but if it gets too hot, turn the heat down.

4. Add the diced chicken and potatoes to the sautéed onion and stir in 3 tablespoons of the parsley along with the flour, salt, and pepper. Pour in the cream. If dry, add about ¼ cup of the poaching broth (or a little water if using leftover chicken).

5. Dump the mixture into the hot skillet, flatten it slightly, and neaten the edges by pushing them inward with a spatula. Poke 5 or 6 small holes into the hash so steam can escape and let brown over moderate heat, without stirring or disturbing, until crusty and deep golden brown, about 20 minutes. Loosen with a spatula and slide onto a large plate. Add remaining 1 tablespoon oil to pan. Invert another plate over the hash and slide it back into the pan, crust side up. Brown about 5 minutes longer and slide onto serving plate. Garnish top with remaining tablespoon chopped parsley and serve hot.

Spaghetti with Chicken and Green Olive Sauce

MAKES 2 MAIN-COURSE SERVINGS OR

4 PASTA-COURSE SERVINGS

- **1** pound chicken breast, split, or 1½ cups shredded cooked chicken (if using cooked chicken you will also need 2 cups chicken broth)
- **2** slices smoked bacon, cut into small squares
- **1** large onion, peeled and chopped
- **1** large garlic clove, peeled and minced or crushed through a press
- **1** teaspoon dried basil, crumbled
- **1** teaspoon dried oregano, crumbled
- **1** teaspoon ground cumin
- **1** teaspoon salt
- **¼** teaspoon black pepper
- **¼** cup all-purpose flour
- **¼** cup dry sherry or white wine
- **½** cup sliced pimiento-stuffed green olives
- **6** tablespoons chopped fresh parsley
- **½** pound thin spaghetti or vermicelli
- **½** to 1 cup (2 to 4 ounces) coarsely shredded medium Cheddar cheese

1. Put the chicken breast in a heavy medium pot; add 2 cups of cold water. Cover and bring to a boil over moderate heat. Lower the heat and simmer until cooked through to the center when cut with a knife, 15 to 18 minutes. Take out and let cool slightly on a plate. Pull off and discard the skin and bones; tear the meat into coarse shreds. Reserve the broth. (If starting with

Originally I concocted this simple and delicious dish from ingredients that I found in the refrigerator during a moment when I had to put together an impromptu dinner. Now I make it all the time. If you don't want to cook a chicken breast you can make it with leftover cooked chicken and canned broth. If you have some mushrooms you can add them, browned in butter. The Cheddar cheese is a welcome change from Parmesan in a pasta dish.

cooked chicken and canned broth, measure and reserve until needed.)

2. Put the bacon in a heavy medium skillet and cook over moderate heat until crisp and golden brown, 3 to 5 minutes. Add the onion and sauté to soften and lightly brown, 3 to 5 minutes. Add the garlic, basil, oregano, cumin, salt, and pepper; sauté for 1 minute. Stir in the flour (the mixture will be dry) and cook for 1 minute, stirring. Add the 2 cups broth and the sherry or wine. Stirring constantly, bring to a boil; simmer for a minute, until thick. Stir in the olives, 1/4 cup of the parsley, and the shredded chicken; return to the boil, remove from the heat, and cover to keep hot.

3. Bring a large pot of lightly salted water to a boil over high heat. Drop in the spaghetti. Stirring constantly, quickly return to the boil. Stirring frequently, boil until tender but firm to the bite, according to package directions. Drain in a colander and dump into a big bowl. Add the sauce and toss. Add 1/2 cup of the cheese and quickly toss. Serve topped with the remaining 2 tablespoons parsley and additional Cheddar if desired.

Crispy Breaded Cutlets

These tender, juicy chicken cutlets with their golden crumb crust are great served solo, or with lemon or

MAKES 4 SERVINGS

4 skinless boned chicken breast halves, 4 to 6 ounces each
1/4 cup all-purpose flour
2 large eggs
1 cup plain dry bread crumbs

¼ cup grated Parmesan cheese (optional)
1 teaspoon dried oregano, crumbled
½ teaspoon salt
3 tablespoons olive oil
3 tablespoons butter

1. Splash a little cold water over both sides of each chicken breast half and place them smooth side down on separate sheets of waxed paper or heavy plastic wrap; fold out the flap (fillet) to one side; top with a second sheet of waxed paper and pound with a mallet or meat pounder, working gently from the center outward, until the cutlets are between ⅛ and ¼ inch thick. Immediately peel off the top sheets of paper and discard them; pick up the cutlets to prevent them from sticking, but return them to their sheets of paper.

2. Choose three pie pans or shallow dishes for the coating ingredients: Put the flour in one, whisk the eggs in a second, and stir together the bread crumbs, Parmesan, oregano, and salt in the third. Do not coat the cutlets until you are ready to cook them.

3. Place a large heavy skillet over moderately high heat. Add 1½ tablespoons each of the olive oil and butter.

4. Dip one cutlet in flour, turning it to coat both sides lightly. Dip quickly into egg, turning once to coat both sides, and then put into the bread crumb mixture; tap it several times and turn to coat evenly. Put the cutlet into the hot pan, then coat a second cutlet and add it to the pan. Fry until crisp and golden brown, about 2 minutes. It may be necessary to regulate the heat between moderate and moderately high as you cook. Turn and cook until no longer pink in the center, 1 to 2 minutes longer (the only way to tell is by cutting into one). Drain on paper towels. Add the remaining 1½ tablespoons each of olive oil and butter to the pan. Coat and cook the remaining two cutlets in the same manner.

mayonnaise, or when made into Chicken Parmigiana (page 116). When you serve them without tomato sauce, sliced tomatoes are good alongside, and zucchini is always welcome. You can eliminate the grated Parmesan cheese and still cook up beautiful crisp cutlets.

Chicken Parmigiana

You might want to serve spaghetti or linguine with this classic Italian-American favorite; it is also good with a salad and with greens such as Swiss chard, spinach, or Belgian endive browned in olive oil. The sauce can be made a day ahead but the cutlets are best when made fresh. Of course you can also turn this into hero sandwiches by serving on crusty toasted Italian rolls.

MAKES 4 SERVINGS

4 Crispy Breaded Cutlets (page 114)

Tomato Sauce:

1 28-ounce can whole Italian tomatoes, with juice
2½ tablespoons olive oil
2 medium onions, peeled and chopped
1 large garlic clove, peeled and minced or crushed through a press
1 teaspoon dried basil, crumbled
½ teaspoon dried oregano, crumbled
1 bay leaf
2 teaspoons sugar
½ teaspoon salt, or more to taste
¼ teaspoon black pepper
½ cup dry white wine
1 cup (4 ounces) coarsely shredded mozzarella cheese
¼ cup grated Parmesan cheese (preferably Parmigiana Reggiano), plus more for serving, if desired

1. Prepare the chicken cutlets and cover them with aluminum foil until needed.

2. Prepare the tomato sauce: Place a medium sieve over a bowl and pour in the tomatoes and juice. Force tomatoes through with a stiff whisk or a large spoon. Discard the seeds and reserve the juicy purée.

3. Spoon 1½ tablespoons of the olive oil into a heavy medium noncorrosive saucepan and place over moderate heat. Add the onions and sauté to soften but not brown, 3 to 5 minutes. Add the garlic and cook 1 minute longer. Stir in the basil, oregano, bay leaf, sugar, salt, pepper, white wine, and strained tomatoes; bring to a boil over moderate heat. Lower the heat and simmer, stirring once in a while, until slightly thickened and reduced to 2½ cups, 25 to 30 minutes.

4. Meanwhile, combine the shredded mozzarella and remaining 1 tablespoon olive oil in a small bowl and let marinate for at least 15 minutes at room temperature.

5. Prepare the chicken parmigiana: Adjust an oven shelf to the top third of the oven and preheat to 400° for at least 15 minutes. Spread ¼ cup of the tomato sauce in a shallow 13-by-9-inch baking pan.

6. Arrange the four breaded cutlets in the pan and spoon on ½ cup of the tomato sauce. Sprinkle with the marinated mozzarella and spoon on ½ cup more sauce. Sprinkle with grated Parmesan and bake until sizzling hot and the cheese is melted, 10 to 15 minutes. Heat the remaining sauce and serve separately, along with more grated Parmesan, if desired.

Pizza Rustica

Here is a deep-dish double-crusted pie, sometimes called torta rustica, made with yeast dough and a thick hearty filling. The pie can be made hours or even a day ahead of time and is especially suited for an Italian picnic in the countryside, or for a party. You will need a 10-inch springform pan, but in a pinch a cake pan lined with aluminum foil will do. Refrain from adding any salt to the filling because the generous amount of Parmesan will take care of that.

MAKES 8 TO 12 SERVINGS

Dough:

- **1** tablespoon sugar
- **3/4** cup warm water (105° to 115°)
- **1** 1/4-ounce package active dry yeast
- **3** cups all-purpose flour
- **2** tablespoons olive oil
- **1/2** teaspoon salt

Filling:

- **2** tablespoons olive oil
- **2** medium onions, peeled and chopped
- **2** large garlic cloves, peeled and minced or crushed through a press
- **1** pound skinless boned chicken breasts, cut into 3/4-inch cubes
- **1/2** pound (2 to 3 links) sweet Italian sausage
- **1/4** cup (1 1/2 ounces) thinly sliced pepperoni, quartered
- **1/2** pound fresh mushrooms, sliced
- **2** teaspoons dried basil
- **1** teaspoon dried oregano
- **1/2** teaspoon dried thyme
- **1/4** cup all-purpose flour
- **1** cup milk
- **1** large egg, slightly beaten
- **1/4** teaspoon black pepper
- **1** 14- to 16-ounce can whole peeled tomatoes, halved, seeded, drained, and coarsely chopped
- **1** 6-ounce can whole pitted medium or large black olives, drained and sliced

1 cup (about 4 ounces) grated Parmesan cheese
⅓ cup chopped parsley
¼ cup plain dry bread crumbs

Topping:

1 egg yolk
1 teaspoon water
1 tablespoon sesame seeds

1. Make the dough: Spoon the sugar into a small bowl and pour in ½ cup of the warm water; stir once or twice and sprinkle the yeast over the surface. Wait a minute and then stir to dissolve. Let proof until foamy and doubled in bulk, about 5 minutes.

2. Place the flour in a food processor (or a large bowl if mixing by hand). Add the olive oil and salt. Stir the proofed yeast and add it to the flour. With motor running, pour in the remaining ¼ cup water to make a soft sticky dough. If the dough does not hold together, add a tablespoon more water; process to knead for about 2 minutes and then knead on a lightly floured surface by hand for a minute, adding a tablespoon more flour if necessary to prevent sticking (but the dough should remain very soft). If making the dough by hand, knead on a floured surface for about 10 minutes, until smooth. Put in a large lightly oiled bowl, turning once to oil the top. Cover and let rise in a warm draft-free place until doubled in bulk, 1 to 1½ hours. Punch down and let rest until ready to shape. If it rises again, punch down and let rest a few minutes before rolling.

3. Make the filling: Spoon 1 tablespoon of the olive oil into a large heavy skillet and place over moderate heat. Add the onions and sauté to soften, about 3 minutes. Add the garlic and cook a minute longer. Scrape onto a plate and reserve. Add the remaining tablespoon of olive oil to the skillet and turn the heat to moderately high. Add the chicken cubes and brown, stirring once or twice after one side has browned, 2 to 3 minutes (don't cook the chicken completely through, as it will finish cooking when the pie bakes). Turn onto the plate with the onions and reserve.

4. With a knife, slit the sausage links lengthwise and crumble the meat into the skillet; brown well over moderate heat and spoon off and discard the fat. Add the pepperoni and cook for a minute. Again, spoon off any fat or blot with a paper towel. Add the mushrooms, basil, oregano, and thyme. Stir in 2 to 3 tablespoons of water and cook until the mushrooms are tender and the liquid has evaporated, about 3 minutes. Stir in the flour and cook for a minute. Pour in the milk and cook, stirring, until thickened and boiling. Stir in the chicken and onion mixture and cook for another minute. Spoon into a large bowl and let cool for 10 minutes. Stir in the egg and pepper. Fold in the tomato pieces, olives, Parmesan cheese, and parsley. Cool to room temperature.

5. Assembly: Position an oven shelf in the center of the oven and preheat to 375°. Lightly oil a 10-inch springform pan. Punch the dough down and let rest for 5 minutes. On a lightly floured surface, roll the dough to a 12-inch round. Now, don't roll the center anymore; you want it to remain slightly thicker. Roll the dough to an 18- to 20-inch round slightly thicker in the center. Fold into quarters; place in the pan, point in the center, and unfold so the dough hangs over the pan all around. Gently pull and push the dough to conform to the inside of the pan. Sprinkle the bread crumbs in the bottom and spoon in all of the filling. Bring the overhanging dough up and over the filling from two opposite sides, then from the two other opposite sides; bring the rest in, pleating evenly and pinching so the filling is covered but there is a 1-inch steam hole in the center. It's okay if it looks a little sloppy; it will bake up beautifully.

6. Topping: In a small bowl stir together the egg yolk and water. Dip a pastry brush into water and then paint the top of the pizza rustica with the egg yolk glaze, using most of it. Sprinkle with the sesame seeds and bake for 1 hour and 15 minutes, until deep golden brown and hollow-sounding when tapped. Cool in the pan on a rack for at least 1 hour before serving (this pie remains hot for a long time and is perfect, to my taste, after 3 hours). Remove pan sides and cut the pie into wedges. Serve hot, warm, or at room temperature. Refrigerate any leftovers. If you make it a day ahead, cool completely before refrigerating.

Chicken Rollatini with Polenta and Chunky Tomato Sauce

This is a rustic home-style Italian dinner of savory chicken rolls stuffed with ham and cheese, surrounded with polenta (pan-fried cornmeal cakes) and chunky tomato sauce. You can make it as much as a day ahead. Consider serving a seafood antipasto and braised fennel bulbs or green beans on the side.

MAKES 4 SERVINGS

Polenta:

- 3/4 cup coarse yellow cornmeal
- 1 1/2 teaspoons salt
- 1/3 cup grated Parmesan cheese
- 2 tablespoons butter

Chicken Rollatini:

- 3 tablespoons butter, softened
- 1 medium garlic clove, peeled and minced or crushed through a press
- 1/3 cup grated Parmesan cheese
- 1/3 cup chopped Italian parsley leaves
- 1/3 cup (1 3/4 ounce) finely chopped smoked ham or prosciutto
- 4 large skinless boned chicken breast halves (1 1/2 pounds total)

Tomato Sauce:

- 1/4 cup olive oil
- 1 large 8-ounce onion, peeled and chopped
- 2 large garlic cloves, peeled and minced or crushed through a press
- 2 teaspoons dried basil, crumbled
- 1 teaspoon dried oregano, crumbled
- 1/2 teaspoon dried rosemary, crumbled
- 1 bay leaf
- 1/2 teaspoon salt

1/4 teaspoon black pepper
1 28-ounce can whole Italian tomatoes, with juice
1 cup dry white wine
3 tablespoons tomato paste
2 teaspoons sugar (optional)
2 tablespoons chopped parsley
2 tablespoons grated Parmesan cheese

1. Prepare the polenta: In a medium bowl stir the cornmeal with 3/4 cup cold water. In a heavy medium pot combine 2 cups of water with the salt and bring to a boil over high heat. Stir the cornmeal mixture and add it all at once, stirring the water in the pan as you add it. Stirring constantly, bring to a boil over low heat. Cook until very thick and beginning to pull away from the sides of the pan, stirring constantly, for 10 to 15 minutes. Remove from the heat and stir in the Parmesan cheese and the butter. Pour into an ungreased 12-by-8-inch glass platter or onto a porcelain dish and spread so it is about 1/2 inch thick. Cool to room temperature so the polenta sets. The polenta can be made a day ahead, covered, and refrigerated.

2. Prepare the chicken rollatini: In a small bowl stir together the butter, garlic, Parmesan, parsley, and ham to make a filling.

3. Splash each chicken breast half with cold water and place each one smooth side down on a separate square of waxed paper; fold out the flap of flesh to one side. Top each with a second sheet of waxed paper and pound with a mallet or a meat pounder, working gently from the center outward, until between 1/8 and 1/4 inch thick. Remove the top sheets of paper and discard. Spread each cutlet with a scant 3 tablespoons of the filling. Staring with one small end, roll up tightly, jelly roll fashion, with the aid of the waxed paper, unpeeling it as you roll.

Secure each roll by piercing it directly with three toothpicks through the center and one at each end (be sure to count them so you will know to remove all 20 before serving).

4. Prepare the tomato sauce: Spoon 2 tablespoons of the olive oil into a large heavy noncorrosive skillet and place over moderately high heat. Add all the chicken rolls and brown very well, about 3 minutes per side. Take them out with a spatula and transfer them to a plate to catch any juices.

5. Add the onion to the skillet and sauté over moderate heat to soften and color lightly, about 5 minutes. Stir in the garlic, basil, oregano, rosemary, bay leaf, salt, and pepper. Cut up the tomatoes and add them along with their juice and the white wine. Stir in the tomato paste and bring to a boil. Taste for acidity and add the sugar if desired. Return the chicken and any juice that has accumulated on the plate. Spoon the sauce up over the rolls; cover and simmer until the chicken is cooked through, 30 to 35 minutes. Scoop out the chicken rollatini and remove all 20 toothpicks. Return the chicken to the sauce to keep hot.

6. Using a 2-inch round cutter, cut out as many cakes of polenta as possible, overlapping the cuts by about 1/4 inch so that there is as little waste as possible (it doesn't matter if they are not perfectly round; the dish is a rustic one and this just adds to that quality). You will have 24 irregular rounds.

7. Spoon 1 tablespoon of the remaining olive oil into a large heavy skillet, preferably with a nonstick surface, and place over moderately high heat. Add half the polenta cakes and brown well, 3 to 4 minutes. Carefully turn with a spatula (they are delicate) and brown the other side for about 3 minutes. The first side of browning is the most important since they are turned only once. They should be speckled brown. Repeat with the remaining 1 tablespoon olive oil and remaining cakes of polenta.

8. Take the rollatini from the sauce and transfer to a board.

Cut each into 7 slices. Spread 4 dinner plates with the sauce, using about 1 cup for each. Arrange a sliced rollatini in the center and 6 slices of polenta around the edges of each plate. Sprinkle each with 2 teaspoons each of the chopped parsley and grated Parmesan. Serve hot.

Chicken Ravioli with Tomato Sauce

MAKES 8 DOZEN (6 TO 8 SERVINGS)

1¼ pounds fresh Homemade Pasta (page 366) or 8 dozen fresh wonton skins (see Note).

Chicken Filling:

- 1 pound skinless boned chicken breasts, cut in 1-inch cubes
- ¼ cup all-purpose flour
- 2 tablespoons olive oil
- ½ pound (3 medium links) sweet Italian sausage
- ½ teaspoon dried basil, crumbled
- ¼ teaspoon grated nutmeg
- ½ teaspoon salt
- ¼ teaspoon black pepper
- ½ cup dry white wine
- ¾ cup light cream or half and half
- 1 large egg
- ¼ cup grated Parmesan cheese

These tender little pockets of pasta have a filling and sauce of double chicken that is double-browned for double the flavor. You can make the pasta, filling, and sauce a day or two ahead of time. This dish makes a delicious dinner when the antipasto is stuffed clams or celeries, and a green vegetable such as escarole, broccoli, or spinach is served alongside. If you don't want to make homemade pasta you can substitute wonton skins and make triangular-shaped ravioli. Be sure to buy 4 ounces extra chicken breast for the sauce when you buy for the stuffing.

Tomato Sauce:

¼ cup olive oil

2 medium onions, peeled and finely chopped

4 ounces skinless boned chicken breast, finely minced with a knife or in the food processor

3 large garlic cloves, peeled and minced or crushed through a press

2 28-ounce cans whole peeled Italian tomatoes

¼ cup tomato paste

1 cup dry white wine

1 bay leaf

2 teaspoons dried basil, crumbled

1 teaspoon dried oregano, crumbled

1 teaspoon salt

¼ teaspoon black pepper

1 teaspoon sugar (optional)

For Serving:

½ cup grated Parmesan cheese

1. If the pasta has been made ahead of time, remove from the refrigerator and allow to return to room temperature.

2. Prepare the chicken filling: Toss the chicken cubes in a bag with 3 tablespoons of the flour. Spoon the olive oil into a large heavy skillet and place over moderately high heat. Add all of the chicken cubes and brown very well without stirring, until deep golden brown, 3 to 4 minutes. Turn the cubes and brown 2 to 3 minutes longer. Remove from the heat.

3. Remove the sausages from their casings and crumble into a heavy medium skillet. Place over moderate heat and brown well, about 5 minutes, stirring occasionally. Scoop out with a slotted spoon and drain on paper towels. Add sausage to the pan of chicken. Add the remaining 1 tablespoon flour to the pan containing the chicken-sausage mixture and stir over moderate heat for a minute or two. Add the basil, nutmeg, salt, pepper, and wine. Stirring, bring to a boil and cook until very thick, 1 to 2 minutes. Add the light cream and stir until very thick, 3 to 4 minutes. Cool to room temperature.

4. Transfer the chicken-sausage mixture to a food processor and grind finely (alternatively, put through a meat grinder). Add the egg and Parmesan and blend briefly (or stir into the ground mixture if you used a meat grinder). Cover and chill until needed. The stuffing should be stiff.

5. Prepare the tomato sauce: Spoon 2 tablespoons of the olive oil into a large noncorrosive saucepan and place over moderate heat. Add the onions and sauté to soften and lightly color, about 5 minutes. Turn onto a plate and reserve. Spoon 1 tablespoon of the remaining olive oil into the pan and place over moderately high heat. Add the minced chicken breast and stir well so all the pieces are coated with oil, then let brown very well without stirring for 3 to 4 minutes. Stir and brown a minute or two longer. Reduce the heat to low; add the garlic and sauté for 30 seconds. Return the onions and cook for a minute. Remove from the heat.

6. Place a strainer over a bowl. Working over the strainer, cut the tomatoes, one at a time, in half crosswise and gently squeeze out the seeds. Cut each half in 3 or 4 pieces and add to the pan of sautéed onions and chicken. Measure the strained tomato juice and add 2 cups to the pan (reserve the rest for another use). Stir in the tomato paste and wine. Add the bay leaf, basil, oregano, salt, pepper, and optional sugar. Bring to a boil over moderate heat, stirring occasionally. Lower the heat and simmer until slightly thickened and the flavor intensifies, about 30 minutes. Stir in the remaining 1 tablespoon olive oil. If making ahead, cool to room temperature and then chill, covered.

7. Shape the ravioli: Shape the pasta into a rectangle and cut into 4 equal pieces. Dust them with flour and pat each into a 3-by-5-inch rectangle. Working on a large lightly floured surface, and using a pasta machine (either hand-cranked or electric rollers), pass the pieces of pasta through the widest setting 3 times to knead further. Continue passing them through, reducing the space between the rollers each time, until the pasta is very thin. As they become too long to handle, cut the pieces in half. You will have 8 pieces about 4 inches wide and 24 inches long. Keep them covered while not working with them to prevent drying (if you stack them, lightly dust with flour so they don't stick together).

8. Using a spoon or a pastry bag fitted with a plain ½-inch tip, shape 1½-teaspoon mounds of the chicken filling and place them on one strip of the dough in two long rows, ¾ inch in from the outside edges; leave 1 inch between mounds. Dip a brush into water and lightly moisten the dough around the filling (this is easiest to do by painting lengthwise along the two edges and the center and then crosswise between the mounds). Carefully place a second sheet of dough on top, starting at one end and using your finger to press it in the center. Press around each mound, pressing out any air. Cut filled dough into 2-inch squares with a pastry wheel or sharp knife. Lightly dust a baking sheet with coarse cornmeal or flour. One at a time, pick up the ravioli and squeeze all around to make sure they are sealed. Place on floured baking sheet. Repeat to use all the dough. Let dry for about an hour, turning them once or twice, or cover and refrigerate until needed.

9. Fill one or two large pots with water and add a little salt to each. (A large dutch oven will comfortably hold about 4 dozen.) Cover and bring to a boil over high heat. Quickly add the ravioli one at a time, stir once or twice, cover again, and return to the boil as quickly as possible. Uncover once the full boil has returned and then lower the heat slightly to keep at a gentle boil. Stir once in a while; cook until tender but firm to the bite (al dente). This will vary from between 4 and 6 minutes to 8 to 12, depending on their thickness and how long they have dried. To test, remove one with a slotted spoon and cut off a corner; bite into it to check for doneness. Drain ravioli in a large colander or scoop out with a strainer.

10. To serve: Toss all of the ravioli with about 4 cups of the hot tomato sauce. Mound on a platter and spoon the remaining sauce over the top. Sprinkle with 2 tablespoons of the grated Parmesan cheese and pass the remainder separately.

NOTE: Instead of making fresh pasta you can start with 8 dozen wonton skins of medium thickness (available in oriental markets). Instead of sealing with water, mix 1 egg yolk with 1 teaspoon water and brush along 2 edges after putting filling in center; then fold over and make triangular-shaped ravioli. Boil only 3 to 5 minutes, just until tender.

Chinese Chicken and Asparagus Salad

Totally addictive, this simple-to-make dish, slightly sweet and sour and a little hot, is good for a summer picnic.

MAKES 4 SERVINGS (6 CUPS)

2 pounds thin to medium fresh asparagus
2 tablespoons vegetable oil
3 large garlic cloves, peeled and minced or crushed through a press
1 pound skinless boned chicken breasts, thinly sliced across the grain (partially freeze to facilitate slicing if desired)
3 tablespoons sugar
3 tablespoons rice vinegar
2 tablespoons oriental sesame oil
1/2 teaspoon dried hot red pepper flakes
1 teaspoon salt
1/4 teaspoon black pepper

1. Snap off the toughest portion of the asparagus stems where the stalks easily break. Cut the stalks on the diagonal into 2- to 3-inch lengths. Drop into a large pot of lightly salted boiling water and cook 1 minute after the boil returns. Drain and re-fresh under cold running water. Drain again.

2. Spoon the vegetable oil into a large heavy wok or skillet and place over moderately high heat. Add the garlic and cook 10 seconds. Add the chicken and stir-fry until cooked, 2 to 3 minutes. Remove from the heat.

3. In a large bowl stir together the sugar, rice vinegar, sesame oil, hot pepper flakes, salt, and pepper. Add the chicken and asparagus; toss to coat the chicken and asparagus with dress-ing. Cover and chill 1 to 2 hours. Serve cold.

Maryland Chicken Cakes

MAKES 6 LARGE CAKES

1½ pounds skinless boned chicken breasts and/or thighs, or 4 cups shredded cooked chicken
2 large garlic cloves, peeled and sliced
4 tablespoons (½ stick) butter
1 medium onion, peeled and finely chopped
3 large eggs
1 teaspoon Tabasco sauce
½ cup Mayonnaise (page 383)
1¼ cups fine soda cracker crumbs, ground in a food processor or rolled between sheets of aluminum foil
¼ cup chopped fresh parsley leaves
2 tablespoons fresh lemon juice
1 teaspoon salt
¼ teaspoon black pepper
3 tablespoons olive oil

I used to make these savory patties with crabmeat, but now that it's $23.00 a pound I've switched to chicken, producing a whole new dish. I like to start by poaching breasts and thighs but once in a while I make them to use up leftovers.

1. Put the chicken breasts and/or thighs and garlic in a medium saucepan and add water to almost cover. Bring to a boil over moderate heat. Lower the heat, cover the pot, and poach until just cooked, 8 to 10 minutes. Take out and let cool. Reserve the broth for another use. Tear the chicken into shreds with your fingers; they should be about ¼ inch wide and 2 inches long.

2. Melt 2 tablespoons of the butter in a small skillet over moderate heat. Add the onion and sauté to soften, 3 to 5 minutes. Let cool.

3. In a large bowl whisk together the eggs and Tabasco sauce. Stir in the shredded chicken, sautéed onion, mayonnaise, ¼ cup of the cracker crumbs, parsley, lemon juice, salt, and pepper. Put the remaining 1 cup cracker crumbs on a plate.

4. Spoon 1 tablespoon each of butter and olive oil into a heavy medium skillet and place over moderate heat.

5. Using a ½-cup measure, scoop ½ cup of the chicken mixture and turn it out onto the crumbs. Tap so the crumbs adhere and turn carefully with a spatula to coat the other side with crumbs. Using the spatula, put the cake into the hot pan. Repeat twice more and cook 3 chicken cakes at once, turning them after they are golden brown, 4 to 5 minutes per side. Keep them warm while you repeat with remaining ingredients, to make 6 chicken cakes. Serve hot with cold Cole Slaw (page 376).

Cold Sesame Noodles with Chicken and Roasted Peanuts

This platterful of cold noodles is always welcome during the hot summer days and nights. It can be made well in advance of serving and is good for outdoor barbecues and picnics. By the way, always store sesame seeds and sesame paste in the refrigerator so they remain fresh longer.

MAKES 6 SERVINGS (ABOUT 8 CUPS)

1½ pound whole chicken breast, split
¼ cup dry sherry
3 tablespoons grated fresh ginger
4 large garlic cloves, peeled, 2 sliced and 2 minced
3 whole cloves
¼ cup soy sauce
1 tablespoon peanut oil
½ teaspoon dried hot red pepper flakes
¼ cup sesame paste (tahini) or sesame butter
3 tablespoons chunky or smooth peanut butter
1 tablespoon oriental sesame oil
2 tablespoons rice vinegar
1 tablespoon sugar
½ pound dried thin linguine or spaghetti

5 medium Kirby pickling cucumbers, or 2 large cucumbers
¼ cup coarsely chopped peanuts
1 tablespoon sesame seeds
2 medium scallions, thinly sliced, including green parts

1. Put the chicken breast halves into a heavy medium pot; add 1 cup cold water along with the sherry, 1 tablespoon of the grated ginger, the two sliced garlic cloves, and the 3 whole cloves. Place over moderate heat and bring to a boil. Cover and simmer over low heat, turning once or twice, just until cooked to the bone, 20 to 25 minutes. Take out and transfer to a plate until cool enough to handle. Add 1 tablespoon of the remaining ginger to the broth and boil over high heat until reduced to ⅔ cup, about 5 minutes. Strain, pressing on the solids with the back of a spoon. Spoon off the fat from the top of the broth. You should have ½ cup strong broth. Cool to room temperature.

2. Pull the skin from the chicken and pull the meat from the bones. Discard the skin and bones. Tear the chicken into shreds about ¼ inch wide. Toss with 1 tablespoon of the soy sauce and ¼ cup of the reduced broth. Cover and reserve.

3. Spoon the peanut oil into a small heavy skillet. Add the 2 minced garlic cloves and the hot pepper flakes; sizzle over low heat for a minute to soften but not color. Let cool.

4. In a medium bowl stir together the sesame paste, peanut butter, and sesame oil until blended. In a cup combine the remaining ¼ cup reduced broth, 2 tablespoons soy sauce, rice vinegar, and sugar; gradually stir into the sesame mixture to make a dressing; stir in the garlic-pepper oil.

5. Break the linguine in half and drop into a large pot of lightly salted boiling water. Stir constantly with a long fork until the boil resumes and frequently thereafter until tender but firm to the bite, 7 to 8 minutes. Drain; rinse under cold water and drain again.

6. In a large bowl toss the noodles with the sesame dressing and shredded chicken.

7. Cut off the ends of each cucumber and peel. Cut in half lengthwise and scoop out the seeds with a spoon. Cut the cucumbers crosswise into ¼-inch slices.

8. In a small dry skillet combine the chopped peanuts and sesame seeds; toast over moderate heat, tossing, until golden, 1 to 2 minutes.

9. Arrange the pasta-chicken salad on a large platter; scatter the cucumber slices over the top and sprinkle with the peanuts, sesame seeds, and sliced scallions. Serve cold, sprinkled with the remaining 1 tablespoon soy sauce.

Chicken Lo Mein

Lo mein indicates soft stir-fried noodles (as opposed to chow mein, which are crisp-fried). As they cook they are scooped and lifted from the wok and tossed back. Here the chicken is velvetized in water to make it delectable. The slurpy noodles are a good

MAKES 2 TO 4 SERVINGS

Velvetized Chicken:

½ pound skinless boned chicken breast
1 egg white
1 tablespoon dry sherry
1 tablespoon cornstarch
½ teaspoon salt
1 tablespoon vegetable oil

Stir-fried Noodles:

10 dried Chinese mushrooms
¾ pound fresh thin egg noodles or ½ pound dried thin spaghetti

1 tablespoon oriental sesame oil
2 tablespoons soy sauce
2 tablespoons vegetable oil
1 large garlic clove, peeled and sliced
8 medium scallions, cut into 1-inch lengths
2 cups fresh bean sprouts
1/2 teaspoon salt

contrast to the crunchy bean sprouts and deep Chinese mushroom flavor. You can start with soft fresh noodles or dried thin spaghetti.

1. Velvetize the chicken: Cut the chicken into thin strips about 2 inches long and 1/4 inch wide. In a medium bowl stir together the egg white, sherry, cornstarch, and salt; add the chicken and let marinate at room temperature for about 30 minutes.

2. Pour 3 cups of water into a medium saucepan and bring to a boil over high heat. Turn off the heat, add the vegetable oil, and slide in the chicken. Stir a couple of times and let stand for 30 seconds. Drain in a sieve and reserve on a plate.

3. Prepare the stir-fried noodles: While the chicken is marinating, put the dried mushrooms in a small bowl; add 1 cup boiling water. Let soften for about 30 minutes. Drain, reserving 1/4 cup of the soaking liquid. Cut off and discard the stems. Cut the caps into 1/4-inch slices.

4. Bring a large pot of lightly salted water to a boil over high heat. Drop in the fresh egg noodles and, stirring frequently, cook until tender but firm to the bite, 2 to 3 minutes. Drain and rinse with cold water. (If using thin spaghetti, boil until tender but firm, 8 to 10 minutes.) Toss in a large bowl with the sesame oil and 1 tablespoon of the soy sauce.

5. Place a large heavy wok or skillet on high heat. Spoon in the vegetable oil and tilt the pan to coat. Add the garlic and stir-fry for 10 to 30 seconds, to lightly color. Scoop out garlic and discard. Add the scallions, bean sprouts, and reserved sliced mushrooms; stir-fry for 30 seconds. Add the noodles and stir-fry, scooping them with two big spoons, lifting them and turning them, for 1 minute over high heat. Add the chicken, reserved mushroom liquid, remaining 1 tablespoon soy sauce, and the salt; toss about 30 seconds longer. Turn out onto a platter and serve hot.

Chinese-American Chicken Chow Mein

This is the kind of chicken chow mein that most people are familiar with. To me it's 1950s comfort food and takes me straight back to my childhood and the days when my father used to take our family to dinner in L.A.'s Chinatown. It's not stir-fried at all, but cooked in broth, so it's not very high in calories. If you're looking for the authentic way to make

MAKES 4 SERVINGS

4 cups (½ pound) coarsely shredded Napa cabbage
3 medium ribs celery, cut into sticks ¼ by 2 inches
1 large onion, peeled and cut lengthwise into ¼-inch-wide shreds
1½ cups Basic Chicken Stock (page 47) or canned broth
1 garlic clove, peeled and minced or crushed through a press (optional)
1 to 2 tablespoons light soy sauce
1 teaspoon salt
3 cups (½ pound) fresh bean sprouts
2 tablespoons cornstarch
½ pound skinless boned chicken breast, cut into strips ⅛ by ½ by 2 inches
2 teaspoons oriental sesame oil
4 ounces crisp Chinese noodles

1. In a large bowl combine the cabbage, celery, and onion; pour 6 cups boiling water over them and let stand 3 minutes. Drain in a colander.

2. In a large heavy wok or dutch oven combine the chicken broth, garlic, soy sauce, and salt; bring to a boil over high heat. Add the bean sprouts and return to the boil. Add the reserved vegetable mixture and return to the boil. Dissolve the cornstarch in 2 tablespoons cold water. Add to the pot along with the chicken and bring to a boil, stirring, to thicken the sauce and just cook the chicken. Remove from the heat and stir in the sesame oil. Serve hot, over the crisp Chinese noodles.

chow mein, see the next recipe.

Chicken Chow Mein

MAKES 4 SERVINGS

Sauce:

1½ tablespoons cornstarch
1 cup Basic Chicken Stock (page 47) or canned broth
1 tablespoon dry sherry
1 teaspoon salt

Velvetized Chicken:

1 tablespoon cornstarch
2 tablespoons dry sherry
1 egg white
5 thin slices fresh ginger
½ teaspoon salt
½ pound skinless boned chicken breast, sliced ⅛ inch thick across the grain
1 tablespoon peanut oil

People conjure up the wrong image when chicken chow mein is mentioned. Chow mein refers to fried noodles, usually well browned on both sides, and topped with a stir-fry of meat and vegetables. If you can't find fresh egg noodles, substitute dried angel hair pasta (capelli d'angelo).

Noodle Pancake:

3/4 pound thin fresh egg noodles or ½ pound dried angel hair pasta

3 tablespoons peanut oil

2 teaspoons soy sauce

Stir-Fry:

2 tablespoons peanut oil

2 large garlic cloves, peeled and sliced

2 medium ribs celery, cut in ¼-by-2-inch sticks

2 medium onions, peeled and cut lengthwise into ¼-inch slivers

¼ pound fresh snow peas, trimmed and cut lengthwise into ¼-inch-wide strips

2 cups coarsely shredded Napa cabbage or green cabbage

1 8-ounce can sliced water chestnuts, or 1 cup sliced fresh peeled water chestnuts

2 tablespoons chopped leaves of celery heart

1 teaspoon oriental sesame oil

1. Make the sauce: In a small bowl stir together the cornstarch, chicken stock, sherry, and salt.

2. Velvetize the chicken: In a medium bowl stir together the cornstarch and sherry. Stir in the egg white, ginger, and salt. Add the chicken and let marinate at room temperature for 30 minutes.

3. Pour 3 cups of water into a medium saucepan and bring to a boil over high heat. Turn off the heat. Add the peanut oil and slide in the chicken. Stir once or twice and let stand for 30 seconds. Drain in a sieve and then reserve on a plate.

4. Make the noodle pancake: Bring a large pot of lightly salted water to a boil over high heat; add the pasta and cook for a minute if using fresh. If using dried pasta, cook until tender but firm to the bite, about 3 minutes. Drain thoroughly. Toss in a large bowl with 1 tablespoon of the peanut oil and all the soy sauce.

5. Place a large cast-iron skillet or wok over high heat. Add the remaining 2 tablespoons peanut oil. Swirl in a handful of the pasta, then add the remainder, patting it down to make an even layer. Poke a wooden spoon handle in 6 spots to make steam vents. Reduce the heat to moderately high and cook until the pancake is golden brown on the bottom, 3 to 5 minutes. Loosen the edges and flip over with a spatula. Cook until golden brown on the second side, about 3 minutes longer. Slide the pancake onto a plate. Cover and keep warm. Cut into quarters before topping.

6. Stir-fry: Place a large heavy wok over high heat. Add the peanut oil and garlic; sizzle for 5 to 10 seconds, then scoop out the garlic with a slotted spoon and discard it. Add the celery, onions, and snow peas; stir-fry for 1 minute. Add the cabbage, water chestnuts, and celery leaves; stir-fry from 30 seconds to a minute longer. Add the chicken. Give the sauce a good stir and add it, too; cook, stirring, until the sauce boils and thickens; stir in the sesame oil. Spoon over the noodle pancake and serve hot.

Cold Chicken with Potatoes and Tomatoes

Here is one of my favorite cold dishes for hot-weather entertaining. It is a salad-like main dish layered with sliced potatoes, chicken breast, and creamy cilantro dressing. The topping is a colorful scattering of little peeled cherry tomatoes. If you have enough leftover cooked chicken breast you can skip Step 2 of the recipe.

MAKES 6 SERVINGS

- **8** medium red-skinned potatoes (2 pounds)
- **1½-** to 1¾-pound whole chicken breast
- **2** large garlic cloves, peeled and sliced
- **¾** cup sour cream
- **½** cup Mayonnaise (page 383)
- **2** tablespoons lime juice
- **¼** cup chopped cilantro, plus 12 sprigs for garnish
- **3** medium scallions, finely minced, including green parts
- **3** medium fresh jalapeño chile peppers
- **1½** teaspoons salt
- **¼** teaspoon black pepper
- **1** pint cherry tomatoes

1. Put the potatoes in a large saucepan and add enough cold water to cover by 1 inch. Bring to a boil over high heat; partially cover and boil until tender, 25 to 30 minutes. Drain and cool to room temperature.

2. Place the chicken breast in a heavy medium pot with the garlic and 3 cups of cold water. Bring to a boil over moderate heat. Cover and simmer over low heat just until cooked through, about 20 minutes. Remove and cool to room temperature.

3. In a medium bowl whisk together the sour cream, mayonnaise, and lime juice. Stir in the chopped cilantro and scallions.

4. Wearing protective gloves if desired, slice off the stem ends from the chile peppers. Cut lengthwise in quarters and slice off the seeds and ribs flush with the peppers. If a hot dressing is desired, chop and reserve about ½ teaspoon of the seeds (this is where the heat is contained); discard the remainder. Cut the peppers lengthwise in fine slivers, then chop finely. Add to the dressing along with the salt and pepper. The dressing should taste a little salty because the potatoes will absorb most of it.

5. Bring a large pot of lightly salted water to a boil over high heat. Drop in the tomatoes and time for 20 seconds. Drain and rinse in a bowl of cold water. Drain again. With a paring knife, remove the stems and peel the tomatoes, taking care to leave them whole. Chill them.

6. Peel the potatoes and cut them into ¼-inch slices. Spread about a quarter of the dressing on a large (about 10-by-14-inch) platter. Arrange all of the potato slices over the dressing in an overlapping pattern. Spoon half of the remaining dressing over them.

7. Pull the skin from the chicken, then pull the meat from the bones, keeping each half intact. Discard the skin and bones. Cut the chicken across the grain into ¼-inch-thick slices. Arrange all of the chicken over the potatoes and spread the remaining dressing over the top. Cover and chill for at least 1 hour, or as long as a day. Uncover and scatter the peeled tomatoes over the top, adding a pinch of salt to the top of each. Garnish with the cilantro sprigs. Serve cold.

Spicy Grilled Citrus Chicken

In a sense, the zesty marinade used to flavor the chicken breasts is related to Mexican *sangrita*, because tomato, orange, and lime are combined to make a luscious barbecue sauce with a kick of hot pepper and a lick of honey. Note that the chicken needs lengthy marination; this isn't a spur-of-the-moment recipe.

MAKES 6 SERVINGS

1 6-ounce can frozen orange juice concentrate, thawed
1/2 cup canned tomato purée
1/4 cup honey
1 teaspoon minced or grated orange zest (see Note)
1 teaspoon minced or grated lemon zest
1 teaspoon minced or grated lime zest
3 tablespoons fresh lemon juice
3 tablespoons fresh lime juice
4 garlic cloves, peeled and crushed through a press
1 teaspoon dried thyme, crumbled
3/4 teaspoon cayenne pepper
3/4 teaspoon freshly ground black pepper
1 teaspoon salt
6 chicken breast halves (about 1/2 pound each), with skin and bones

1. In a large bowl, combine the orange juice concentrate, tomato purée, honey, orange, lemon, and lime zest, lemon and lime juice, garlic, thyme, cayenne, black pepper, and salt. Mix to blend well. Add the chicken pieces and turn to coat; cover and refrigerate 12 hours or overnight.
2. Light a charcoal fire. When the coals are glowing, place a lightly oiled grill about 5 inches above them and heat for 5 minutes. Remove the chicken from the marinade; reserve the marinade. Place the chicken, bone side down, on the grill. Cook for 5 minutes.
3. Meanwhile, pour the marinade into a small nonaluminum saucepan and bring to a boil over moderate heat. Boil for 1 minute. After the chicken has grilled for 5 minutes, spoon some

of the marinade over each piece and turn. Grill, basting with marinade and turning every 5 minutes, for 20 to 30 minutes, until the chicken is white throughout but still juicy.

NOTE: Zest, the outer layer of orange, lemon, or lime peel, is easiest to remove with a zester, a tool that has 5 tiny holes designed for scraping the peel. Finely mince the strands of zest with a knife. If you don't have this tool, simply grate the rind.

Greek Feta Chicken

MAKES 4 SERVINGS

4 skinless boned chicken breast halves, about 6 ounces each
1 cup plain yogurt
2 tablespoons olive oil
1 large garlic clove, peeled and minced or crushed through a press
1 teaspoon dried rosemary or oregano, crumbled
½ teaspoon salt
½ teaspoon black pepper
1 cup (about 4 ounces) crumbled feta cheese
2 tablespoons chopped fresh parsley

1. Trim any fat and tendons from the chicken.
2. In a shallow glass dish stir together the yogurt, olive oil, garlic, rosemary, salt, and pepper. Add the breast halves, turning to coat, and marinate at room temperature for 30 minutes (or up to an hour in the refrigerator).
3. Preheat the broiler. Take the chicken from the marinade

I think that this simple dish tastes best at room temperature so I often contribute it to picnics. It is especially good served with sliced tomatoes, cucumbers, and Greek olives. Of course crusty bread is welcome, too. If you are cutting calories, leave out the olive oil and this will be a tasty diet dish.

(reserve the marinade) and place the halves smooth side down on a foil-lined broiler pan (or heavy flameproof metal platter). Broil 5 to 7 minutes. Turn and spoon reserved marinade over the chicken. Top with the crumbled feta and broil until the tops are lightly browned and the breasts are no longer pink when you cut into one, 5 to 7 minutes longer. Remove from the broiler, sprinkle with parsley, and serve hot, or cool to room temperature and serve.

Chicken alla Francese

This is a popular dish in New York Italian restaurants. The light egg coating soaks up some of the tangy lemon-wine and broth, and it holds up well so you can prepare the dish well in advance of serving. Pasta or roasted potatoes are good accompaniments, as are green beans amandine.

MAKES 4 SERVINGS

- 4 skinless boned chicken breast halves, 4 to 6 ounces each
- 1/3 cup all-purpose flour
- 2 large eggs
- 2 tablespoons vegetable oil
- 1 tablespoon olive oil
- 2 large garlic cloves, peeled and minced or crushed through a press
- 1 cup dry white wine
- 1 cup Basic Chicken Stock (page 47) or canned broth
- 3 tablespoons chopped parsley
- 1 tablespoon fresh lemon juice
- 1 tablespoon butter
- 1/2 teaspoon salt
- 1/8 teaspoon black pepper
- 4 thin lemon slices

1. Splash a little cold water over both sides of each breast half and place smooth side down on separate sheets of waxed paper or heavy plastic wrap, folding the flap (fillet) out to one side; top each with a second sheet of paper and pound gently with a mallet or meat pounder, working from the center outward, until the cutlets are between ⅛ and ¼ inch thick. Immediately peel off the top sheets of paper and discard them; pick up each cutlet to prevent sticking but return them to their papers.

2. Choose two pie pans or shallow dishes; put the flour in one and the eggs in another. Add 1 teaspoon of the flour to the eggs along with 1 teaspoon water; whisk to blend. Remove 1 teaspoon flour for the sauce and reserve it.

3. Place a large heavy noncorrosive or nonstick skillet over moderately high heat. Add 1 tablespoon of the vegetable oil and ½ tablespoon of the olive oil. As you cook the cutlets, regulate the heat between moderate and moderately high. Dip a cutlet into the flour, turning and tapping to coat both sides. Dip into the egg to coat completely and place in the hot oil. Repeat, cooking 2 cutlets at once. When bottoms of cutlets are golden brown, turn and sauté the other sides just until cooked through (about 1 to 2 minutes per side). The first side is the most important for color. Transfer to a plate. Add remaining oil and cook the remaining 2 cutlets in the same manner; remove and hold with the other cutlets.

4. Add the garlic to the skillet and cook over low heat to soften and lightly color, about 1 minute. Stir in the reserved 1 teaspoon flour to moisten. Pour in the wine and chicken stock; stirring constantly, bring to a boil over moderate heat; boil until reduced by half, about 5 minutes. Stir in 2 tablespoons parsley, the lemon juice, butter, salt, and pepper. Return the cutlets to the pan, spooning some of the sauce up over them to coat. Let stand 5 to 10 minutes, then serve hot, garnished with the remaining 1 tablespoon parsley and the lemon slices.

Chicken Margarita

All the flavors of a classic Mexican margarita cocktail are here in a simple but elegant dinner dish. For drama, you can flambé at the table if you're in that kind of mood.

MAKES 4 SERVINGS

- **4** skinless boned chicken breast halves, 4 to 6 ounces each
- **2** limes
- **2** tablespoons butter
- **2** teaspoons all-purpose flour
- **1/2** cup chicken stock or canned broth
- **1/2** teaspoon salt
- **1/8** teaspoon black pepper
- **2** tablespoons Cointreau or other orange-flavored liqueur
- **1** tablespoon tequila

1. Splash each breast half with a little cold water and place smooth sides down on separate squares of waxed paper. Top with additional sheets of waxed paper and flatten to about 1/4-inch thickness by pounding with a meat mallet or rolling pin. Peel off the top sheets of paper and discard. Pick up each cutlet to make sure it doesn't stick to the paper.

2. Using a special zesting tool if you have one, remove the green outer zest from the limes in tiny strips and reserve for garnish. Lacking this tool, slice off a few very thin layers of zest and cut into fine shreds, or simply remove with a lemon grater. Cut the limes in half and squeeze out the juice. You will need 1½ to 2 tablespoons of juice.

3. Melt 1 tablespoon of the butter in a large heavy nonaluminum skillet over moderately high heat. Add two breast halves and cook about 1½ minutes on each side, until lightly browned and cooked through. Transfer to a warm platter and cover with foil. Add the remaining butter to the pan and cook the remaining breast halves in the same manner.

4. Add the flour to the pan drippings and cook for 1 minute, stirring. Add the chicken broth, salt, and pepper and stir constantly, bringing to a boil. Lower the heat and simmer for 1 to 2 minutes, stirring. Stir in the Cointreau and 1½ tablespoons lime juice; return the chicken to the pan. Pour in the tequila to one side; carefully avert face and ignite with a long match; shake and let flames die down. Serve the chicken with the sauce (adding a little more lime juice if desired), and garnish the top with the reserved lime zest.

Chicken Piccata

MAKES 4 SERVINGS

- **1** cup Basic Chicken Stock (page 47) or canned broth
- **1** lemon
- **4** skinless boned chicken breast halves, 4 to 6 ounces each
- **1½** tablespoons olive oil
- **1½** tablespoons butter
- **¼** cup all-purpose flour
- **¼** cup finely chopped shallots
- **1** garlic clove, peeled and minced or crushed through a press
- **½** cup dry white wine
- **3** tablespoons chopped parsley
- **¼** teaspoon salt
- **⅛** teaspoon black pepper

These chicken breasts are tender-juicy, tangy, and fragrant. Either mashed potatoes or spaghetti will make a good accompaniment, and broccoli rabe or broccoli florets and sliced tomatoes are welcome, too.

1. Pour the chicken broth into a small saucepan and boil until reduced by half, 5 to 8 minutes over moderate heat. Grate the zest from the lemon and reserve. Cut the lemon in half and squeeze the juice; you will need 1 tablespoon.

2. Splash a little cold water over both sides of each breast half and place, smooth side down, on separate sheets of waxed paper or heavy plastic wrap; fold the flap (fillet) out and top with a second sheet of paper. Pound gently with a mallet or meat pounder, working from the center outward, until the cutlets are between ⅛ and ¼ inch thick. Immediately peel off the top sheets of paper and discard them; pick up each cutlet to prevent sticking but return them to the papers.

3. Place a large heavy nonaluminum skillet over moderately high heat. Add 1 tablespoon olive oil and 1 tablespoon butter. Put the flour on a plate and dredge 2 cutlets, 1 at a time, coating both sides lightly. Put them in the skillet. Brown the first side very well, 1 to 2 minutes. Turn and cook a minute longer, just until done. Transfer to a plate. Add the remaining olive oil and butter to the pan and cook the remaining two cutlets in the same way. Reserve all cutlets on the plate.

4. Add the shallots to the skillet and sauté over moderate heat to soften, 2 to 3 minutes. Add the garlic and cook a minute longer. Pour in the wine and the ½ cup reduced chicken stock. Boil over high heat until reduced by half, 2 to 3 minutes. Add the 1 tablespoon lemon juice, the grated zest, 2 tablespoons of the parsley, the salt, and pepper. Return the cutlets, spooning the sauce over them. Serve hot, sprinkled with the remaining 1 tablespoon parsley.

Chicken Florentine

1 pound fresh spinach or one 10-ounce package frozen, thawed

4 skinless boned chicken breast halves, about 6 ounces each

1 cup dry white wine

3 tablespoons butter

¼ cup finely chopped shallots or onion

¼ cup all-purpose flour

1 cup strong Basic Chicken Stock (page 47) or double-strength canned broth

½ cup light cream

¼ teaspoon grated nutmeg

½ teaspoon salt

¼ teaspoon black pepper

2 egg yolks

6 tablespoons grated Parmesan cheese

In this recipe, the creamy spinach sauce spooned over slices of chicken breast bubbles and browns under the broiler. Thin spaghetti and cherry tomatoes are good alongside. If you want to peel the cherry tomatoes, which makes them especially elegant, see the instructions on page 141.

1. Rinse fresh spinach in a large bowl or sinkful of cool water. Pull off and discard the large tough stems. Put the spinach, with just the water clinging to the leaves, in a large heavy non-aluminum pot. Cover tightly and place over high heat. Cook until barely wilted down, turning once or twice, 2 to 3 minutes. Place in a strainer over a bowl and let cool slightly. Press out the juice and reserve for another use. Chop the spinach and reserve; you should have about 1 cup. If using defrosted frozen, simply squeeze lightly and chop.

2. Put the chicken breast halves in a single layer in a nonaluminum skillet just large enough to hold them. Add the wine; cover and bring to a boil over moderate heat. Lower the heat and simmer, turning once, just until cooked through, 10 to 12

minutes. Transfer to a plate and cover with aluminum foil to keep warm. Reserve the wine.

3. Melt the butter in a heavy medium saucepan over moderate heat. Add the shallots and sauté to soften, 3 to 5 minutes. Stir in the flour to moisten and cook a minute longer. Pour in the chicken stock, ½ cup of the reserved poaching wine, and the cream. Stirring constantly, bring to a boil. Add the nutmeg, salt, and pepper; simmer 2 to 3 minutes over low heat, stirring.

4. Whisk the egg yolks in a medium bowl; gradually whisk in about half of the cream sauce; return all to the pan and cook, stirring, 1 to 2 minutes longer at a bare simmer. Remove from the heat and stir in ¼ cup of the grated Parmesan cheese and all of the spinach. Preheat the broiler.

5. Slice each breast half horizontally. Arrange two halves in each of four individual gratin dishes (or all of them on one large one that will fit under your broiler). Top each slice with about ⅓ cup of the spinach sauce and sprinkle lightly with the remaining 2 tablespoons Parmesan. Broil until hot, bubbly, and golden brown, about 2 minutes for individual portions and slightly longer if broiling all of them together. Serve hot.

Crepas ala Poblana

These rich and creamy Mexican stuffed crêpes can be assembled an hour ahead of time and baked just before serving. They

MAKES 18 (6 SERVINGS OF 3 CREPAS)

1½   pound whole chicken breast, split

 2   large peeled garlic cloves, 1 sliced and 1 minced

 1   bay leaf

1½   pounds (6 to 8 large) fresh *poblano* chile peppers or three 4-ounce cans whole roasted peeled chiles

4	tablespoons (½ stick) butter
1½	teaspoons ground cumin
1½	teaspoons dried oregano, crumbled
½	cup all-purpose flour
1½	cups milk
½	cup heavy cream
2	teaspoons salt
¼	teaspoon black pepper
2	cups corn kernels, fresh (cut from 4 to 5 medium ears) or frozen, thawed slightly
18	Corn Crêpes (page 367)
½	cup sour cream
2	cups (½ pound) shredded Monterey Jack cheese
2	large ripe tomatoes, finely diced

are perfect for brunch or dinner. You can make the crêpes a day or two ahead. Although you can substitute canned roasted peeled chiles for the fresh poblanos in a pinch, I urge you to try it with fresh peppers; the flavor will be superior.

1. In a heavy medium saucepan, combine the chicken with 1½ cups cold water, the halved garlic clove, and the bay leaf. Cover and bring to a boil over moderate heat. Reduce the heat to low and simmer until the chicken is just cooked through, about 20 minutes. Transfer the chicken to a plate and set aside until cool enough to handle. Strain the broth through a sieve and reserve 1½ cups (if you have less, add water to make 1½ cups). Pull the skin and bones from the chicken and discard. Tear the meat into fine shreds.

2. Roast the fresh poblanos by placing them directly on the burners of a gas stove (with burners turned to high), or as close to the heat source as possible under an electric broiler; turn frequently with tongs until they are blistered and black all over. Let them cool for a minute or two and put them in a plastic bag; twist the top to enclose and chill them for at least 10 minutes. Rub away the skins (this is easiest done over a colander under slowly running water, though you will lose some juice) and pull out the stems, seeds, and ribs. If using canned chiles, rinse and drain. Coarsely chop the chiles.

3. Melt the butter in a heavy medium saucepan over moderate heat. Add the minced garlic, cumin, and oregano; sauté for a minute. Stir in the flour and cook for a minute or two longer, stirring. Pour in the reserved 1½ cups broth, milk, and cream; stirring constantly, bring to a boil. Lower the heat and simmer, stirring, 1 to 2 minutes longer. Stir in the salt and pepper. Spoon 1 cup of the sauce into a medium bowl and reserve. Add all of the corn kernels and half the poblanos to the sauce in the saucepan; simmer for 2 minutes, stirring frequently. Remove from the heat.

4. Add the shredded chicken and the remaining poblanos to the reserved 1 cup sauce to make a filling for the crêpes.

5. Preheat the broiler. Position a shelf in the top third of the oven. Lightly grease 6 individual gratin dishes (or one or two larger ones that will fit in your broiler).

6. To assemble, place 1 corn crêpe on a work surface speckled side down. Spoon 2 tablespoons of the filling in a line across the lower third of the crêpe and loosely roll up. Place in gratin dish seam side down. Repeat with remaining crêpes and filling, arranging 3 in each dish if you are using 6 dishes, more per dish for larger gratin dishes.

7. Spoon a scant ¼ cup of the chile-corn sauce over each crêpe. Spoon tiny dabs of the sour cream over all the crêpes and top with shredded cheese. (The recipe can be prepared to this point up to 1 hour ahead and kept covered at room temperature.) Place 2 dishes on the top shelf of the oven for about 3 minutes, until heated through. Place under the broiler for about 1 minute to melt and lightly brown the cheese. Repeat with the remaining crêpes. Garnish with the diced tomato and serve hot.

Chicken Enchiladas

MAKES 12 (4 TO 6 SERVINGS)

Chicken Filling:

1½ pound whole chicken breast, with skin and bone
2½ cups Basic Chicken Stock (page 47) or canned broth
1 bay leaf
1 teaspoon dried oregano, crumbled
1 large garlic clove, peeled and sliced
3 whole cloves
½ teaspoon salt
⅛ teaspoon black pepper

Enchilada Sauce:

2 tablespoons vegetable oil
1 large garlic clove, peeled and minced or crushed through a press
3 tablespoons chili powder
½ teaspoon ground cumin
½ teaspoon dried oregano, crumbled
⅛ teaspoon ground cinnamon
3 tablespoons all-purpose flour
½ cup tomato sauce
½ teaspoon salt

Assembly:

½ cup vegetable oil
12 6-inch corn tortillas
½ cup thinly sliced scallions, including green parts
2 cups (½ pound) shredded mild Cheddar cheese such as longhorn

This is my simplified version of really tasty enchiladas. In Mexico you'd have to roast, soak, and grind dried chiles, peel tomatoes, toast spices and garlic; here I have used ground chili powder and abbreviated the cooking procedures to create a delicious but practical variation. The chile sauce is mild.

1. Prepare the chicken filling: Put the chicken breast in a heavy medium pot. Add the chicken broth, bay leaf, oregano, garlic, and whole cloves; cover and bring to a boil over moderate heat. Lower the heat and simmer until the chicken is cooked through, 25 to 30 minutes. Remove the breast and let it cool on a plate. Strain the broth; you should have 2½ cups. If there is less, add water to make that amount.

2. Pull off the chicken skin and discard. Pull the meat from the bones. Discard the bones and tear the meat into shreds about ½ inch wide and 2 inches long. Put them in a bowl and stir in ½ cup of the broth and all of the salt and pepper.

3. Make the enchilada sauce: Spoon the vegetable oil into a heavy medium skillet. Add the garlic and chili powder; sauté over moderate heat for 1 minute. Add the cumin, oregano, cinnamon, and flour; cook, stirring, for 1 minute. Pour in the reserved 2 cups broth and the tomato sauce. Stirring constantly, bring to a boil. Lower the heat and simmer for 3 to 5 minutes to thicken slightly and blend the flavors. Stir in the salt.

4. Assemble the enchiladas: Preheat the oven to 425°. Pour the vegetable oil into a heavy medium skillet and place over moderately high heat until just beginning to smoke. Using tongs, lower one tortilla into the oil, swish it back and forth and turn it frequently until softened and barely beginning to stiffen, 10 to 20 seconds. Drain on a paper towel. Repeat, stacking the tortillas between paper towels.

5. Lightly oil a 13-by-9-by-2-inch baking pan. If necessary, reheat the enchilada sauce so it is warm, adding 1 or 2 tablespoons of water if it is too thick; it should be the consistency of creamy soup.

6. Dip one tortilla into the sauce to lightly coat, and put it in the pan. Repeat with a second tortilla. Assemble the enchiladas directly in the pan, arranging them in two crosswise rows. Spoon 3 tablespoons of the chicken filling in a line across the lower quarter of each tortilla; sprinkle with about 2 tablespoons of the scallions and roll up tightly; place seam side down. Repeat to make 12 enchiladas. Spoon any remaining sauce over the ends of the enchiladas. Top with the cheese and bake until bubbly around the edges and the cheese has melted, 10 to 12 minutes. Serve hot.

Crispy-Creamy Chicken Breasts

MAKES 4 SERVINGS

Poached Chicken:
- **4** skinless boned chicken breast halves (about 4 ounces each), trimmed of fat and gristle
- **½** cup dry white wine
- **1** bay leaf
- **1** teaspoon dried basil
- **1** large garlic clove, peeled and sliced

Coating Sauce:
- **4** tablespoons (½ stick) butter
- **½** cup all-purpose flour
- **1** cup milk
- **¼** teaspoon grated nutmeg
- **¾** teaspoon salt
- **⅛** teaspoon black pepper
- **¼** cup chopped fresh parsley leaves

A crisp coating of golden bread crumbs clings to a creamy parsley-wine sauce spread over poached chicken breasts. For a delicious variation, add ⅓ cup minced smoked ham to the sauce with the parsley and reduce the salt to ½ teaspoon. The frying temperature is important, because you don't want the coating to brown before the chicken is hot.

Crumb Coating and Frying:

Vegetable oil for frying
1 large egg
½ cup plain dry bread crumbs

1. Prepare the poached chicken: Put the chicken breast halves in a heavy medium saucepan. Add ½ cup water, the white wine, bay leaf, basil, and garlic. Cover and bring to a boil over moderate heat. Lower the heat and poach for 5 minutes, until almost cooked through. Remove from the broth, cover, and let cool to room temperature. Meanwhile boil the poaching broth over high heat until it is reduced to a generous ½ cup, about 3 minutes. Strain; you will need ½ cup strong broth (add a little water to make ½ cup if you have less).

2. Prepare the coating sauce: Melt the butter in a small heavy saucepan over moderate heat. Stir in the flour and cook for a minute; the mixture will be dry. Stir in the milk and the ½ cup reserved strong broth. Whisking constantly, bring to a boil over low heat, simmering until very thick and smooth. Stir in the nutmeg, salt, and pepper; cook about 2 minutes longer, stirring. Remove from the heat and turn into a small bowl. Cool to room temperature, stirring frequently.

3. When the sauce has cooled to room temperature but is not yet set, coat the poached breast halves one at a time. Using a quarter of the coating for each, spread the rough side of each first so the coating is about ¼ inch thick. Place a sheet of plastic wrap on a dinner plate and arrange the breasts, coated side down, on it. Spread the remaining coating smoothly over the top and sides. Chill until set, at least 1 hour or as long as 8.

4. Crumb coating and frying: Pour about ½ inch vegetable oil into a heavy medium skillet and heat until it registers 370°, or slightly below the smoking point.

5. Whisk the egg in a shallow dish or pie pan and put the bread crumbs in another. Carefully pick up one coated chicken breast, patching coating as necessary. Dip it into the egg, rolling to coat, and then roll it in the crumbs to coat evenly, pressing lightly. Put chicken into the hot oil and repeat with a second breast. Fry 2 at a time, for 3 to 4 minutes per side, until crisp and golden brown and cooked to the center. Drain on paper towels and repeat with the remaining chicken breasts. Serve hot.

Crispy Chicken Strips with Lemon-Soy Dipping Sauce

MAKES 4 SERVINGS

- ½ cup thin or light soy sauce
- ¼ cup fresh lemon juice
- 1 medium garlic clove, peeled and minced or crushed through a press
- 1 tablespoon sugar
- 1 tablespoon oriental sesame oil
- 2 medium scallions, thinly sliced
- 1½ pounds skinless boned chicken breast halves
- ¼ cup all-purpose flour

About ¼ cup vegetable oil

- ½ teaspoon freshly ground black pepper

When strips of chicken breast are quickly pan-fried over high heat the outside becomes crisp and golden brown while the inside remains tender and succulent.

1. Make a dipping sauce in a small bowl by combining the soy sauce, lemon juice, garlic, sugar, sesame oil, and scallions; stir to dissolve the sugar.

2. Trim away any fat or tendons from the chicken breasts. Cut into 3- by ½-inch strips.

3. In a paper or plastic bag combine the chicken with the flour; shake to coat the chicken. In a large heavy skillet, heat 2 tablespoons of the oil over moderately high heat. The key to cooking these is to keep the temperature of the oil just below the smoking point. Add as much of the floured chicken as will fit in a single layer without crowding. Brown well without stirring over moderately high heat until crisp and golden brown, about 2 minutes. Turn quickly with tongs and cook the remaining side until just cooked through, about 15 seconds. Drain on paper towels. Fry the remaining chicken in batches, adding more oil as needed. Sprinkle the chicken with the pepper and serve hot with 4 individual bowls of dipping sauce.

Pasta Shells with Chicken, Collard Greens, and White Beans

Soupy but not a soup, this saucy, slurpy pasta dish, reminiscent of pasta e fagioli but with added chicken and luscious collard greens, is comforting for lunch or supper on a cold day.

MAKES 4 TO 6 SERVINGS (10 CUPS)

1½ pound whole chicken breast, split
4 cups Basic Chicken Stock (page 47) or canned broth
1 cup dry white wine
1 bay leaf
1 tablespoon dried basil
1 teaspoon dried oregano
1½ pounds fresh collard greens, or one 10-ounce box frozen, thawed
2 tablespoons olive oil

1 tablespoon butter
1 medium onion, peeled and chopped
2 large garlic cloves, peeled and minced or crushed
  through a press
¼ cup all-purpose flour
1½ teaspoons salt
⅛ teaspoon pepper
1 16-ounce can small white beans, rinsed and drained
½ pound medium pasta shells
4 to 6 tablespoons grated Parmesan cheese

Toasted Italian bread is a good accompaniment for sopping up the sauce.

1. Put the chicken breast in a heavy 3-quart saucepan and pour in the chicken stock and white wine; add the bay leaf, basil, and oregano and place over moderate heat. Bring to a boil; lower the heat, cover, and simmer gently just until cooked through, about 20 minutes. Transfer to a plate until cool enough to handle. Then pull off and discard the skin and bones; tear the chicken with the grain into ½-inch-wide shreds.

2. Rinse the collard greens and pull the leaves to strip them from their stems. Discard the stems and cut the leaves roughly into 1-inch squares. Add the chopped leaves to the stock, cover, and simmer until tender, 10 to 15 minutes. If using frozen, cook for 5 minutes. Remove from the heat and reserve.

3. Spoon the olive oil and butter into a heavy 3-quart saucepan and place over moderate heat. Add the onion and sauté to soften but not brown, about 5 minutes. Add the garlic and cook a minute longer. Stir in the flour and cook 1 minute more. Pour in the stock and collard greens and, stirring constantly, bring to a boil. Add the salt and pepper and simmer for about 2 minutes. Add the shredded chicken and the white beans and return to the simmer. Remove from the heat. This recipe may be prepared up to a day ahead to this point.

4. Bring a medium pot of lightly salted water to a boil over high heat. Add the pasta shells and, stirring constantly, return to the boil. Stirring frequently, cook until tender but firm to the bite, about 10 minutes. Drain in a colander and add to the sauce. Serve hot in shallow soup dishes, sprinkling each serving with 1 tablespoon grated Parmesan cheese.

Pasta with Chicken and Spinach Sauce

Hearty, creamy, and satisfying, this jade green pasta dish reminds me somewhat of macaroni and cheese, but flavored with good Parmesan.

MAKES 4 MAIN-COURSE OR
8 PASTA-COURSE SERVINGS

1½	pound whole chicken breast, split
¾	cup dry white wine
1	large garlic clove, peeled and sliced
1	teaspoon dried basil, crumbled
1	teaspoon dried oregano, crumbled
1	bay leaf
1	pound fresh spinach, or 1 cup cooked, or one 10-ounce package frozen, thawed
3	tablespoons olive oil
3	tablespoons all-purpose flour
1½	teaspoons salt
¼	teaspoon black pepper
¼	teaspoon grated nutmeg
1	8-ounce package cream cheese, softened to room temperature
½	cup grated Parmesan cheese
1	pound dried penne, ziti, or large elbow macaroni

1. Place the chicken breast in a large heavy nonaluminum saucepan. Pour in 1 cup cold water and ½ cup of the white wine. Add the garlic, basil, oregano, and bay leaf; bring to a boil over moderate heat. Cover and simmer over low heat until cooked to the bone, 18 to 20 minutes. Remove and put on a plate until cool enough to handle. Strain the broth and reserve it. Pull the skin from the chicken and pull the meat from the bones. Discard the skin and bones. Tear the meat lengthwise into shreds about ½ inch wide and 2 inches long, and set aside.

2. Rinse the spinach in the sink or a large bowl of cool water. Pull off just the thick tough stems. Place in a large nonaluminum pot with just the water clinging to the leaves, and place over high heat, covered. Cook, turning once or twice, until the leaves have wilted down, about 3 minutes. Drain, reserving the juice for another purpose. Coarsely chop the spinach (it will be puréed in the sauce).

3. Spoon 2 tablespoons of the olive oil into a large heavy non-aluminum saucepan and place over moderately high heat. Stir in the flour and cook 1 to 2 minutes, stirring. Pour in the reserved broth and add the salt, pepper, and nutmeg. Bring to a boil, stirring constantly, until thickened. Let cool sightly, add the chopped spinach, and purée the mixture in a food processor or blender. Return the purée to the pot and add the cream cheese, stirring over low heat until it has melted. Add the Parmesan, shredded chicken, remaining ¼ cup white wine, and the final 1 tablespoon olive oil.

4. Cook the pasta in plenty of lightly salted boiling water to the *al dente* stage. Drain thoroughly, toss well with the sauce, and serve hot.

Curried Chicken with Potatoes and Peas

Here is my simple version of a way with favorite flavors and textures. The sauce will be best if you make it several hours ahead and then add the chicken and sour cream shortly before serving. If desired, serve with steamed white rice, preferably Indian basmati rice, which has a nutty grain flavor.

MAKES 4 SERVINGS

2 tablespoons vegetable oil
2 large onions (1 pound), peeled and chopped
¼ cup finely minced peeled fresh ginger
3 large garlic cloves, peeled and minced or crushed through a press
2 tablespoons curry powder
½ teaspoon ground cumin
¼ teaspoon cayenne pepper (optional)
2 tablespoons tomato paste
1 cup plain yogurt
2 teaspoons salt
¼ teaspoon black pepper
1 3-inch cinnamon stick
2 cups Basic Chicken Stock (page 47) or canned broth
1 pound (3 to 4 medium) red-skinned potatoes, peeled and cut into 1-inch chunks
1 10-ounce package frozen green peas
1 pound skinless boned chicken breasts, thinly sliced across the grain
½ cup sour cream, at room temperature

Optional Toppings:

Sliced fresh mango
Mango chutney
Chopped peanuts
Chopped fresh cilantro leaves

1. Spoon the vegetable oil into a large heavy nonaluminum saucepan and place over moderately high heat. Add the onions and brown-fry for 12 to 15 minutes, adjusting the heat from high to moderately high and stirring frequently, until they become soft and medium caramel brown. Any time that they become dry, add 1 to 2 tablespoons water and continue cooking. This browning is important for the flavor of the curry.

2. Add the ginger and garlic and cook 2 minutes longer, stirring over moderately high heat. Stir in the curry, cumin, and cayenne; cook 2 minutes longer. Stir in the tomato paste and cook for a minute; the mixture will be thick and pastelike. Stir in the yogurt, salt, and pepper. Cook for 1 minute. Cool slightly and then purée in a blender or food processor. Return to the pan. Add the cinnamon stick and gradually stir in the stock. Bring to a boil over moderate heat, then lower the heat. Add the potatoes and simmer, covered, until they are tender, about 30 minutes. The curry will taste best if you let this mixture cool and reserve it for several hours; reheat and proceed.

3. Add the peas to the potato mixture and simmer for 2 to 3 minutes, until hot. Add the chicken and simmer 2 to 3 minutes, until cooked. Stir in the sour cream and simmer for a minute, but do not boil. Serve hot, with any of the optional toppings.

Aztec Pie

This hearty make-ahead casserole of layered corn tortillas, chicken, mild *poblano* chile peppers, cheese, and salsa verde is like one that they serve at buffets on the rooftop terrace of the old Majestic Hotel in the colonial section of downtown Mexico City.

MAKES 8 SERVINGS

- **2** cups Salsa Verde (page 380)
- **1½** pounds (6 to 8 medium) fresh *poblano* chile peppers, or three 4-ounce cans whole roasted peeled chiles, drained
- **1½** pound whole chicken breast
- **1½** teaspoons salt
- **1** teaspoon dried oregano, crumbled
- **½** teaspoon ground cumin
- **¼** teaspoon black pepper
- **1** cup plain yogurt
- **½** cup light cream

Vegetable oil
- **18** 6-inch corn tortillas (about 1 pound)
- **4** medium tomatoes (¾ pound), thinly sliced
- **½** cup (4 to 6 medium) thinly sliced scallions
- **½** pound medium Cheddar cheese, such as longhorn, coarsely shredded to make 2 cups
- **½** pound Monterey Jack cheese, coarsely shredded to make 2 cups
- **½** cup canned tomato sauce

1. Prepare the *salsa verde*, leaving out the jalapeño chile peppers if you do not want your casserole to be spicy hot.

2. Roast the *poblanos* by placing them directly on the burners (over high flame) of a gas stove or as close to the heat source as possible under a broiler; turn with tongs frequently until they are blistered and black all over. Let them cool for a minute or two and put them in a plastic bag; twist the top to enclose and chill them for at least 10 minutes. Rub the skins away and cut out the stems. Pull out the seeds and veins. (This is easiest to do over a colander under gently running water, but some of the juices will be lost.) If using canned chiles, simply drain and discard seeds. Cut the chiles into 1½-inch squares. Reserve.

3. Put the chicken breast in a heavy medium saucepan and add 1½ cups cold water. Bring to a boil over moderate heat. Cover the pan, lower the heat, and simmer until cooked through, 20 to 25 minutes. Transfer the chicken to a plate until cool enough to handle. Reserve the broth for another use. Pull off and discard the skin and bones and tear the chicken along the grain into ½-inch-wide shreds. Put in a bowl and toss with 1 teaspoon of the salt and the oregano, cumin, and pepper.

4. In a small bowl stir together the yogurt, light cream, and remaining ½ teaspoon salt.

5. Preheat the oven to 350°. Lightly oil a 13-by-9-by-2-inch baking dish. Cut 5 paper towels into quarters and have them nearby. Pour ¼ inch of vegetable oil into a heavy medium skillet and place over high heat. When the oil is hot and just beginning to smoke, lower the heat slightly. As you work, keep the temperature just below the smoking point. With tongs, dip one tortilla into the oil and cook it till it softens and just begins to firm up, about 10 seconds per side. Put on a paper towel on a small plate. Continue cooking the tortillas, stacking them between sheets of paper towels.

6. Spread ¼ cup of the *salsa verde* in the prepared pan. Tear 6 of the tortillas into quarters and arrange them in an overlapping layer in the pan. Scatter with half the shredded chicken, half the poblanos, and half the tomato slices. Spoon on ½ cup of the *salsa verde* and sprinkle with half of the scallions. Spoon on in dabs ½ cup of the yogurt mixture. Toss together the Cheddar and Monterey Jack cheeses and sprinkle ⅓ of the mixed cheeses in the casserole. Repeat all the layers. Quarter the remaining 6 tortillas and arrange over the top. In dabs, spoon on the remaining *salsa verde* interspersed with the remaining ½ cup yogurt mixture. Scatter the remaining cheese over the sauces and spoon on the tomato sauce. Bake uncovered for 50 minutes to 1 hour, until hot and bubbly and lightly browned. Let cool at least 15 minutes before cutting into squares and serving. A green salad is a good accompaniment.

Tamale Pie

This hearty pie is a good choice for a party because it can be made well in advance (even a day ahead) and just gets better when reheated. It is low in fat compared to traditional tamales and has double the corn flavor and texture. You can start with canned chicken broth here because the chicken breast boosts the flavor and makes it taste better. Be sure to prepare all the ingredients so the pie can be

MAKES 8 SERVINGS

1½ pound whole chicken breast, split
4 cups Basic Chicken Stock (page 47) or canned broth
4 large peeled garlic cloves, 2 sliced and 2 minced or crushed through a press
1 bay leaf
3 tablespoons butter
2 medium onions, peeled and chopped
1 tablespoon chili powder
1½ teaspoons dried oregano, crumbled
1 teaspoon ground cumin
1 teaspoon sugar
1 tablespoon salt
¼ teaspoon black pepper
3 tablespoons all-purpose flour
2 4-ounce cans whole peeled green chiles, drained and coarsely chopped
1½ cups yellow cornmeal
3 cups corn kernels (fresh from 4 to 5 ears, or frozen, thawed slightly)
1 6½-ounce can large whole pitted black olives, drained and sliced

½ pound Monterey Jack or Muenster cheese, coarsely grated
½ pound longhorn Cheddar cheese or other mild Cheddar, coarsely grated
2 large ripe tomatoes, sliced ¼ inch thick
½ cup canned tomato sauce

assembled quickly after you cook the cornmeal.

1. Put the chicken breast halves (with skin and bones) in a 3-quart heavy saucepan; add the chicken stock, sliced garlic, and bay leaf. Place over moderate heat. Cover and bring to a boil. Lower the heat and simmer until almost cooked through, 20 to 25 minutes (it's better to let it remain just slightly pink rather than overcook it, since the casserole will bake for an hour to complete the cooking). Remove the chicken, transfer it to a plate, and let cool to room temperature. Strain the broth; you need 4 cups (if necessary, add water to make 4 cups). Reserve. Pull the skin and bones from the chicken. Tear the meat into large shreds about ¾ inch by 2 to 3 inches.

2. Melt 2 tablespoons of the butter in a large heavy skillet over moderate heat. Add the onions and sauté to soften, about 5 minutes; add the 2 reserved minced garlic cloves along with the chili powder, oregano, cumin, sugar, 1 teaspoon of the salt, and pepper; sauté for about 1 minute. Add the remaining 1 table-spoon butter and stir in the flour to moisten; cook a minute longer. Pour in 1 cup of the reserved chicken broth and, stirring constantly, bring to a boil (the mixture will be very thick). Stir in the canned green chiles and simmer for 2 to 3 minutes over low heat. Remove from the heat and reserve.

3. Preheat the oven to 350°. Lightly grease a 13-by-9-by-2-inch baking pan (4-quart capacity).

4. Pour the remaining 3 cups chicken broth into a large heavy saucepan; add the remaining 2 teaspoons salt and bring to a boil over moderately high heat. Measure the cornmeal into a bowl and stir in 2 cups cold water. When the broth boils, add the cornmeal-water mixture all at once, stirring constantly. Lower the heat and boil over moderate heat, stirring constantly, until very thick, about 8 minutes. Stir in the corn kernels and cook about 2 minutes longer.

5. Spread two-thirds of the cornmeal batter (keep the remainder covered) in the baking pan. Add all of the chicken shreds and olives. Top with three-fourths of the grated cheese (the two varieties mixed together). Cut the tomato slices in half and arrange them over the cheese. Spread with all of the green chile sauce and press lightly. Spread the remaining cornmeal batter over the top (if it should happen to set before you spread it, stir in ¼ cup water and cook, stirring constantly, to soften). Spoon on the tomato sauce in diagonal lines and top with the remaining cheese. Bake in the center of the oven for about 1 hour, until bubbly and lightly browned. Let cool at least 30 minutes before serving. If making ahead, cool completely; top with a little more cheese, cover tightly with aluminum foil, and bake at 350° for an additional hour. Serve hot.

Tandoori Chicken Kebobs with Raita and Smoky Dal

I have paired the accompanying dishes with the main course because I want you to taste these dishes together on the same plate. The deep, com-

MAKES 6

¼ cup chopped fresh cilantro leaves

2 large garlic cloves, peeled and minced or crushed through a press

1 tablespoon minced fresh ginger

1 teaspoon ground cumin

1 teaspoon ground coriander seeds

1 teaspoon curry powder
1 teaspoon paprika
1/2 teaspoon cayenne pepper
2 tablespoons fresh lemon juice
1 cup plain yogurt
2 pounds skinless boned chicken breasts, cut in 1 1/2-inch cubes
2 tablespoons vegetable oil
Raita (recipe follows)
Smoky *Dal* (recipe follows)
Steamed *basmati* rice (optional)
Indian breads, such as *roti*, *chapati* or *paratha* (optional)

1. In a large bowl combine the cilantro, garlic, ginger, cumin, coriander, curry, paprika, and cayenne. Pound with a pestle or the bottom of a spice jar, working in the lemon juice to make a paste. Stir in the yogurt. Add the chicken cubes; cover and marinate in the refrigerator 1 to 4 hours.

2. Thread the chicken cubes onto six 10-to-12-inch skewers. Light a charcoal fire. When the coals are glowing but covered with gray ash, brush the kebobs with a little of the vegetable oil and place on a grill about 5 inches above the coals. Grill, brushing with oil and turning every 3 to 4 minutes, until cooked through, 12 to 15 minutes (the best way to check is to cut into the center of a center piece). Do not overcook, or the chicken will be dry. Serve hot or at room temperature with the *raita*, *dal*, rice, and bread.

plex flavor of the yogurt marinade penetrates the tender chicken breasts. (Be sure not to overmarinate or the chicken will become mushy.) Make the accompaniments ahead of time and serve with Indian basmati rice and bread if desired. Since most homes do not own a tandoori oven, this recipe is adapted for grilling. If you are using bamboo skewers for the charcoal grilling, soak them in cold water for 30 minutes before threading the chicken cubes onto them.

Raita

The cool and refreshing flavor of cucumber and yogurt enhances the fragrant tandoori kebobs. Make ahead and chill.

MAKES ABOUT 4 CUPS

3 large 8-inch cucumbers, peeled and halved lengthwise
2 teaspoons salt
1 teaspoon ground cumin
1½ cups plain yogurt
1 cup sour cream
¼ cup chopped fresh mint leaves
¼ teaspoon black pepper

1. Using a spoon, scoop the seeds from the cucumber halves and discard. Slice the cucumbers crosswise into ⅛-inch slices and put them in a colander; add 1 teaspoon of the salt and toss to coat. Let drain in the sink for 30 minutes. Lightly press with the back of a spoon.

2. Put the cumin in a small heavy dry skillet and toast over moderate heat until fragrant, shaking the pan, about 1 minute. Turn into a large bowl. Whisk in the yogurt, sour cream, mint, pepper, and remaining 1 teaspoon salt. Stir in the cucumbers. Cover and chill until serving. May be prepared a day ahead.

Smoky Dal

Not exactly your traditional Indian *dal*, this one I dreamed up to complement the tandoori chicken and raita. It contains a good variety of tex-

MAKES ABOUT 8 CUPS

8 slices (about 6 ounces) hickory-smoked bacon
1 cup dried pinto beans
½ cup dried yellow split peas
½ cup dried brown lentils
1 16-ounce can whole tomatoes
2 tablespoons minced fresh ginger

2 large garlic cloves, peeled and minced or crushed through a press
1 teaspoon ground cumin
1 teaspoon ground coriander
1 teaspoon curry powder
2 teaspoons salt
¼ teaspoon black pepper

tures and flavors and is quite fragrant.

1. Cut the bacon into ½-inch squares, cutting directly through the stack of chilled slices. Put them in a 3-quart heavy saucepan and cook over moderate heat, stirring frequently. As the bacon begins to brown, after 5 to 7 minutes, increase the heat and stir constantly until the pieces are crisp and golden brown, about 1 minute longer. Pour off all but 3 tablespoons of the fat.
2. Rinse the pinto beans, picking them over to remove any grit. Add to the bacon along with 6 cups of cold water. Bring to a boil over moderate heat. Partially cover and simmer over low heat for 1 hour, stirring occasionally.
3. Combine the split peas and lentils in a medium bowl; cover generously with cool water and rinse, pouring off the water from the top but leaving the legumes behind in the bowl. Drain and rinse in a strainer. Add to the pot of pinto beans.
4. Drain the tomatoes, reserving the juice for another use. Cut them in half crosswise and gently squeeze out the seeds. Cut the tomatoes into 1-inch pieces and add to the pot along with the ginger and garlic. In a small dry skillet combine the cumin, coriander, and curry; stir over moderate heat for a minute to toast until fragrant. Add to the pot. Simmer, stirring occasionally, for 30 minutes.
5. Preheat the oven to 325°. Stir the salt and pepper into the dal. Cover and bake about 45 minutes, until tender, stirring gently once or twice. If the dal becomes too thick add ¼ to ½ cup water. Serve hot.

Cool Japanese Chicken with Baby Eggplant

I like exotic picnics and this is a good choice for one. The flavors blossom as the dish cools. You will need 2 cups of dashi (Japanese stock) for this, but the instant kind that you simply dissolve in boiling water is quite fine. If you want to make your own, there is a recipe on page 174.

MAKES 6 TO 8 SERVINGS

- **2** pounds (20 to 30 3-inch) baby eggplants
- **7** tablespoons vegetable oil
- **½** pound large fresh mushrooms, sliced ¼ inch thick
- **2** cups dashi, homemade (see page 174) or instant
- **1** cup sake (rice wine)
- **⅓** cup sugar
- **¼** cup Japanese soy sauce, such as Kikkoman
- **½** teaspoon dried hot red pepper flakes
- **1½** pounds skinless boned chicken breasts, cut into strips about ½ by 3 inches
- **1** small red bell pepper, cut into slivers
- **1** tablespoon cornstarch

1. Trim the stem ends from the eggplants and cut them in half lengthwise. Cut two diagonal slits halfway into the cut sides of each half so the flavors permeate.

2. Spoon 2 tablespoons of the vegetable oil into a large heavy skillet and place over moderately high heat. Add a third of the eggplant, cut sides down, and cook until deep golden brown, 3 to 5 minutes. Turn and cook 2 to 3 minutes longer. Take out and transfer to a bowl. Repeat twice more, adding 2 tablespoons of the oil for each batch.

3. Spoon the remaining 1 tablespoon oil into the pan; add the mushrooms, and brown lightly over moderately high heat. Remove and reserve with the eggplant.

4. In a large heavy nonaluminum saucepan combine the dashi, sake, sugar, soy sauce, and hot pepper flakes; bring to a boil over moderate heat. Add the eggplant and mushrooms and simmer, uncovered, over low heat for 10 minutes. Add the chicken and red pepper slivers and simmer until cooked, about 2 minutes. In a cup, dissolve the cornstarch in 1 tablespoon cold water. Pour into the sauce and stir gently until thickened slightly, 1 minute. Pour into a bowl and cool to room temperature. Cover and chill for 1 or 2 hours before serving. Serve cold.

Chicken Sukiyaki

MAKES 6 SERVINGS

12 dried shiitake mushrooms
 4 ounces fine bean threads (cellophane noodles)
 2 quarts *dashi* (recipe follows)
 1 cup *sake* (rice wine)
 1 cup *mirin* (sweet rice wine)
 ½ cup Japanese soy sauce, such as Kikkoman
 1 tablespoon sugar
 5 slices fresh ginger, each the size of a half dollar
 1 medium onion, peeled and sliced
 6 cups coarsely shredded Napa cabbage, including stem end
 4 cakes grilled or fresh bean curd (tofu), cut in 1-inch cubes
 ½ pound fresh spinach, rinsed, cut in 1½-inch squares
 ¼ pound large fresh mushrooms, sliced
 1 pound skinless boned chicken breast, thinly sliced across grain
12 medium scallions, cut in 2-inch lengths

1. Put the shiitake mushrooms in a small bowl; pour 1 cup boiling water over them and allow to soften for 1 hour. Drain,

You'll make acceptably slurpy sounds as you suck up the slippery noodles in this festive Japanese one-dish supper, a carnival of tastes and textures perfect for a dinner party. Traditionally, sukiyaki is cooked at the table and it can be lots of fun, but I find that most people don't want to bother, so here it is cooked in the kitchen. If you want to cook at the table, prepare the cooking broth and have it on a burner at the table; arrange the remaining ingredients on a large tray so guests can dip and cook their own. You'll need homemade or instant dashi.

reserving the soaking liquid. Slice off the stems and discard. If desired, slice out a grooved X in the top center of each cap to make them decorative. Put the bean threads in a medium bowl; add hot tap water to cover and let soak for 1 hour. Drain, discarding the water.

2. In a large heavy soup pot combine the *dashi, sake, mirin*, soy sauce, sugar, ginger, onion, and reserved mushroom liquid; bring to a boil over moderate heat. Keep the broth simmering as you cook the remaining ingredients. As each is done, remove with a slotted spoon and reserve on a hot deep platter. Cook in the following order: cabbage (4 to 5 minutes), bean curd (4 minutes), spinach (4 minutes), mushrooms (3 minutes), chicken (3 to 4 minutes), scallions (3 minutes), bean threads and shiitake (2 minutes). To serve, discard the ginger slices and ladle hot dashi into 6 large shallow sukiyaki dishes, soup dishes, or shallow casseroles. Arrange the cooked ingredients in groupings in each bowl. Serve hot.

Dashi

You will need two special ingredients for making this light Japanese seafood stock but they are easily obtainable from a Japanese grocer (and they have a very long shelf life). Be sure to follow the directions accurately.

MAKES 2 QUARTS

2 15-inch-long pieces dried sea kelp (*dashi konbu*)
2½ cups loosely packed dried bonito shavings (*katsuo bushi*)

1. Put the sea kelp into a large heavy pot and pour in 2½ quarts of cold water. Place over moderately high heat and bring to a boil. Immediately take out the kelp with tongs (do not let it boil more than a few seconds).
2. Bring the stock to a full boil and remove from the heat. Add the dried bonito shavings and let them settle for 1 minute. Line a colander with damp cheesecloth and strain the stock. In Japan the kelp and bonito are used to make a second, weaker stock that can be used for soups and for cooking vegetables, and you can do that too; otherwise, discard them.

Chicken Thighs

Many connoisseurs of fine food consider the thigh to be the choicest part of the chicken. I don't take sides because I love all the parts. It's simply a matter of personal taste and timing, but the tender dark meat is packed full of fine flavor and juice, perfect for all the popular cooking techniques.

The meat remains moist after cooking and has a good deep flavor. I like the combination of breast and thigh, as many people do, so I alternate slices of them on my dinner plate when I have a roast bird.

Chinese cooks like to use thighs for many of their crunchy stir-fries. They cut them into cubes, marinate them, coat them in egg white and cornstarch, and fry them until the coating is crunchy and golden brown. The meat inside is tender and moist and the crisp coating soaks up a succulent sauce.

Italian cooks turn thighs into heart-warming, soothing cannelloni, while East Indians roast them in a tandoori oven. Japanese cooks marinate them and grill them *yakitori*-style over their hibachis. Thais skewer and grill morsels of thigh and serve them with spicy peanut sauce and cool cucumbers. Vietnamese cooks grill them over smoke and present them with fragrant mint and cilantro in deep bowls of chicken broth; with lime, chile, and fish sauce the bouquet is great. The choice is yours.

Crispy Orange Chicken

This sensational Chinese dish is crispiest when freshly made but I find it addictively delicious at room temperature or cold, so it is perfect for an exotic midnight picnic. It is good served with shrimp lo mein and broccoli or green beans in garlic sauce. You can also serve the succulent cubes of chicken on picks as an hors d'oeuvre. There's no getting around the deep-frying; it's necessary to create the crunchy coating. You will need dried orange peel, which is available in Chinese markets.

MAKES 4 SERVINGS

1½ pounds skinless boned chicken thighs (start with 3 pounds with skin and bones; see page 13)

Marinade:

2 tablespoons Chinese rice wine or dry sherry
1 tablespoon soy sauce
1 tablespoon rice vinegar
2 teaspoons sugar
1 teaspoon oriental sesame oil

Sauce:

2 teaspoons cornstarch
½ cup chicken stock or canned broth
2 tablespoons Chinese rice wine or dry sherry
2 tablespoons frozen orange juice concentrate, thawed
2 tablespoons soy sauce
2 tablespoons sugar
1 teaspoon rice vinegar
1 teaspoon oriental sesame oil
¼ to ½ teaspoon hot red pepper flakes

Crispy Chicken:

3 cups peanut oil
3 pieces dried orange peel, about 1 by 2 inches each
3 large egg whites
1 cup cornstarch
4 medium scallions, thinly sliced, including the green parts
¼ cup finely diced (¼ inch) red bell pepper
1 tablespoon minced fresh ginger

1 medium garlic clove, peeled and minced or crushed through a press

4 scallion brushes (optional garnish)

1. Cut the chicken into 1-inch cubes.

2. Prepare the marinade: In a large bowl stir together the rice wine, soy sauce, rice vinegar, sugar, and sesame oil; add the chicken cubes, toss well, and let marinate at room temperature for 30 to 60 minutes, or in the refrigerator for up to 24 hours.

3. Prepare the sauce: In a small bowl stir together the cornstarch and chicken stock to dissolve. Stir in the rice wine, orange juice concentrate, soy sauce, sugar, rice vinegar, sesame oil, and hot pepper flakes to taste.

4. Prepare the crispy chicken: Pour the peanut oil into a large heavy wok and place over high heat until it reaches 375° (just slightly under the smoking point). Add the orange peel and fry until medium dark brown, about 15 seconds. Scoop out with a slotted spoon and reserve. As you work, adjust the heat as needed to maintain the 375° temperature.

5. Whisk the egg whites with a fork in a pie pan or shallow dish. Put ⅓ cup of the cornstarch in a separate pie pan or shallow dish. Have a sheet of waxed paper nearby. Drain the chicken, discarding any remaining marinade. Put a third of the chicken cubes into the egg whites; as you take them out one by one, roll them in the cornstarch to coat and put on the waxed paper. Repeat with remaining chicken cubes and cornstarch, in 2 more batches.

6. One at a time, quickly drop the coated cubes into the hot oil. Do not crowd the wok. Stirring once in a while to submerge and brown them all over, fry until crisp and deep golden brown, 4 to 5 minutes. Remove one piece and cut into it to make sure it is cooked through. Scoop out all the cubes with a strainer or slotted spoon when done and drain on paper towels. Repeat with the remaining chicken cubes.

7. Carefully pour out all the oil into a clean, dry stainless steel bowl (this is dangerous so use caution) *or* use a second wok to proceed and wait until the oil is cool to pour it out. Coarsely crush the orange peel in a mortar and pestle, or with a hammer.

8. Wipe out the wok and return 1 tablespoon of the oil to it; place over high heat. Add the scallions, red bell pepper, ginger, garlic, and crushed orange peel; stir-fry for 30 seconds. Stir the sauce well and pour it in all at once; stirring, bring to a boil. Add the chicken and heat for a minute or two. Turn out onto a serving dish and garnish with scallion brushes if desired.

SCALLION BRUSHES: Cut a 3-inch length from each of 4 medium scallions (the portion toward the bulb end but not including the bulb). Make parallel lengthwise cuts about 1/8 inch apart and 1 inch long, cutting toward the center; do this at both ends of each scallion. Spread the petals slightly with your fingers and put in ice water for 10 minutes to fluff.

Thai Chicken Satay with Peanut Sauce and Pickled Cucumbers

Strips of chicken are marinated in curried coconut milk, threaded onto skewers, and grilled over charcoal or under the broiler. Though they

MAKES 4 MAIN-COURSE SERVINGS OR
12 APPETIZER SERVINGS

Marinated Chicken:

1 1/2 pounds skinless boned chicken thighs (start with 3 pounds thighs if you must bone your own)
3/4 cup unsweetened coconut milk (see Note)
2 tablespoons fresh lime juice

1 tablespoon sugar
2 teaspoons curry powder
1 garlic clove, peeled and minced or crushed through a
  press
1/2 teaspoon salt

Pickled Cucumbers:

1/3 cup rice vinegar
2 tablespoons sugar
1/2 teaspoon dried hot red pepper flakes
1 1/2 teaspoons salt
2 large cucumbers
1 small onion, sliced paper-thin and separated into rings
3 tablespoons chopped cilantro (fresh coriander)

Peanut Sauce:

3/4 cup unsweetened coconut milk (see Note)
1/3 cup chunky peanut butter
1 tablespoon Thai fish sauce (*nam pla*), or soy sauce
1 tablespoon fresh lime juice
1 teaspoon sugar
1 teaspoon oriental sesame oil
1/8 teaspoon cayenne pepper
2 tablespoons peanut oil, for grilling

1. **Marinate the chicken:** Cut the boneless chicken into strips about 3/4 inch wide and 3 inches long. Soak twelve 12-inch or twenty-four 8-inch bamboo skewers in cold water until needed.

2. In a medium bowl stir together the coconut milk, lime juice, sugar, curry powder, garlic, and salt; add the strips of chicken and marinate in the refrigerator for 1 to 4 hours.

3. **Pickle the cucumbers:** In a medium bowl stir together the rice vinegar, sugar, hot pepper flakes, and salt. Peel

are often an appetizer, I like to serve them as the main course (with rice and broccoli with red peppers) for an outdoor barbecue. The spicy sweet-tart cucumbers punctuate the rich peanut sauce and light smoky chicken. You can make the sauce without *nam pla* (fish sauce) but I urge you to locate some; it will keep on your kitchen shelf for years and will add authentic flavor to all of your Thai dishes. The unsweetened coconut milk is available in cans and is an excellent product well worth buying, but instructions follow for making your own in case you can't find the canned version.

the cucumbers and cut them in half lengthwise. With a small spoon, scoop out the seeds. Thinly slice crosswise and add to the dressing along with the onion and fresh cilantro. Toss and chill at least 1 hour.

4. Prepare the peanut sauce: Pour the coconut milk into a small heavy saucepan, bring to a simmer over moderate heat, and simmer 5 minutes. Remove from the heat and stir in the peanut butter to melt. Stir in the fish sauce, lime juice, sugar, sesame oil, and cayenne pepper. Cool to room temperature.

5. Assemble and grill the satay: Light a charcoal fire or preheat the broiler. Thread the chicken strips onto the bamboo skewers without packing them too tightly together; each strip will become an S shape as it threads onto the skewer. Grill them over charcoal, brushing lightly with the peanut oil and turning several times, until cooked through, 10 to 15 minutes (this will vary tremendously, depending on your charcoal and cooking conditions; test one for doneness). Or broil the chicken strips, turning frequently, until cooked through, 6 to 8 minutes. Serve hot, with pickled cucumbers and peanut sauce on the side.

NOTE: A 12- or 13-ounce can of coconut milk (nam katee) is perfect for this recipe. It is available in oriental grocery stores and can be kept in the cupboard indefinitely. To make your own, peel and grate enough fresh coconut to make 3 cups. Bring 3 cups milk to a simmer; add the coconut and let stand until mixture reaches room temperature. Line a sieve with about 6 layers of cheesecloth and pour in the mixture. Pick up the bundle, twist the top and squeeze out as much coconut milk as possible; discard the solids.

Yakitori

- **1** pound skinless boned chicken thighs (if you must bone your own, start with 2 pounds)
- **½** to ¾ pound chicken livers

Marinade:

- **⅓** cup *sake*
- **⅓** cup *mirin* (see Note)
- **⅓** cup Japanese soy sauce, such as Kikkoman
- **1** tablespoon sugar
- **1** tablespoon minced fresh ginger
- **1** large garlic clove, peeled and minced or crushed through a press

Assembly:

- **2** bunches medium-large scallions
- **2** large green bell peppers
- **20** medium mushrooms (8 to 12 ounces)
- **3** tablespoons peanut oil, for grilling

1. Cut the chicken into strips about ¾ inch wide and 3 inches long. Cut the livers in half, or into quarters if very large. Soak twenty 10- to 12-inch bamboo skewers in cold water until needed.

2. Prepare the marinade: In a medium bowl stir together the *sake*, *mirin*, soy sauce, sugar, ginger, and garlic. Add the chicken and livers; marinate in the refrigerator 1 to 4 hours.

3. Light a charcoal fire or preheat your broiler.

4. Assemble the yakitori: Trim the ends from the scallions and cut most of the white and light green parts, and any of the dark green that will hold together, into 1-inch lengths.

These are delicious teriyaki shish kebobs, made with strips of marinated chicken and grilled with vegetables. If you cannot find *mirin* (sweet rice wine), follow the alternative instructions in the note below. Yakitori make a tasty contribution to a barbecue or picnic. Serve with white rice or steamed dumplings and asparagus, broccoli, or green beans sprinkled with toasted sesame seeds.

Onto 8 of the skewers, thread the chicken strips, piercing them on to resemble S-shapes as you thread; intersperse scallion pieces, sideways, between the chicken pieces. Thread the livers onto 4 skewers, dividing them equally.

5. Cut the bell peppers lengthwise into quarters. Cut out the stems and ribs and shake out the seeds. Cut each quarter into 3 pieces (24 in all) and thread them onto 4 skewers. Thread the mushrooms, end to end, onto 4 skewers. Brush everything with a little of the peanut oil and grill over charcoal, turning frequently and basting with marinade until browned and cooked through, 10 to 15 minutes. Time will vary greatly depending on your charcoal and cooking conditions. Alternatively, broil, turning several times, until cooked through, 8 to 10 minutes, or until done. The bell peppers and mushrooms will take slightly longer to cook than the chicken, and the livers will be done sooner than the chicken. Serve hot.

NOTE: If you cannot obtain *mirin*, use this formula for the marinade: ⅔ cup sake, ½ cup soy sauce, 3 tablespoons sugar, 1 tablespoon ginger, and 1 large garlic clove.

Chicken "Blasto" with Egg Noodles

Here is a recipe designed for the microwave (but it defies analysis of cooking technique). There is

MAKES 4 SERVINGS

⅓ cup Dijon or brown mustard
¼ cup honey
2 tablespoons lemon juice
1 tablespoon soy sauce

¼ teaspoon cayenne pepper, or hot red pepper flakes
½ teaspoon salt
¼ teaspoon black pepper
4 medium-large chicken thighs (about 1 pound)
½ cup heavy cream
½ pound wide egg noodles
4 medium scallions, thinly sliced
¼ cup chopped fresh parsley leaves or cilantro

1. In a 9-inch round microwave dish or glass pie pan, stir together the mustard, honey, lemon juice, soy sauce, cayenne pepper, salt, and black pepper.

2. Pull the skin from the thighs and discard it. Put them in the sauce, turning several times to coat, and arrange spoke-fashion with thickest parts outward. Cover with waxed paper and microwave at full power for 5 minutes (tested in a 700-watt oven). Turn and cook 5 minutes longer. Test for doneness. If meat is still pink near center cook for 1-minute increments. Take the chicken from the sauce and put it on a cutting board until cool enough to handle. Slice very thinly across the grain. Discard bones. Add the sliced chicken meat to the sauce. Stir in the heavy cream. (The recipe can be prepared well ahead of time to here.)

3. Bring a large pot of lightly salted water to a boil over high heat. Drop in the noodles and stir until a full boil returns. Cook to the al dente stage (tender but firm to the bite), or to taste. Drain well. Heat the chicken sauce, covered, for 2 minutes on high (full) power. Toss with the noodles, scallions, and parsley or cilantro. Serve hot.

heat from the mustard, cayenne, and black pepper and a blast from the microwave.

Crispy Chicken with Candied Walnuts and Watercress

The remarkable thing about this dish, besides the crispy coated chunks of chicken, is the combination of bright green peppery watercress with a slightly sweet and sour sauce topped with crisp candied walnuts.

MAKES 4 TO 6 SERVINGS

Marinated Chicken:

- **2** tablespoons dry sherry
- **2** tablespoons white vinegar
- **1** tablespoon soy sauce
- **1** teaspoon oriental sesame oil
- **1½** pounds skinless boned chicken thighs, cut into 1-inch cubes (start with 3 pounds with skin and bones)

Candied Walnuts:

- **1** cup (4 ounces) large walnut pieces or small halves
- **3** tablespoons honey
- **3** tablespoons sugar
- **1** tablespoon vegetable oil

Sauce:

- **2** teaspoons cornstarch
- **½** cup chicken stock or canned broth
- **2** tablespoons dry sherry
- **2** tablespoons soy sauce
- **2** tablespoons ketchup
- **1** tablespoon white vinegar
- **3** tablespoons sugar
- **1** teaspoon oriental sesame oil

For Deep-frying the Crispy Chicken:

- **3** cups peanut oil
- **3** large egg whites
- **1** cup cornstarch

Stir-fry:

- **3** tablespoons peanut oil
- **1** pound fresh watercress (about 3 bunches), rinsed and dried on paper towels
- **1** tablespoon minced fresh ginger
- **1** large red bell pepper, trimmed and cut into 1-inch squares

1. Marinate the chicken: In a large bowl combine the sherry, vinegar, soy sauce, and sesame oil. Add the chicken and marinate at room temperature for 1 hour, or longer in the refrigerator.

2. Make the candied walnuts: Put the walnuts in a small heavy saucepan. Add 1 cup water and stir in the honey and sugar. Bring to a boil over moderate heat and then simmer over low heat for 10 minutes. Drain in a strainer and let dry, shaking occasionally.

3. Spoon the vegetable oil into a heavy medium skillet and place over moderately high heat. Add the walnuts and stir-fry 1 to 2 minutes, until toasted. Reserve.

4. Make the sauce: In a small bowl stir together the cornstarch, chicken stock, sherry, soy sauce, ketchup, and vinegar. Add the sugar and sesame oil and stir well to dissolve the cornstarch and sugar.

5. Make the crispy chicken: Pour the peanut oil into a large heavy wok or deep-fryer and place over high heat until it reaches 375° (slightly under the smoking point).

6. Meanwhile put the egg whites in a shallow dish or pie pan and whisk to blend. Put ⅓ cup of the cornstarch in another shallow dish or pie pan. Have a sheet of waxed paper nearby. Drain the chicken. Put a third of the chicken into the egg whites and as you take them out, one by one, roll them in the cornstarch to coat and put them on the waxed paper. One at a time, drop the coated chicken cubes into the hot oil and fry until crisp, deep golden brown, and cooked through, 4 to 5 minutes (cut into one to see if it is cooked to the center). Scoop out with a slotted spoon and drain on paper towels. Repeat, using ⅓ cup of the cornstarch to dredge each batch, until all the chicken is cooked.

7. Stir-fry: Carefully pour the oil from the wok into a clean, dry metal bowl or pot (this is dangerous, so be careful) or use a second wok. (I suppose ideally one could use the deep-fryer and a cool wok.) Place the wok over high heat. Add 2 tablespoons of the fresh peanut oil and when it is hot, stir-fry the watercress until wilted, 1 to 1½ minutes; scoop out to a large warm platter.

8. Add the remaining 1 tablespoon oil to the wok. Add the ginger and stir-fry 10 seconds. Add the bell pepper and stir-fry 30 seconds. Add the crispy deep-fried chicken and stir-fry 30 seconds. Give the sauce a good stir and pour into the wok; cook, stirring, until thickened and clear, 30 seconds to 1 minute. Spoon over the bed of stir-fried watercress and sprinkle with the candied walnuts. Serve hot.

Chinese Hot and Sour Chicken Soup

This famous peppery Szechuan soup is very popular in restaurants across this country. It is always

MAKES ABOUT 12 CUPS

10	dried Chinese mushrooms
2	tablespoons small dried Chinese tree ear mushrooms
½	pound skinless boned chicken thighs (start with 1 pound before skinning and boning)

Marinade:

- **1** tablespoon dry sherry
- **1** tablespoon soy sauce
- **2** teaspoons rice vinegar
- **2** teaspoons oriental sesame oil
- **1** teaspoon sugar
- **1** teaspoon cornstarch
- **¼** teaspoon black pepper

Soup:

- **6** cups Chinese Chicken Broth (page 49) or canned broth
- **5** slices fresh ginger, each the size of a half dollar
- **1** garlic clove, peeled and minced or crushed through a press
- **4** ounces small fresh mushrooms, sliced
- **2** cups diced (½ inch) fresh firm tofu
- **¼** cup rice vinegar
- **¼** cup soy sauce
- **1** 8-ounce can bamboo shoots, drained and cut into matchsticks
- **1** teaspoon ground black pepper, plus more for topping
- **⅓** cup packed cornstarch
- **3** large eggs
- **1** tablespoon oriental sesame oil, plus more for topping
- **8** medium scallions, thinly sliced

made with pork, but I've found that a chicken version is a very welcome change. Besides serving it with the usual Chinese accompanying dishes, try it with a hearty seven-grain bread and butter.

1. Put the dried mushrooms in a small bowl; add 1 cup boiling water and let soften 30 to 60 minutes. Put the tree ears in another small bowl; add 1 cup very hot tap water and let soften 30 to 60 minutes. Drain both, reserving the liquid from just the mushrooms. Cut off the stems from the mushrooms and discard; slice the caps into ¼-inch strips. Cut off any hard spots from the tree ears and discard. Slice them into ¼-inch slivers. Reserve.

2. Meanwhile, partially freeze the chicken to facilitate slicing. Slice into ¼-by-2-inch matchsticks.

3. Prepare the marinade: In a medium bowl stir together the sherry, soy sauce, rice vinegar, sesame oil, sugar, cornstarch, and pepper. Add the chicken shreds and marinate at room temperature for 30 minutes.

4. Prepare the soup: Pour the chicken broth and the reserved liquid from the mushrooms into a large nonaluminum soup pot or dutch oven. Add the ginger and garlic and bring to a boil over moderate heat. Cover and simmer for 5 minutes. Remove ginger slices and discard.

5. Add the chicken (along with any marinade), sliced fresh mushrooms, and tofu; cover and bring to a boil over moderate heat. Uncover and add the rice vinegar, soy sauce, bamboo shoots, pepper, reserved soaked tree ears, and soaked dried mushrooms. Cover and bring to a boil.

6. In a small bowl dissolve the cornstarch in ⅓ cup cold water. Stir into the soup, pouring it in a wide circle and stirring constantly as you pour. Bring to a boil, stirring to thicken. Keep at a simmer.

7. Whisk the eggs in a bowl with 1 tablespoon sesame oil; pour into the soup, ⅓ at a time; heat briefly, then stir in. Add all but 2 of the sliced scallions and serve hot, topped with the remaining sliced scallions, a little black pepper, and a splash of sesame oil.

Chicken Wonton Soup

MAKES 8 DOZEN

(8 MAIN-COURSE OR 16 SOUP-COURSE SERVINGS)

1 tablespoon vegetable oil
2 cups finely chopped green cabbage
1 tablespoon minced fresh ginger
½ cup chopped cooked spinach, well drained
½ cup finely chopped water chestnuts
¾ pound skinless boned chicken thighs (or 1½ pounds before skinning and boning), roughly diced
2 thin pork chops (½ pound), boned and diced
2 large whole eggs, plus 2 egg yolks
2 tablespoons soy sauce
1 teaspoon oriental sesame oil
1 12-ounce package (8 dozen) thin wonton wrappers
2 quarts Chinese Chicken Broth (page 49)

A moist chicken filling flavored with pork, spinach, and cabbage is simple to put together. And you start with packaged wonton wrappers, so it's mostly a matter of assembling the wontons. Be sure to make the broth ahead of time.

1. Spoon the vegetable oil into a heavy medium skillet or wok and place over moderately high heat. Add the cabbage and sauté until well browned, 4 to 5 minutes. Add the ginger and cook a minute longer. Turn into a bowl and stir in the spinach and water chestnuts. Cool to room temperature.

2. Combine the chicken and pork in a food processor and grind to a medium consistency (alternatively, put through a meat grinder or finely mince with a knife). Turn into the bowl with the sautéed vegetables. Add the 2 whole eggs, soy sauce, and sesame oil; stir to blend evenly.

3. In a cup stir the 2 egg yolks with 1 tablespoon cold water.

4. Place one wonton wrapper on a flat surface in front of you. Spoon or pipe (with a pastry bag fitted with a plain round tip) 2 teaspoons of the filling in the center. Dip a fingertip into the egg yolk mixture and coat two edges of the wrapper. Fold the wrapper up over the filling to make a triangle with the top two points slightly askew, and pinch to enclose the filling, squeezing out any air as you do so. Dab a little of the egg on the point to the right side and bring the left and right points together, overlapping them by about ½ inch. Pinch together so the wonton resembles a nurse's cap. Place on a plate or board lightly dusted with cornstarch. Repeat with the remaining ingredients. If making ahead, cover and refrigerate.

5. Heat the broth in a large soup pot or tureen.

6. Bring a large pot of lightly salted water to a boil over high heat. One at a time, quickly drop in half the wontons. Reduce the heat slightly and boil gently until tender but slightly firm to the bite, about 3 to 4 minutes. Scoop out with a strainer or slotted spoon. Drain and add to the broth. Repeat with the remaining wontons. Serve hot. For main course servings you'll want 1 dozen wontons in 1 cup of the broth; for soup course servings, 6 wontons in ½ cup broth.

Vietnamese Grilled Chicken Soup

The fragrant culinary palette of the Vietnamese is composed of fresh mint, cilantro, charcoal smoke, lemon, ginger, garlic, chile, and fish sauce. These ingredients are the essence of their

MAKES 4 MAIN-COURSE SERVINGS

Marinated Chicken Thighs:

¼ cup Vietnamese or Thai fish sauce (*nuoc nam* or *nam pla*)

¼ cup fresh lemon juice

2 tablespoons sugar

1 tablespoon soy sauce

8 slices fresh ginger, each the size of a quarter

1 small onion, peeled and sliced

1 large garlic clove, peeled and sliced

8 medium chicken thighs (2½ pounds)
1 tablespoon vegetable oil

Soup:

3 quarts unsalted Basic Chicken Stock (page 47) or
Superior Chicken Broth (page 48)

⅓ cup Vietnamese or Thai fish sauce (nuoc nam or nam pla)

5 slices fresh ginger, each the size of a quarter

2 large garlic cloves, peeled and minced or crushed
through a press

4 medium scallions, cut into 1-inch lengths, including
green parts

¾ pound thin fresh egg noodles, or ½ pound dried
extra-thin spaghetti

4 cups fresh bean sprouts

2 cups finely shredded romaine lettuce hearts

½ cup chopped fresh mint

½ cup chopped fresh cilantro

½ cup chopped peanuts

4 to 8 teaspoons Vietnamese chili sauce (optional)

1 lemon, cut into 8 wedges

fresh cooking style, and all are employed in this addictive soup. It is best served in oversized soup bowls. Note that the chicken must be marinated 12 hours.

1. Marinate the chicken: In a large bowl stir together the fish sauce, lemon juice, sugar, soy sauce, ginger, onion, and garlic; add the chicken thighs, turning to coat them. Cover and marinate in the refrigerator 12 hours or overnight, turning once or twice.

2. Light a charcoal fire. When the coals are glowing but covered with gray ash, drain the chicken thighs. Brush the undersides lightly with the vegetable oil and place on a grill about 5 inches above the coals, skin side up. Grill, turning every 5 minutes, until cooked through, 20 to 30 minutes. Alternatively, the chicken can be broiled.

3. Prepare the soup: Pour the chicken stock into a large saucepan. Add the fish sauce, ginger, and garlic. Bring to a boil over moderate heat, then simmer over low heat for 5 minutes. Remove from the heat and add the scallions. (Before serving, fish out and discard the ginger.)

4. Bring a large pot of lightly salted water to a boil over high heat. Boil the pasta until tender but firm to the bite, 2 to 3 minutes for fresh or 7 to 9 minutes for dried. Drain.

5. To serve, pour 3 cups of the hot broth into each of four very large (1½ to 2-quart) bowls; add a quarter of the noodles, 1 cup bean sprouts, ½ cup romaine shreds, 2 tablespoons mint, 2 tablespoons cilantro, and 2 tablespoons peanuts. Top with two chicken thighs. To one side, spoon 1 to 2 teaspoons of the chili sauce. Serve 2 wedges of lemon at one side of each bowl. Serve hot with chopsticks and soup spoons.

Chicken Minestrone

This main-dish country-style Italian soup is best finished an hour before you serve it. It is hearty and robust and exactly what I want on a cold Saturday evening. You can add macaroni to each serving if you want. If

MAKES 20 CUPS

2	tablespoons olive oil
3	medium carrots, peeled and cut into ½-inch dice
2	medium onions, peeled and chopped
2	ribs celery, cut in ½-inch dice
2	large garlic cloves, peeled and minced or crushed through a press
1½	teaspoons dried oregano, crumbled
1	teaspoon dried basil, crumbled
1	bay leaf
1	16-ounce can whole tomatoes, with juice
1½	cups dry white wine

6 cups Basic Chicken Stock (page 47) or canned broth
2 pounds chicken thighs (6 medium), skin pulled off
1 tablespoon salt
1 tablespoon sugar
3 medium red-skinned potatoes (1 pound), peeled and cut into ½-inch dice
2 medium zucchini, cut into ½-inch slices and quartered
1 16-ounce can red kidney beans, rinsed and drained
1 16-ounce can white kidney beans (cannellini), rinsed and drained
¼ cup chopped parsley leaves
¼ teaspoon black pepper
Grated Parmesan cheese

not, be sure to add grated Parmesan cheese, at least. Crusty bread and sweet butter are welcome accompaniments.

1. Spoon the olive oil into a heavy 6-quart nonaluminum soup pot or dutch oven and place over moderate heat. Add the carrots, onions, and celery; sauté to soften and lightly brown, 5 to 7 minutes. Add the garlic, 1 teaspoon of the oregano, basil, and bay leaf; sauté for 1 minute. Pour in the tomatoes and juice, breaking up the tomatoes with a spoon. Add the white wine, chicken stock, and 4 cups of hot water. Add the chicken thighs and bring to a boil over moderate heat. Simmer over low heat, stirring occasionally, for 30 minutes. Take out the chicken with tongs and put the pieces on a plate until cool enough to handle.
2. Add the potatoes and simmer for 15 minutes. Add the zucchini and simmer 10 minutes longer.
3. Pull the chicken meat from the bones and tear into ½-inch shreds. Add to the soup along with the red and white kidney beans and simmer 5 minutes longer. Stir in the parsley, pepper, and remaining ½ teaspoon oregano. Add a bit more salt to taste if needed and let stand 1 hour. Reheat gently over low heat and serve hot, topped with grated Parmesan cheese.

Chinese Pan-fried Dumplings

These dumplings are called pot stickers, because they are browned on their bottoms before they are steamed. The filling is composed of chicken thighs with spinach and ginger. You can make them ahead and resteam with a splash of water. The sauce can be made a day or two ahead. You will need wonton wrappers for this recipe.

MAKES 48

Dipping Sauce:

- **2** tablespoons oriental sesame oil
- **1** tablespoon grated fresh ginger
- **1** garlic clove, peeled and minced or crushed through a press
- **½** cup chicken broth
- **3** tablespoons soy sauce
- **1** tablespoon rice vinegar
- **2** teaspoons sugar
- **1** medium scallion, thinly sliced, including green part

Dumplings:

- **1** pound skinless boned chicken thighs, cut in 1-inch cubes (start with 2 pounds with skin and bone)
- **1** cup chopped cooked (see Note) well-drained spinach, or one 10-ounce package frozen, thawed and lightly squeezed
- **1** large egg
- **1** tablespoon grated fresh ginger
- **1** tablespoon soy sauce
- **1** tablespoon oriental sesame oil
- **½** teaspoon salt
- **1** egg yolk
- **48** medium wonton wrappers
- **2** tablespoons vegetable oil

1. Make the dipping sauce: Spoon the sesame oil into a small heavy saucepan. Add the ginger and garlic. Place over low heat and sizzle for 10 to 15 seconds. Add the chicken broth, soy sauce, vinegar, and sugar. Bring just to a simmer. Remove from the heat and cool to room temperature. Stir in the sliced scallion. If making ahead, cover and chill.

2. Make the dumplings: Put the chicken cubes in a food processor and grind to a fine texture (or put through a meat grinder, or mince very finely with two sharp heavy knives). Turn the chicken into a bowl and add the spinach, egg, ginger, soy sauce, sesame oil, and salt; mix well with your hands, beating the mixture vigorously in a circle to blend.

3. In a cup, stir the egg yolk with 2 teaspoons cold water. Place one wonton wrapper in front of you (keeping the remainder covered so they don't dry out). Spoon about 1 tablespoon of the filling in the center. Dip your fingertip into the egg and brush two of the edges of the wrapper. Fold the wrapper up over the filling to make a triangle with the top two points slightly askew, and pinch to enclose, squeezing out the air as you do so. Dab a little of the egg on the point on the right side and bring the left and right points together, overlapping them by about ½ inch. Pinch together so the dumpling resembles a nurse's cap. Repeat, shaping all the dumplings, and keeping them covered as you assemble them.

4. Cook the dumplings in two batches, or use two skillets and cook simultaneously. Spoon 1 tablespoon of the vegetable oil into a heavy 10-inch well-seasoned or nonstick skillet and place over moderate heat. Add half the dumplings, points upward, and fry until deep golden brown on the bottom, 2 to 3 minutes. Add ½ cup water; cover and steam until the water evaporates, 2 to 3 minutes longer. If the tops seem dry, splash with a few drops of water. Continue cooking, uncovered, until the bottoms have recrisped, about 1 minute longer. Shake the pan occasionally while they cook, so they don't stick. Invert a plate over the pan and invert both the plate and pan so the dumplings are unmolded, browned side up. Repeat with the remaining tablespoon oil and dumplings. Serve hot, with shallow dishes of the dipping sauce.

NOTE: Wash 1 pound spinach and put in a large pot with just the water clinging to the leaves; cover and cook over high until wilted, about 3 minutes: drain, cool, and finely chop.

Crunchy Spring Rolls

These are the type of crisp-fried rolls favored in Vietnam rather than the egg rolls made in China. However, you can also use the filling to make delicious Chinese egg rolls by following the instructions that follow. You will need edible rice paper rounds for the Vietnamese version or egg roll skins to make the Chi-

MAKES TWENTY 4-INCH ROLLS

½ pound skinless boned chicken thighs (2 medium), or 1 pound with skin and bone
7 thin slices fresh ginger
2 large peeled garlic cloves, 1 sliced and 1 minced
3 tablespoons peanut oil, plus more for frying
2 cups finely shredded green cabbage
2 cups fresh bean sprouts
½ cup fine julienne of canned bamboo shoots
1 tablespoon minced fresh ginger
4 ounces fresh mushrooms (4 large), finely chopped
¼ cup dry sherry
1 tablespoon cornstarch
1 tablespoon soy sauce
1 teaspoon oriental sesame oil
¼ cup sugar
Dipping Sauce (page 264)
20 6-inch rounds edible rice paper

Optional Accompaniments:

10 small romaine lettuce leaves, halved crosswise
20 small mint sprigs
20 small cilantro sprigs

1. Combine the chicken thighs with 1 cup cold water in a medium saucepan; add the sliced ginger and sliced garlic and bring to a boil over moderate heat. (If you are using whole chicken thighs, add an extra ½ cup of water.) Lower the heat, cover the pot, and simmer until cooked through, about 15 minutes (cook 5 to 8 minutes longer for chicken with bones). Let cool completely. Cut the thighs into fine julienne matchsticks about ⅛ by 2 inches.

2. Spoon 1 tablespoon of the peanut oil into a heavy medium skillet and place over moderate heat. Add the cabbage and sauté to lightly brown, about 5 minutes. Remove and reserve. Spoon in 1 tablespoon more oil and add the bean sprouts; stir-fry for 1 minute. Add the bamboo shoots and cook a minute longer. Spoon sprouts and bamboo shoots over the cabbage.

3. Spoon the remaining 1 tablespoon oil into a large heavy skillet or wok. Add the minced ginger and minced garlic; stir-fry over high heat for about 10 seconds. Add the chicken shreds and sizzle for about 1 minute. Add the mushrooms and stir-fry a minute longer. Pour in the sherry and boil until it evaporates. Stir in the reserved cabbage, bean sprouts, and bamboo shoots and heat for a minute.

4. In a small bowl stir together the cornstarch and 2 tablespoons cold water and the soy sauce; add to the filling and cook until thick, about 30 seconds. Stir in the sesame oil and 1 teaspoon of the sugar. Turn into a bowl and cool to room temperature.

5. Make the dipping sauce (it can be made days ahead of time if you wish).

nese version. By the way, the rice paper softens quickly and easily in sweetened water. The rolls are also exceptionally delicious *without* frying so you can serve them cold with just the dipping sauce and eliminate extra calories and work.

6. Pour 2 cups of very warm tap water into a shallow bowl or pie pan and stir in the remaining sugar.

7. The rice paper is brittle and fragile. Work with one sheet at a time. Dip one into the sweetened water and let soften until pliable, about 20 seconds. Take it out and place it on a paper towel. Spoon about 2 tablespoons of the filling across the lower third; fold the bottom rounded edge of the rice paper up over the filling; fold the ends inward, then roll up tightly and place seam side down on a paper towel. Continue making rolls, arranging them on the paper towel so they do not touch each other. If serving unfried, cover with a damp paper towel.

8. Pour ½ inch peanut oil into a large heavy skillet and place over moderate heat until the oil reaches 325° on a thermometer (this is a well below the smoking point). Place the spring rolls in the oil without crowding the pan and fry, turning frequently, until they are crisp and golden brown, about 8 minutes. Do not try to brown too quickly or they won't be crisp. Drain on paper towels. Serve hot with the dipping sauce.

9. Optional accompaniments: To serve in traditional Vietnamese style, place one spring roll on half a lettuce leaf along with a sprig each of mint and cilantro, then roll up the lettuce, tucking the ends in. The rolls are dipped into the sauce as they are eaten.

NOTE: Rice paper and the fish sauce used to make the dipping sauce are available in oriental grocery stores.

Chinese Egg Rolls

MAKES 8

1. Use the above filling and eight 6-inch square egg roll skins. You will also need a "glue" mixture of 1 egg yolk, 2 tablespoons cornstarch, and 2 tablespoons water.

2. Place one egg roll skin on a flat surface in front of you so one point is at the bottom, diamond fashion. Spoon a scant ⅓ cup of the filling in a 4½-inch log across the center. Fold the bottom point up over the filling. Brush some of the "glue" over the two side points and fold them inward over the filling. Paint the top point and sides (like an envelope flap) and tightly roll the egg roll away from you to enclose and seal. Assemble them as you fry them, 2 or 3 at a time.

3. Heat about 4 cups peanut oil in a wok to about 370°. Fry until crisp and golden brown, about 4 minutes. You can fry 2 or 3 at a time. Drain on paper towels. If making ahead, recrisp in 375° oil for a minute or two. Serve with hot Chinese mustard and duck sauce, if desired.

Italian Chicken Sausages

Really great Italian sausages can be made from chicken. Parmesan cheese and parsley contribute good flavors, along with the expected fennel seeds. You will need a meat grinder and sausage stuffer or a food processor and a pastry bag with a large plain tip. Sausage casings are available at some butcher shops; they are packed in salt and keep indefinitely in the refrigerator.

MAKES ABOUT 2 POUNDS
(3 WHEELS OR SIXTEEN 4-INCH LINKS)

- **1** tablespoon whole fennel seeds
- **2** pounds skinless boned chicken thighs (start with 4 pounds with skin and bones), cut in 1-inch cubes
- **5** slices smoked bacon (about 4 ounces), cut in ¹⁄₂-inch pieces
- **2** tablespoons Rendered Chicken Fat (page 337)
- **1** cup grated Parmesan cheese
- **1** cup chopped fresh parsley leaves
- **1** tablespoon coarse kosher salt
- **¹⁄₂** teaspoon black pepper
- **3** 3-foot lengths sausage casing

1. Coarsely grind the fennel seeds in a mortar with a pestle or in a spice grinder; put in a small bowl and add ¹⁄₄ cup boiling water. Let cool in the refrigerator.
2. Partially freeze the chicken until firm but not frozen; combine in a food processor with the bacon and grind to a coarse texture; or force through the coarse blade of a meat grinder. Transfer to a large bowl and stir in the soaked fennel seeds, chicken fat, Parmesan cheese, parsley, salt, and pepper.
3. Rinse the sausage casings in a bowl of cold water and then let cold water run through them directly from the tap. Thread one casing onto a sausage stuffer (attached to the meat grinder) or a ¹⁄₂- to ³⁄₄-inch plain round tip on a large pastry bag.
4. Put the sausage mixture back into the meat grinder (minus the cutting blade) or fill the pastry bag if using. Tie a knot at the end of the casing. As you hold the casing, let 2 inches remain unstuffed near the knot to allow for expansion; let the

mixture grind through into the casing (or squeeze the pastry bag). The sausage should be about 1 inch wide and even throughout. Tie a knot at the other end, leaving a little space for expansion. You can use your hands to shape the sausage evenly and let it coil naturally. If desired, use small pieces of string to tie as you shape into 4-inch links. Place on a rack. Repeat to use all the sausage mixture and casing. Let air-dry on racks in the refrigerator for about 12 hours. Then cover and keep refrigerated for up to 3 days.

5. Put one coil of sausage (or the links) in a large heavy skillet over low heat. Prick several times with a fork and cook, turning several times, until well browned, about 20 minutes. Drain on paper towels.

Chicken Strudel

Sheets of phyllo pastry (fresh or frozen) make it so simple to create magically light and flaky strudels with a savory chicken and creamy mushroom filling. These are good for a party or for a special dinner.

MAKES 2

- **1** pound skinless boned chicken thighs or breasts
- **1** to 2 tablespoons olive oil
- **1** medium onion, peeled and finely chopped
- **1** large garlic clove, peeled and minced or crushed through a press
- **1** teaspoon dried basil, crumbled
- **1/2** pound fresh mushrooms, finely chopped
- **2** tablespoons all-purpose flour
- **3** tablespoons dry white wine
- **2** teaspoons lemon juice
- **1** 8-ounce package cream cheese, softened to room temperature
- **1/2** teaspoon salt
- **1/8** teaspoon pepper
- **6** tablespoons (3/4 stick) butter, melted
- **14** sheets phyllo pastry, each about 12 by 17 inches
- **2** teaspoons poppy seeds or sesame seeds

1. Cut the chicken into 1/2-inch dice.

2. Spoon 1 tablespoon of the olive oil into a large heavy skillet and place over moderately high heat. Add the chicken and sauté just until cooked through, 3 to 5 minutes. Take out with a slotted spoon and reserve in a bowl.

3. If you have used chicken thighs, there will probably be plenty of melted fat in the skillet; spoon off all but about 2 tablespoons. If you have used breasts, add the remaining tablespoon of olive oil. Add the onion and sauté over moderate heat to soften, about 3 minutes. Add the garlic and basil; cook a minute longer. Add the mushrooms and sauté about 3 minutes longer. Stir in the flour; the mixture will be dry. Pour in the wine and lemon juice and cook until very thick, a minute longer. Turn into the bowl with the chicken and stir in the cream cheese and salt and pepper. Let cool to room temperature.

4. Preheat the oven to 375°. Line a baking sheet with aluminum foil and lightly butter the foil.

5. Working on a kitchen towel or a board, place one sheet of phyllo in front of you (keep the remainder covered with a towel or with plastic wrap so they do not dry out). Dip a pastry brush into melted butter and dab all over (do not attempt to cover completely by brushing). Repeat with 4 more sheets of phyllo to make 5 layers. Spoon half of the filling along one short side, leaving about 1½ inches at each end and along the front. Roll up tightly, tucking in the ends as you roll. Dab with butter and roll one of the remaining sheets of pastry around, again tucking in the ends. Repeat so the roll has 7 sheets of pastry. Place on the prepared baking sheet. Repeat to make a second strudel and place on the same baking sheet. Prick the tops of each with a fork 8 or 10 times.

6. Brush each strudel with a little melted butter and sprinkle with the poppy seeds. Bake about 35 minutes, until golden brown. Let cool for a few minutes before cutting into 1½-inch slices.

Ziti with Chicken and Sun-dried Tomatoes

With rich, rustic flavors, this hearty pasta dish needs no herbs. It is meant to be simple. The intense flavor of Italian sun-dried tomatoes is enough to carry the chicken and the ziti. I hope that media overexposure hasn't ruined sun-dried tomatoes for everyone. They are splendid and classic. The sauce simmers just 15 to 20 minutes. Serve with browned mushrooms and buttered greens.

MAKES 4 MAIN-COURSE OR 8 PASTA-COURSE SERVINGS

- **2** tablespoons vegetable oil
- **1½** pounds skinless boned chicken thighs, cut into ½-inch dice (start with 3 pounds with skin and bone)
- **1** medium onion, peeled and finely chopped
- **2** large garlic cloves, peeled and minced or crushed through a press
- **2** cups dry white wine
- **2** 8-ounce cans tomato sauce
- **½** cup packed slivered sun-dried tomatoes in olive oil
- **¼** cup olive oil
- **2** teaspoons salt
- **½** teaspoon black pepper
- **¼** teaspoon cayenne pepper
- **1** pound ziti, rigatoni, or penne

1. Spoon 1 tablespoon of the vegetable oil into a large heavy skillet and place over moderately high heat. Add half the chicken and brown well without stirring, increasing the heat to high if necessary, about 4 minutes. Stir and brown about 2 minutes longer. Scoop out with a slotted spoon and transfer to a plate. Add the remaining 1 tablespoon vegetable oil and the rest of the chicken and brown in the same way. Scoop out. Add the onion and garlic and sauté over low heat for about 2 minutes to soften. Return all the chicken to the skillet and pour in the white wine. Boil briefly, stirring, to deglaze the pan.

2. Transfer mixture to a heavy medium saucepan. Add the tomato sauce, sun-dried tomatoes, olive oil, salt, black pepper, and cayenne pepper. Simmer, stirring occasionally, 15 to 20 minutes, to blend the flavors and soften the tomatoes.

3. Meanwhile, place a large pot of lightly salted water over high heat and bring to a boil. Drop in the pasta and, stirring constantly, return to the boil. Stirring frequently, boil until tender but firm to the bite, about 10 minutes. Drain and put in a large bowl. Add the sauce; toss and let stand 3 to 5 minutes. Serve hot.

Japanese Soy Chicken with Pickled Cucumbers

MAKES 6 SERVINGS

Pickled Cucumbers:

- **3** 8-inch cucumbers, peeled and halved lengthwise
- **1** tablespoon salt
- **2** tablespoons white vinegar
- **1** tablespoon sugar
- **1** tablespoon oriental sesame oil
- **¼** to ½ teaspoon dried hot red pepper flakes
- **1** small red bell pepper, trimmed and cut into strips ¼ by 1½ inches
- **2** medium scallions, sliced

Here's another re-freshingly simple rec-ipe from my Hawaiian cousins, Betty and Anthony, in which chicken thighs are coated with a beauti-ful shimmering glaze. It is best made with Japanese sweet rice wine, mirin, but is also delicious when made with sake. It is a good dish to make in an electric skillet as my cousins do. Prepare the cucumbers first so they can pickle lightly.

Soy Chicken:

1 tablespoon vegetable oil
12 medium chicken thighs (about 4 pounds)
1 small onion, peeled and finely chopped
1 tablespoon minced fresh ginger
3 medium garlic cloves, peeled and minced or crushed through a press
1/2 cup plus 2 tablespoons dry sherry
1/2 cup turbinado sugar (raw sugar)
1/2 cup Japanese soy sauce, such as Kikkoman
1/4 cup *mirin*, or *sake*
1 tablespoon white vinegar
1 teaspoon oriental sesame oil
1/8 teaspoon white pepper
1 tablespoon cornstarch
2 medium scallions, thinly sliced
2 tablespoons chopped fresh cilantro

1. Prepare the pickled cucumbers: With a spoon, scoop the seeds from the cucumbers and discard. Slice into 1/4-inch half-rounds and put in a large bowl with the salt, 1 tray of ice cubes, and 1/4 cup cold water; toss and let stand for 1 hour. Drain, reserving 2 tablespoons of the liquid.

2. In a medium bowl combine the reserved 2 tablespoons liquid with the vinegar, sugar, sesame oil, and hot pepper flakes; mix together and add the cucumbers, red pepper, and scallions. Cover and chill until ready to serve.

3. Prepare the soy chicken: Spoon the vegetable oil into a large heavy skillet and place over moderately high heat. Add half of the chicken thighs, skin side down, and brown well, 4 to 5 minutes. Turn and brown the other side for 3 to 4 minutes. Take out and transfer to a plate. There should be enough oil in the pan to cook the remaining chicken. Brown as before and remove.

4. Pour off all but 1 tablespoon of the fat from the skillet. Add the onion, ginger, and garlic; sauté over moderate heat to soften, 2 to 3 minutes. Pour in ½ cup sherry and deglaze the pan, scraping the bottom. Add the sugar, soy sauce, *mirin*, vinegar, sesame oil, and pepper; pour in 1 cup water and bring to a boil. Return the chicken and simmer, uncovered, turning occasionally, for 30 to 35 minutes, until cooked. Remove the chicken and hold on a platter, covered with aluminum foil to keep warm.

5. Boil the cooking liquid over high heat for 3 minutes. Strain; you should have 1½ cups. Return the liquid to the pan. In a small bowl dissolve the cornstarch in the remaining 2 tablespoons sherry and pour it into the sauce; cook to thicken, stirring. Return the chicken and toss to coat with the glaze. Serve hot, sprinkled with the scallions and cilantro, accompanied by the pickled cucumbers and white rice or simple noodles.

Teriyaki Chicken Thighs

MAKES 4 SERVINGS

- ½ cup *sake* (Japanese rice wine)
- ½ cup *mirin* (Japanese sweet rice wine)
- ½ cup Japanese soy sauce, such as Kikkoman
- 2 tablespoons sugar
- 2 tablespoons minced fresh ginger
- 1 large garlic clove, peeled and minced or crushed through a press
- 8 medium chicken thighs (about 2½ pounds)
- 2 teaspoons cornstarch

Chicken thighs marinate in a fragrant sauce that later becomes a glaze. You will need *mirin* (sweet rice wine), which is available in stores selling Japanese ingredients. Serve with a nippy vinegary salad, stir-fried green cabbage or broccoli, and white rice. The chicken can be done under the broiler or over charcoal as you desire.

1. In a large bowl combine the *sake, mirin,* soy sauce, sugar, ginger, and garlic; stir to dissolve the sugar.

2. Grasp the skin of one thigh with a paper towel and pull off and discard; repeat with all thighs. With a sharp knife, score the meaty side of each thigh with cuts about ¼ inch deep in a ½-inch diamond pattern. Place thighs, scored side down, in the marinade. Marinate about 30 minutes, turning twice.

3. Preheat the broiler and set the rack about 5 inches from the heat source, or light a charcoal fire outdoors.

4. Remove the thighs from the marinade; drain, letting the excess marinade run back into the dish. Strain the marinade and reserve 1 cup for the glaze. Place the thighs scored sides down under the broiler (or scored side up over the charcoal) and cook for 7 minutes.

5. Meanwhile, make the glaze: Pour the reserved 1 cup cool marinade into a small heavy saucepan. Add the cornstarch and stir to dissolve. Place over moderate heat and, stirring constantly, cook until the mixture thickens and comes to a boil. Remove from the heat.

6. Turn the thighs with tongs and broil 5 to 7 minutes, until they begin to brown and the meat is cooked through. Test for doneness. Before serving, spoon a little of the glaze over each thigh.

Chicken Stew with Corn and Beans

MAKES 4 SERVINGS

- **1** tablespoon vegetable oil
- **8** chicken thighs (about 2 pounds)
- **1** medium onion, peeled and chopped
- **1** large garlic clove, peeled and minced or crushed through a press
- **1½** teaspoons ground cumin
- **1** teaspoon dried oregano, crumbled
- **2** tablespoons all-purpose flour
- **1** cup dry white wine
- **1** cup Basic Chicken Stock (page 47) or canned broth
- **1** cup light cream
- **1½** teaspoons salt
- **¼** teaspoon black pepper
- **1** pound fresh green beans, ends trimmed
- **1½** cups fresh corn kernels or one 10-ounce package frozen
- **¼** cup chopped fresh cilantro

Favorite ingredients of South America are used here to create a good, simple stew that tastes best if made at least an hour before you serve it. Small boiled potatoes make a fine side dish.

1. Spoon the vegetable oil into a large heavy flameproof casserole or dutch oven and place over moderately high heat. Add the chicken, skin side down, and brown well, about 5 minutes. Turn and brown 3 to 5 minutes longer. Take out and transfer to a platter.

2. Add the onion to the pan and sauté over moderate heat to soften, about 5 minutes. Add the garlic, cumin, and oregano; cook 1 minute. Stir in the flour to moisten it. Pour in the white wine, stirring to deglaze the pan, and add the chicken stock and light cream. Add the salt and pepper and stir over moderate heat until thickened and simmering. Return to the skillet the chicken and any juices on the platter. Cover and simmer until the chicken is cooked to the bone, about 15 minutes.

3. Meanwhile, drop the green beans into a large pot of lightly salted boiling water. Blanch until tender, 4 to 5 minutes. Drain and add to the stew along with the corn. Simmer 2 to 3 minutes to cook the corn. Remove from the heat and stir in the cilantro. Serve hot.

Mid-Eastern Grilled Chicken with Tabbouleh and Hummus

Chicken thighs are marinated and grilled with whole scallions to become part of a Mid-Eastern feast. The accompaniments are important because the flavors have been designed to complement the chicken and each other on the same plate. Prepare the hummus and tabbouleh before grilling the chicken.

MAKES 6 SERVINGS

2 medium onions, peeled and grated
1/2 cup fresh lemon juice
2 large garlic cloves, peeled and minced or crushed through a press
12 chicken thighs (about 4 pounds)
1/4 cup olive oil
18 to 24 large scallions, roots trimmed but 4 inches of green stems left attached
Salt and pepper
Hummus (recipe follows)
Tabbouleh (recipe follows)

1. In a large bowl stir together the grated onions, lemon juice, and garlic; add the chicken thighs, turning them to coat. Cover and marinate 12 hours or overnight. Take out the thighs and reserve 1/4 cup of the marinade. In a small bowl combine the reserved 1/4 cup marinade with the olive oil for basting.

2. Light a charcoal fire (or preheat the broiler). When the coals are glowing but covered with gray ash, brush the chicken thighs with a little of the basting sauce and place them on the grill about 5 inches above the coals (or under the broiler). Also brush the scallions and put them on the grill as well. Grill the chicken for 25 to 30 minutes, turning and basting every 5 minutes, until cooked. The scallions will take 10 to 15 minutes. The thighs should be charred but tender and no longer pink at the bone. Sprinkle lightly with salt and pepper. Serve hot with the cold hummus and tabbouleh, and if desired, black olives, feta cheese, and pita bread.

Tabbouleh

MAKES ABOUT 8 CUPS

1½ cups medium-grain bulgur wheat
  1 large cucumber, peeled and halved lengthwise
  2 cups diced (½-inch) tomato
  1 medium green bell pepper, trimmed and cut into ½-inch squares
  1 cup thinly sliced scallions (8 to 10 medium), with green parts
  1 cup finely chopped fresh mint leaves
  1 cup chopped fresh parsley leaves
 ⅓ cup olive oil
 ⅓ cup fresh lemon juice
  2 teaspoons salt
 ½ teaspoon black pepper

Fresh and fragrant with plenty of parsley and mint, this big-flavored whole grain and vegetable salad is a Mideast classic. Crunchy cucumbers, bright scallions, and juicy tomatoes are enhanced by aromatic lemons. Bulgur wheat is available in many supermarkets and all health food stores.

1. Put the bulgur wheat in a large bowl and add cold water to cover generously. Swish around the grains with your hand to rinse and pour off the water from the top of the bowl. Repeat several times, until the water is no longer cloudy. Cover with fresh cold water and let soak for 1 hour to soften. Drain.

Squeeze dry by wrapping in several layers of cheesecloth, or by pressing the grains firmly in a fine sieve.

2. Put the bulgur wheat in a large bowl. With a spoon, scoop out the seeds from the cucumber halves and discard. Cut the cucumber into ½-inch dice and add to the bowl. Add the diced tomato, bell pepper, scallions, mint, and parsley; toss to combine. Add the olive oil, lemon juice, salt, and pepper; toss again. Cover and chill until serving time. Serve cold.

Hummus

Here is a rich and earthy garbanzo bean purée flavored with sesame paste, sesame oil, and lemon juice. It is great served cold with fresh hot pita bread.

MAKES ABOUT 4 CUPS

2 16-ounce cans garbanzo beans (chick-peas)
¼ cup olive oil
2 large garlic cloves, peeled and minced or crushed
¾ cup tahini (sesame paste)
¼ cup fresh lemon juice
1 tablespoon oriental sesame oil (optional)
1 teaspoon ground cumin
1 teaspoon salt
½ teaspoon black pepper
1 medium tomato, finely diced

1. Drain the garbanzo beans and rinse them. Put them in a food processor or blender.

2. Spoon 3 tablespoons of the olive oil into a small heavy skillet and place over low heat. Add the garlic and sizzle gently without browning, 1 to 2 minutes. Scrape onto the garbanzo beans. Add the tahini, lemon juice, sesame oil, cumin, salt and pepper; process to a purée, gradually adding ½ cup to ⅔ cup cold water to make a good spreading consistency. Cover and chill. To serve, spread on a large platter, making swirls. Drizzle with the remaining olive oil and sprinkle with the diced tomato. Serve cold.

Chicken Wings

6

Chicken wings—some people love 'em while others don't care for them at all. Me, I love chicken wings and all the good things you can do with them. There's not much meat in proportion to bone, for sure, but what's there is choice. The delicate white meat is tender, juicy, and tasty, and for crispy-crunchy chicken skin lovers, there's plenty of that too.

One thing's for sure, wings take well to all cooking techniques; they can be roasted, barbecued, braised, fried, zapped, steamed, sautéed, battered, dipped, fricasseed, curried, or red-cooked the Chinese way. You can even turn them inside out to make miniature drumstick "lollipops."

Every country in the world shares our love for the clipped wings; in this chapter you'll find international treatments like Mexican green chile, Aztec mole, chicken wings niçoise, Italian marinara, and Chinese wings in oyster sauce.

Wings are a bargain too; I've seen them for as little as 39¢ a pound on sale in quantity (and you'll need a substantial amount if you're going to make a meal from them). They make succulent appetizers and snack foods. Buffalo chicken wings have recently received a lot of attention, and rightfully so; the combination of bleu cheese, spicy fried wings, and crisp celery sticks hits the spot.

Thai Chicken Wings
with Fragrant Rice

You will need Thai fish sauce (*nam pla*) and canned unsweetened coconut milk from Thailand or Vietnam for this luscious recipe. Both keep well on the shelf for a year or more. This dish looks as if it makes a lot more than it really does because there is so little meat on wings. If you'd rather serve noodles than rice, omit the last part of this recipe.

MAKES 4 TO 5 SERVINGS

Thai Chicken Wings:

- **4** pounds chicken wings (about 20)
- **1½** tablespoons vegetable oil
- **2** medium onions, peeled and chopped
- **1** tablespoon minced fresh ginger
- **1** large garlic clove, peeled and minced or crushed through a press
- **½** teaspoon dried hot red pepper flakes
- **1** 12-ounce can unsweetened coconut milk (or see Note on page 180)
- **3** tablespoons Thai fish sauce (*nam pla*)
- **1** 10-ounce package frozen peas, thawed slightly
- **1** 4-ounce red bell pepper, trimmed and cut into strips ¼ by 1½ inches
- **3** tablespoons chopped fresh cilantro
- **1** teaspoon grated lime rind
- **2** tablespoons fresh lime juice
- **¼** teaspoon black pepper

Fragrant Rice:

- **1** cup long-grain white rice
- **1** tablespoon Thai fish sauce (nam pla)
- **2** tablespoons chopped fresh cilantro
- **1** tablespoon vegetable oil

1. Prepare the Thai chicken wings: With a heavy cleaver, knife, or poultry shears, cut off the wing tips from the wings at the first joint. (Reserve tips for making stock, freezing until enough accumulate, if you like.) With a paring knife, cut out the V-shaped flap of skin at the inside of the "elbow" of each wing.

2. Place a large heavy sauté pan or dutch oven over moderately high heat. Spoon in 1 tablespoon of the oil and add half the chicken wings, meaty side down; brown well, regulating the heat as needed, about 5 minutes. Turn and brown the other side over moderate heat for 3 to 4 minutes. Take wings out with tongs and transfer them to a large plate. Add the remaining ½ tablespoon oil and the remaining wings; brown as before and transfer to the plate.

3. Add the onions to the pan and sauté to soften and lightly brown over moderate heat, 3 to 5 minutes. Add the ginger, garlic, and hot pepper flakes; stir for 1 minute. Shake the can of coconut milk; open it and pour in the contents along with the fish sauce; bring to a boil. Return the chicken wings and any juice that has accumulated on the plate. Cover and simmer over low heat, stirring gently several times, until the wings are very tender but not falling apart, about 30 minutes. Add the peas and bell pepper; cover and simmer 2 to 3 minutes, until hot. Remove from the heat and stir in the cilantro, grated lime rind, lime juice, and pepper.

5. Meanwhile, while the wings are simmering, **prepare the fragrant rice:** Pour about 2 quarts of hot tap water into a 3-quart saucepan and bring to a boil over high heat. Slowly add the rice so the boiling doesn't stop and boil until tender, 12 to 14 minutes. Add 1 cup cold water to stop the boiling; pour into a strainer, shake to drain rice, and return to the pan. Stir in the fish sauce, cilantro, and vegetable oil. Cover to keep hot until needed.

6. To serve, take the wings out with tongs and divide them among warm dinner plates. Spoon the sauce, peas, and pepper strips over them, and spoon the rice to one side.

Chicken Wings Niçoise with Spaghetti

Juicy chicken wings in a sauce with a deep, complicated flavor like this are best served up with crusty bread and a side dish of steamed green beans. You might choose an herbed goat cheese as a starter. Be sure to look for true niçoise olives and be careful to warn your guests about the pits (they are very small).

MAKES 4 SERVINGS

- **16** chicken wings (about 3 pounds)
- **3** tablespoons olive oil
- **2** medium onions, peeled and chopped
- **1** large garlic clove, peeled and minced or crushed through a press
- **1½** teaspoons dried basil, crumbled
- **½** teaspoon dried oregano, crumbled
- **¼** teaspoon dried thyme, crumbled
- **3** tablespoons all-purpose flour
- **2** cups Basic Chicken Stock (page 47) or canned broth
- **½** cup dry white wine
- **1** tablespoon Dijon mustard
- **1** 9-ounce package frozen artichoke hearts, thawed
- **½** pound small whole fresh mushrooms, sliced
- **½** cup whole small black niçoise olives
- **½** teaspoon salt
- **⅛** teaspoon black pepper
- **¼** cup chopped fresh parsley
- **½** pound thin spaghetti or vermicelli
- **1** lemon, cut in 4 wedges

1. With a heavy cleaver, knife, or poultry shears, cut off the wing tips at the first joint (reserve or freeze until enough have accumulated for making stock). With a small knife, cut out the V-shaped flap of skin at the inside of the "elbow."

2. Spoon 1 tablespoon of the olive oil into a large heavy sauté pan or dutch oven and place over moderately high heat; add half the chicken wings, meaty sides down, and brown well, regulating the heat as necessary, about 5 minutes. Turn and brown remaining sides about 3 minutes longer. Take out with tongs and transfer to a plate. Add 1 tablespoon more oil if needed and the remaining wings; brown as before and remove.

3. Add the onions to the pan and sauté to soften and lightly brown, 3 to 5 minutes. Add the garlic, basil, oregano, and thyme; cook, stirring for 1 minute. Stir in the flour and cook a minute longer. Pour in the stock and white wine; bring to a boil, stirring constantly until thickened. Return the wings to the pan, cover, and simmer over low heat until they are tender but not falling apart, about 30 minutes, stirring gently once or twice. Stir in the mustard.

4. Add the artichoke hearts, sliced mushrooms, and the niçoise olives; cover and simmer about 10 minutes, until the artichokes are hot. Add the salt, pepper, and parsley; remove from the heat and keep covered to keep hot.

5. Meanwhile, bring a large pot of lightly salted water to a boil; drop in the spaghetti and, stirring constantly, return to the boil. Cook, stirring frequently, until tender but firm to the bite. Drain and then toss with the remaining tablespoon of olive oil. Arrange the spaghetti on 4 warm dinner plates; top each portion with 4 chicken wings, and spoon the sauce, mushrooms, and artichokes over the top. Serve with lemon wedges.

Chile Verde Chicken Wings

This is a chicken version of chile verde, the mild Mexican green chile stew usually made from pork and fresh *poblano* chile peppers. The rich roasted flavor of the peppers is what makes the gravy so tasty. Serve with plenty of steaming hot flour tortillas (or crusty bread if you aren't a purist), a pot of Pinto Beans with Bacon (page 375), and lots of napkins. Steamed white rice flecked with fresh cilantro also makes a good accompaniment.

MAKES 6 SERVINGS

- **3** pounds medium-sized fresh *poblano* chile peppers (12 to 16), or six 4-ounce cans mild roasted peeled green chiles
- **5** pounds chicken wings (about 30)
- **2** tablespoons vegetable oil
- **4** medium onions (1 pound), peeled and slivered lengthwise
- **3** large garlic cloves, peeled and minced or crushed through a press
- **2** tablespoons all-purpose flour
- **1½** teaspoons dried oregano, crumbled
- **1½** teaspoons ground cumin
- **½** teaspoon dried thyme, crumbled
- **1** bay leaf
- **1** 14- to 16-ounce can whole tomatoes, with juice
- **3** cups Basic Chicken Stock (page 47) or canned broth
- **1** teaspoon salt

1. Roast the *poblanos* by placing them directly on the burners (over high heat) of a gas stove or as close to the heat source as possible under a broiler; turn with tongs frequently until they are blistered and black all over. Let them cool for a minute or two and then enclose them in a plastic bag by twisting the top, and chill for at least 10 minutes. Rub the skins away and cut out the stems, ribs, and seeds (this can be done under gently running water in a colander but some of the juices will be rinsed away as well). If using canned green chiles, simply drain and discard seeds. Cut or tear the chilies lengthwise into ½-inch-wide strips.

2. With a heavy cleaver, large heavy knife, or poultry shears, cut off the wing tips (freeze and/or reserve for chicken stock). With a knife, cut out the V-shaped flap of skin at the "elbow" and discard.

3. Spoon 1 tablespoon of the vegetable oil into a large heavy sauté pan or dutch oven and place over moderately high heat. Add about a third of the wings, meaty side down, and brown well, about 5 minutes. Turn and brown the other sides about 3 minutes. Take out with tongs and reserve on a plate. Add ½ tablespoon of the remaining oil to the pan and brown another third of the wings in the same manner; then repeat with the last batch. Discard all but 2 tablespoons of the fat in the pan.

4. Add the onions to the pan and sauté over moderate heat to soften and lightly brown, about 5 minutes. Add the garlic and cook for a minute. Stir in the flour and cook a minute longer. Add the oregano, cumin, thyme, bay leaf, and tomatoes with their juice; break up the tomatoes with a spoon and stir in the chicken stock and the salt. Stirring constantly, bring to a boil. Add the strips of chiles and the browned chicken wings; cover and simmer over low heat, stirring once in a while, until the wings are very tender but not falling apart, 30 to 40 minutes. Serve hot in shallow soup plates.

Chicken Wings Marinara

These juicy tender wings in bright red marinara sauce are good as an appetizer or main course piled atop spaghetti. Either way serve with plenty of grated Parmesan cheese. Arugula with olive oil and balsamic vinegar is a nice addition to the menu.

MAKES 4 TO 6 SERVINGS

20 to 24 chicken wings (about 4 pounds)
2½ tablespoons olive oil
2 medium onions, peeled and chopped
2 large garlic cloves, peeled and minced or crushed through a press
2 teaspoons dried basil, crumbled
1 teaspoon dried oregano, crumbled
½ teaspoon dried rosemary, crumbled
¼ cup tomato paste
1 cup dry white wine
1 35-ounce can whole Italian tomatoes, with juice
1 bay leaf
¼ teaspoon dried hot red pepper flakes
2 teaspoons sugar
2 teaspoons salt
¼ teaspoon black pepper
Thin spaghetti
Grated Parmesan cheese

1. Using poultry shears or a large heavy knife, cut off the wing tips from the wings and reserve for stock. Cut out the V-shaped flap of skin from the joint at each wing, so the flavors can penetrate more easily.

2. Spoon 1½ tablespoons of the olive oil into a large heavy flameproof casserole or dutch oven and place over moderately high heat. Add half the wings, meaty sides down, and brown well, moving them occasionally so they don't stick to the pan, about 5 minutes. Turn with tongs and brown about 3 minutes longer. Take out and hold on a platter. There should be enough fat in the pan to brown the remaining wings in the same manner.

3. Spoon off and discard all but 1 tablespoon of the fat. Sauté the onions over moderate heat to soften, 3 to 5 minutes. Add the remaining 1 tablespoon olive oil and the garlic, basil, oregano, and rosemary; sauté for 1 minute. Stir in the tomato paste and then the wine. Add the tomatoes and juice, breaking up the tomatoes with a spoon. Add the bay leaf, red pepper flakes, sugar, salt, and black pepper; bring to a boil over moderate heat. Simmer uncovered for 30 minutes. Return the wings to the pan and simmer, covered, 30 to 40 minutes longer, until tender. Serve hot with spaghetti cooked al dente and the grated Parmesan cheese.

Buffalo Chicken Wings

Born in the Anchor Bar in Buffalo, New York, these hot and spicy wings were first concocted for some hungry drinkers and they became a real hit. They are usually served with bottled bleu cheese dressing but I don't care much for that so have given my favorite dressing recipe here instead. And to my taste, the classic accompanying celery sticks need crisp carrot sticks alongside for their crunchy sweetness.

MAKES 4 SERVINGS

Bleu Cheese Dressing (recipe follows)
  6 medium ribs celery
  6 medium carrots, peeled
24 medium chicken wings (4½ pounds)
  4 tablespoons (½ stick) butter
  3 tablespoons Durkee Red Hot Pepper sauce or Tabasco
1½ teaspoons paprika
Vegetable oil for deep-frying

1. Prepare the bleu cheese dressing up to several days ahead; cover it and chill until needed.

2. Cut the celery into sticks about 4 inches long and ½ inch wide. Cut the carrots in half crosswise and then into quarters lengthwise. Cover the celery and carrot sticks with plastic wrap and chill until needed.

3. Using a large heavy knife, chop off the tips of the chicken wings and reserve for making stock or soup. Cut the wings in half to separate them at their elbows, to make 48 half-wings.

4. Melt the butter in a small saucepan over low heat. Stir in the hot pepper sauce (this is for medium-hot wings; add 1 tablespoon less or more if desired) and 1 teaspoon of the paprika. Remove from the heat.

5. Pour about 1½ inches of vegetable oil into a deep-fryer and heat to 370°. Add half to a third (this depends on the size of your fryer) of the wing halves and fry until golden brown, 8 to 10 minutes. Drain on paper towels. Repeat with remaining wings.

6. Reheat the hot pepper butter and toss in a large bowl with the wings. Mound on a platter (or individual plates) surrounded by the celery and carrot sticks and the bleu cheese dressing. Serve the wings hot and everything else cold.

Bleu Cheese Dressing

MAKES ABOUT 3 1/2 CUPS

1/2	pound bleu cheese, crumbled (about 2 cups)
1	cup sour cream
1	cup plain yogurt
1/2	cup Mayonnaise (page 383)
2	tablespoons dry white wine
1	tablespoon cider vinegar
1	teaspoon salt
1/4	teaspoon black pepper

Put the bleu cheese in a medium bowl and mash with the sour cream, using a fork. Mash in the yogurt and mayonnaise to make a slightly lumpy dressing. Stir in the dry white wine, vinegar, salt, and pepper. Cover and chill. Serve cold.

This recipe makes a rather large amount because I love it so much and it always disappears fast. Serve it with the Buffalo chicken wings and with your favorite green salad and tomatoes.

Sherry-Lemon Chicken Wings

This is so easy: All you do is combine the sauce ingredients in a blender, bring them to a boil, and braise the wings. Then they are run under the broiler to glaze, so there's no frying mess to clean up. The sauce permeates, tenderizes, and glazes.

MAKES 4 TO 6 SERVINGS

- **1** medium onion, peeled and coarsely chopped
- **2** large garlic cloves, peeled and sliced
- **1** cup dry sherry
- **¼** cup lemon juice
- **2** tablespoons soy sauce
- **2** tablespoons honey, brown sugar, or granulated sugar
- **2** teaspoons ground coriander
- **½** teaspoon turmeric (optional)
- **½** teaspoon hot red pepper flakes
- **4** pounds chicken wings (about 20)
- Salt

1. In a blender or food processor combine the onion, garlic, sherry, lemon juice, soy sauce, honey, coriander, turmeric, and hot pepper flakes; blend to purée. Pour into a large heavy non-aluminum saucepan and bring to a boil over moderate heat.

2. Meanwhile, chop off the wing tips from all the wings and reserve for stock. With a sharp knife, cut out and discard the V-shaped flap of skin from the elbow of each wing. Add the wings to the sauce and boil, uncovered, over moderate heat, turning frequently with tongs, until the sauce has almost completely evaporated and the wings are tender and glazed, 30 to 35 minutes. Let cool slightly or completely. (This recipe can be prepared a day ahead to here.)

3. Preheat the broiler. Working in one or two batches depending on the size of your broiler, put the wings close together meaty side up on a broiler pan, spooning some of the reduced sauce over them. Brown well, about 3 minutes. Do not turn. Serve hot, sprinkled with salt.

Chicken Wings in Mole Rapido

MAKES 4 TO 5 SERVINGS

- **4** pounds chicken wings (about 20)
- **3** tablespoons vegetable oil
- **2** corn tortillas
- **3** cups Basic Chicken Stock (page 47) or canned broth
- **1/3** cup untoasted pumpkin seeds
- **1/4** cup skinless unsalted peanuts
- **1** large garlic clove, peeled and minced or crushed through a press
- **3** tablespoons all-purpose flour
- **1/4** cup chili powder
- **2** tablespoons unsweetened cocoa powder
- **2** teaspoons ground cumin
- **3/4** teaspoon fennel seeds or anise seeds, crushed
- **1/4** teaspoon cayenne pepper (optional)
- **1/8** teaspoon ground cinnamon
- **1/2** teaspoon salt
- **1/4** teaspoon black pepper
- **1** 8-ounce can whole tomatoes with juice
- **1** tablespoon sesame seeds

Traditional Mexican mole *requires a full day's preparation from an ingredient list a mile long. This addictively delicious version is a cinch to make. It reflects my taste after years of sampling mole across Mexico. Serve the wings with white rice, roasted carrots, and steamed green beans, or as an appetizer.*

1. Using a large heavy knife, chop off the tips from the chicken wings and reserve for another purpose, such as stock. With a small sharp knife, cut out the V-shaped flap of skin at the elbow of each wing and discard.

2. Spoon 1 tablespoon of the vegetable oil into a large heavy dutch oven. Place over moderately high heat, add half the chicken wings, meaty side down, and brown well, 5 to 7 minutes. As they first begin to cook, move them several times with tongs so they don't stick to the pan. Turn and brown 3 to 4 minutes longer. Transfer to a platter. Brown the remaining wings in the same manner (if necessary, ½ tablespoon more oil can be added). Remove, reserving the pan drippings in the dutch oven and the wings separately.

3. Spoon the remaining 2 tablespoons oil into a small heavy skillet and place over moderately high heat. One at a time, fry the tortillas, turning several times, until just beginning to stiffen, 15 to 20 seconds. Drain them on a paper towel.

4. Pour the chicken stock into a medium saucepan and bring to a boil over moderate heat. Add the corn tortillas, remove from the heat and let soak until needed.

5. To the pan of chicken drippings, add the pumpkin seeds and peanuts; sauté over moderate heat until they are toasted and beginning to pop, a minute or two. Add the garlic and cook a minute longer. Stir in the flour to moisten it and cook for a minute. Add the chili powder, cocoa, cumin, fennel, cayenne, cinnamon, salt, and pepper; cook a minute longer. Stir in the tomatoes and juice along with the chicken broth and soaked corn tortillas. Bring to a boil, stirring frequently. Simmer 1 to 2 minutes. Let cool slightly, then purée in a blender.

6. Put the chicken wings in the dutch oven, along with any juices that accumulated on the plate; add all the mole sauce and bring to a boil over moderate heat. Lower the heat, cover, and simmer until very tender, 30 to 40 minutes.

7. Toast the sesame seeds in a small heavy dry skillet, shaking the pan, until golden and beginning to pop, about 1 minute. Sprinkle each serving of wings and sauce with some of the seeds and serve hot.

Curried Chicken Wings

MAKES 4 TO 6 SERVINGS

- **20** to 24 chicken wings (about 4 pounds)
- **1** tablespoon vegetable oil
- **3** tablespoons plus 1 teaspoon curry powder
- **1** medium onion, peeled and chopped
- **2** large garlic cloves, peeled and minced or crushed through a press
- **1** tablespoon minced fresh ginger
- **1** teaspoon ground cumin
- **1/8** teaspoon ground cinnamon
- **1/4** cup canned tomato sauce
- **3/4** cup unsweetened applesauce
- **1/2** cup plain yogurt
- **1** cup Basic Chicken Stock (page 47) or canned broth
- **1 1/2** teaspoon salt
- **1/4** teaspoon black pepper

Steamed white rice, noodles, or boiled potatoes with cauliflower and peas make good side dishes to sop up the wonderfully abundant curry sauce. This is messy finger food at its best.

1. Using poultry shears or a large heavy knife, chop off the wing tips. Cut out the V-shaped flap of skin at the joint of each wing so the sauce can penetrate.

2. Spoon the vegetable oil into a large heavy flameproof casserole or dutch oven and place over moderately high heat. Add half the wings, meaty sides down, and brown well, moving them occasionally so they don't stick to the pan; sprinkle with 1/2 tablespoon of the curry powder; turn with tongs and brown the other side about 3 minutes longer. Take out and reserve. Brown the remaining wings in the same manner, though you won't have to add any more oil (but be sure to sprinkle the wings with 1/2 tablespoon curry powder before turning, as before). Remove and reserve.

3. Add the onion, garlic, and ginger to the drippings in the pan and sauté over moderately high heat, stirring constantly, for 2 to 3 minutes. Add 2 tablespoons of the remaining curry powder along with the cumin and cinnamon; cook 1 to 2 minutes longer, stirring. Stir in the tomato sauce and cook for a minute; stir in the applesauce and yogurt to blend. Pour in the chicken stock and bring to a boil. Return the chicken wings and add the remaining 1 teaspoon curry powder and the salt and pepper. Cover and simmer over low heat until very tender, 40 to 45 minutes. Serve hot. The flavors will blossom if the dish is made an hour ahead and reheated.

Peanut-coated Chicken Lollipops

These cute little "drumsticks" are made from chicken wings. You chop off the wing tips (reserve them for stock) and the middle portions (reserve those for Buffalo Chicken Wings, page 224) and then push the remaining meat inside out to resemble drumsticks or

MAKES 20 TO 24

Chicken Lollipops:

20	to 24 chicken wings (about 4 pounds)
¼	cup dry sherry
2	tablespoons soy sauce
2	tablespoons sugar
¼	teaspoon ground cinnamon
1	tablespoon minced fresh ginger
1	large garlic clove, peeled and minced or crushed through a press
¼	cup brown or golden mustard
½	cup cornstarch
2	large eggs
1½	cups (about ½ pound) finely chopped roasted peanuts

Apricot Sauce:

- ⅔ cup apricot preserves
- ¼ cup cider vinegar
- 1 tablespoon soy sauce
- 1 tablespoon oriental sesame oil
- ⅛ teaspoon cayenne pepper

1. Prepare the chicken lollipops: Using poultry shears or a large heavy knife, cut off the tips from the wings (illustration A), then cut off the center section of each drumstick (the ones with double bones).

2. Using a paring knife, cut toward the bone all around at the narrow end of one wing piece, to sever the skin and tendons (illustration B). With the knife, scrape the meat toward the wide end (illustration C), pushing it with the knife so it turns inside out and forms a "lollipop." Repeat with the remaining wing sections.

3. In a large bowl stir together the sherry, soy sauce, sugar, cinnamon, ginger, and garlic. Add the chicken lollipops, tossing to coat. Cover and marinate in the refrigerator for at least 12 hours.

4. Preheat the oven to 375°. Lightly oil a 15-by-10-inch baking sheet. Stir the mustard in a large bowl. Take the lollipops from the marinade and put them in the mustard, tossing to coat. Discard any marinade remaining.

5. Put the cornstarch in a small bowl. In another small bowl whisk the eggs with 2 teaspoons cold water. Put the peanuts in a third bowl.

6. Pick up one lollipop by the bone end and roll the meaty end in cornstarch. Dip it into egg to coat, then roll it in chopped peanuts to coat. Place in the prepared pan. Repeat, placing lollipops about ½ inch apart and alternating directions so all of them fit in the pan. Bake in the top third of the oven for 40 to

lollipops. The marinade is flavored with ginger and cinnamon and there is a sexy apricot dipping sauce. The lollipops are crusted with chopped peanuts and baked in the oven.

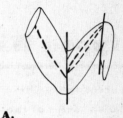

A.

B.

C.

50 minutes until crisp and golden brown. Use a spatula to remove them from the pan and pile onto a serving platter. Serve hot or warm with the apricot sauce.

7. Make the apricot sauce: In a small nonaluminum saucepan combine the apricot preserves, cider vinegar, soy sauce, sesame oil, and cayenne pepper; stir over moderate heat and bring just to a boil. Remove from the heat and stir until smooth. Serve warm.

Clipped Wings in Oyster Sauce

This great saucy Chinese dish tastes of the land and the sea because it is flavored with Chinese oyster sauce. Serve it as an appetizer or as a main course with rice and Chinese vegetables.

MAKES 4 TO 6 SERVINGS

4 pounds chicken wings (about 20)
1 tablespoon vegetable oil
2 tablespoons minced fresh ginger
2 medium garlic cloves, peeled and minced or crushed through a press
1 cup Basic Chicken Stock (page 47) or canned broth
1/3 cup dry sherry
1/3 cup Chinese oyster sauce (see Note)
1 tablespoon cornstarch
2 medium scallions, thinly sliced

1. Using a meat cleaver or poultry shears, clip off the tips of the wings and reserve them for stock. Cut the wings into two pieces at the "elbow" (see page 13).

2. Spoon the vegetable oil into a large heavy flameproof casserole or dutch oven and place over moderately high heat. Add about one-third of the wing pieces, meaty sides down. Cover with a spatter screen if available, otherwise do not cover. Brown well, moving them once or twice with tongs so they don't stick, about 5 minutes. Turn and brown about 3 minutes longer. Take out and hold in a bowl. Repeat with the remaining wings (no more oil will be necessary).

3. Spoon off all but 1 tablespoon of the fat in the pan. Add the ginger and garlic; cook until fragrant, 10 to 15 seconds. Pour in the chicken stock, sherry, and oyster sauce; bring to a boil. Dissolve the cornstarch in ¼ cup cold water and stir in to thicken. Return the wings to the pan. Cover and simmer, stirring occasionally, until very tender, 25 to 30 minutes. Mound on a platter and sprinkle the scallion slices over the top. Serve hot or warm.

NOTE: Oyster sauce is available in many supermarkets and all oriental grocery stores. Hop Sing Lung is my favorite brand. Refrigerated, it will keep indefinitely.

Chinese Red-cooked Chicken Wings

You'll need the red-cooking liquid used for Chinese Chicken Feet, either fresh or leftover, to braise these juicy morsels of white meat. The fragrant braising broth contributes a sweet spice to the wings.

MAKES 4 SERVINGS

20 medium chicken wings (about 4 pounds)
Red-cooking liquid (see page 351)

1. With a heavy cleaver, poultry shears, or a knife, chop off the wing tips at the first joint. (Reserve for making stock or soup, freezing if desired.) With a sharp knife, cut out the V-shaped flap of skin at the inside elbow of each wing.
2. Bring the red-cooking liquid to a boil in a large heavy saucepan. Add the chicken wings and simmer over low heat, uncovered, until very tender, about 45 minutes. Scoop out with a slotted spoon and serve hot. Reserve the cooking liquid for additional braising recipes. It can be kept indefinitely in the refrigerator if you boil it for 5 minutes every 3 days.

Chicken Drumsticks

7

Drumsticks are the perfect finger food because they have their own little handle and are easy to pick up and eat on the go. They are ideal for eating in front of the TV or at a picnic. Children always go for drumsticks, and I do too. They are good to keep on hand, cooked, in the refrigerator because they can quench a hunger pang the minute you walk in the door after a busy day.

They can be down-home drumsticks with red beans and rice or smoky barbecued over a charcoal grill. They can even be deliciously deviled or smoked over Chinese tea in a wok. Teamed with oxymoronic jumbo shrimp, they can star in a paella or they can be minced with sweet crunchy water chestnuts and reassembled back onto the bones to create Chinese inside-out drumsticks with honey mustard and apricot dipping sauce, a sublime dim sum treat with tea.

Not only are drumsticks delicious and versatile, they are plentiful and inexpensive. The more you buy the cheaper they get.

Deviled Drumsticks

The aromatic flavors
of mustard, lemon,
and tarragon crumbs
swaddle drumsticks
that become crisp in a
simple baked dish.
This is a good make-
ahead dish for picnics
and parties.

MAKES 6 SERVINGS

12	medium drumsticks (3 to 3½ pounds)
½	cup Dijon or spicy brown mustard
2	tablespoons dry white wine
6	tablespoons butter (¾ stick), melted
3½	cups fresh soft bread crumbs (see Note)
1	tablespoon paprika
1	teaspoon salt
¾	teaspoon black pepper
½	teaspoon dried tarragon, crumbled
2	large eggs
2	tablespoons fresh lemon juice

1. Starting at the wide end of each drumstick, grasp the skin and yank it downward (if it is slippery, use a paper towel to help your grip); pull off and discard the skin.

2. In a large bowl stir together the mustard and wine. Add the drumsticks and toss to coat. Marinate at room temperature for 30 minutes to an hour (if marinating longer, refrigerate for up to a day).

3. Preheat the oven to 375°. Use 1 tablespoon of the melted butter to coat a 13-by-9-inch shallow baking dish.

4. Put the fresh bread crumbs in a large bowl and stir in the paprika, salt, pepper, and tarragon. In a shallow dish or pie pan whisk the eggs with 1 teaspoon water.

5. Toss the drumsticks to coat again with mustard. One at a time, dip them in egg, roll them in the seasoned crumbs, and place in the pan. The fit will be somewhat snug so juggle them to fit as they are coated. Spoon the remaining melted butter over the tops, and then the lemon juice. Bake, uncovered, until the tops are golden brown and the juices run clear when the flesh of a drumstick is pierced with a fork, 50 to 60 minutes. Let stand at least 10 minutes before serving. Loosen and separate the drumsticks with a knife and scoop out with a spatula. Serve hot or at room temperature.

NOTE: Grind 4 English muffins or enough homestyle firm white bread in a food processor to make 3½ cups.

Sweet and Sour Drumsticks

MAKES 4 TO 6 SERVINGS

12	medium drumsticks (about 3 pounds)
⅓	cup rice vinegar
¼	cup soy sauce
¼	cup dry sherry
3	tablespoons sugar
2	tablespoons vegetable oil
1	cup Basic Chicken Stock (page 47)
1	tablespoon cornstarch
2	tablespoons ketchup
2	teaspoons oriental sesame oil

These are skinless drumsticks marinated in sweet and sour sauce for a deep flavor. They are good hot or at room temperature.

1. Pull the skin from each drumstick, pulling from the wide end and using a paper towel to help grasp as you yank. Discard the skin. In a large bowl stir together the rice vinegar, soy sauce, sherry, and sugar; add the drumsticks and marinate in the refrigerator for 30 to 60 minutes. Drain and reserve ½ cup marinade for the sauce. Discard the remainder.

2. Spoon the vegetable oil into a large deep skillet or dutch oven and place over moderately high heat. Add all of the drumsticks and brown well without turning, but moving them with tongs occasionally to prevent sticking, 4 to 5 minutes. Turn and brown 3 to 4 minutes longer. Pour in ⅔ cup of the broth; cover and boil over moderate heat until drumsticks are cooked through and glazed, 10 to 15 minutes. Uncover and boil the broth for the last 5 minutes to reduce it.

3. In a bowl, dissolve the cornstarch in the remaining ⅓ cup broth. Stir in the reserved ½ cup marinade along with the ketchup and sesame oil. Add it to the drumsticks all at once and stir as you bring it to a boil to thicken and glaze the drumsticks. Serve hot or at room temperature.

Drumsticks with Red Beans and Rice

In New Orleans, Monday is red beans and rice day. I have combined the duo with pan-fried drumsticks to make a tasty trio. Don't use the light pink kidney beans; they cook too quickly and will fall apart. Soak the beans over-

MAKES 6 TO 8 SERVINGS

- **1** pound dried dark red kidney beans
- **4** cups Basic Chicken Stock (page 47) or canned broth
- **1** bay leaf
- **½** pound hickory-smoked bacon, sliced and cut into ½-inch pieces
- **2** medium onions, peeled and chopped
- **2** large garlic cloves, peeled and minced or crushed through a press
- **1** teaspoon dried thyme, crumbled
- **1** large green bell pepper, cored, seeded, and finely chopped

1 cup finely chopped celery
1/2 cup all-purpose flour
1/4 cup yellow cornmeal
1 tablespoon salt
1/2 teaspoon black pepper
3 tablespoons vegetable oil
12 to 16 drumsticks (3 to 4 pounds)
Parsley-Scallion Rice (page 365)

night, and start preparing this early in the day, because the beans cook for 3 hours.

1. Rinse the beans in a large bowl of cool water, picking them over for any sand or grit. Take them out by small handfuls and put them in a strainer; rinse well. Put in a 4- to 5-quart heavy ovenproof pot; add 2 quarts of cold water and let soak overnight.

2. Add to the undrained beans 2 cups of the chicken stock and the bay leaf. Bring to a boil over moderate heat. Lower the heat, cover, and simmer, stirring occasionally, for 1 hour.

3. Put the bacon in a large heavy skillet and cook over moderate heat until crisp and golden brown, about 5 minutes. Spoon off all but 3 tablespoons of the fat. Add half the chopped onions, both garlic cloves, and 1/2 teaspoon of the thyme; sauté to soften the onion, 3 to 4 minutes. Stir the mixture into the pot of beans. Add the remaining 2 cups of chicken stock, 2 teaspoons of the salt, and 1/4 teaspoon of the pepper.

4. Preheat the oven to 325° and bake the beans, covered, for 1 hour. Add the bell pepper, celery, and remaining onion; cover and bake 1 hour longer, stirring occasionally.

5. In a large sturdy paper bag combine the flour, cornmeal, remaining 1/2 teaspoon thyme, and the remaining 1 teaspoon salt and 1/4 teaspoon pepper; shake to blend.

6. Spoon 2 tablespoons of the vegetable oil into a large heavy skillet or dutch oven and place over moderately high heat. Shake half of the drumsticks in the bag to coat, and put in the pan. Brown well, about 5 minutes; turn and brown about 5 minutes longer. Take out and transfer to a plate. Add the remaining 1 tablespoon oil to the pan. Shake the remaining drumsticks to coat as before and brown. Return all the drumsticks to the pan; reduce the heat to low, cover, and cook until done, about 15 minutes longer. Add to the red beans. Prepare the rice and serve hot.

Chinese Inside-out Drumsticks

The inspiration for these easy-to-eat drumsticks came from a Cantonese version of stuffed crab claws. The meat is scraped from the bones, chopped, and mixed with water chestnuts, ginger, and sherry; it is then put back onto the bones to resemble drumsticks, sprinkled with sesame seeds, and fried. These are delicious with the sauce and mustard suggested, or with

MAKES 8

- **8** medium-large drumsticks (about 2 pounds)
- **1** egg white
- **1/2** cup chopped water chestnuts
- **2** tablespoons cornstarch
- **1** tablespoon dry sherry
- **2** teaspoons grated fresh ginger
- **1 1/2** teaspoons oriental sesame oil
- **1** teaspoon salt
- **8** teaspoons sesame seeds

Peanut oil or vegetable oil for frying
Apricot Sauce or Spicy Honey Mustard (page 243)

1. Starting at the wide end of one drumstick, grasp the skin with a paper towel and pull it off; it will turn inside out as you pull. Repeat to skin all 8 drumsticks, and discard the skins. Using a paring knife, make a cut into the flesh all around the narrow bone end of each drumstick. Working from the narrow end, scrape the flesh downward until all is removed from the bones. Pull out any white tendons from the meat and grind the meat in a food processor. Boil the bones in water to cover for 15 minutes; drain and let cool.

2. Put the ground chicken in a bowl and add the egg white, water chestnuts, cornstarch, sherry, ginger, sesame oil, and salt; mix well.

3. Rinse the bones under warm water, working over a colander and pulling off any remaining meat or skin.

4. Dip your hands into cold water and then shape about ¼ cup of the meat mixture around the wide end of each bone, tapering it toward the other end to resemble a drumstick. Shape all 8 drumsticks. Working over a plate, sprinkle each with 1 teaspoon of the sesame seeds, pressing so they adhere.

5. Pour 1 to 1½ inches of oil into a deep-fryer and heat to 370°. Fry about 4 drumsticks at a time, so they aren't crowded, until golden brown and cooked to the bone, about 5 minutes. Drain on paper towels. Serve hot with shallow bowls of apricot sauce and honey mustard for dipping.

Chinese mustard and plum or duck sauce.

Creamy Drumstick Stew

Tarragon-flavored gravy with potatoes and mushrooms round out this hearty stew. You can add small boiling onions if you like. Serve with hot crusty bread and butter or sesame breadsticks.

MAKES 6 SERVINGS

2	tablespoons vegetable oil
12	medium drumsticks (about 3 pounds)
1	pound carrots, peeled and cut into 1-inch chunks
3	tablespoons butter
1/4	cup all-purpose flour
1	teaspoon dried tarragon, crumbled
4	cups Basic Chicken Stock (page 47) or canned broth
1	cup heavy cream
1/2	cup dry sherry
2	teaspoons salt
2	pounds small red-skinned potatoes, peeled and cut into 1-inch chunks
1/4	pound smoked ham, cut in 1/4-inch by 2-inch sticks
1	10-ounce package frozen peas
1/2	pound fresh mushrooms, quartered
1/4	cup chopped parsley leaves

1. Spoon the vegetable oil into a large heavy flameproof casserole or dutch oven and place over moderately high heat. Add the drumsticks in a tight single layer and brown very well, 8 to 10 minutes, turning them with tongs several times. Remove and transfer to a platter. Add the carrots to the pot and brown well, tossing, until they are speckled deep golden brown, 5 to 8 minutes over moderately high heat. Remove and hold with the drumsticks.

2. Add 2 tablespoons of the butter to the pot and melt over moderate heat. Stir in the flour to moisten it (mixture will be dry) and cook for 1 minute. Add 1/2 teaspoon of the tarragon. Pour in the chicken stock, heavy cream, and sherry; stirring constantly, bring to a boil over moderate heat. Add the potatoes and ham. Return the drumsticks and carrots to the pan. Bring to a boil, then simmer over low heat until the potatoes are tender and the chicken is cooked, about 30 minutes. Add the peas and remaining 1/2 teaspoon tarragon; simmer 2 to 3 minutes longer.

3. Melt the remaining 1 tablespoon butter in a large heavy skillet over high heat. Add the mushrooms and brown quickly, 2 to 3 minutes, adding 1 to 2 tablespoons water after 1 minute. Add to the stew along with the parsley. Serve hot.

Crispy Double-cooked Drumsticks with Apricot Sauce and Honey Mustard

MAKES 8

- **1** teaspoon whole black peppercorns
- **8** drumsticks (1½ to 2 pounds)
- **1** tablespoon grated fresh ginger
- **2** medium scallions, minced
- **2** tablespoons dry sherry
- **1/2** cup packed cornstarch
- **1/2** cup all-purpose flour
- **1** teaspoon salt
- **1/2** teaspoon baking soda

Peanut oil or vegetable oil for frying
Apricot Sauce and Spicy Honey Mustard (recipes follow)

Steamed first, then dipped in batter and fried crisp and golden brown, these drumsticks are tasty and fun. The mustard can be made a week or two ahead and it only gets better.

1. Put the peppercorns in a small dry skillet and toast over moderate heat for 4 to 5 minutes, shaking, until they swell and pop. Cool slightly, then pulverize with mortar and pestle or in a spice grinder.

2. Put the drumsticks in a large bowl. Sprinkle with the pepper. Add the ginger, scallions, and sherry; toss to coat and marinate at room temperature for 1 hour or cover and refrigerate up to 12 hours. Return to room temperature.

3. Rig a makeshift steamer by propping up a shallow dish or pie pan on trivets or tuna cans (open at both ends) set in a dutch oven with a tight-fitting lid. Remove the dish and add about 1 inch of water. Return the dish. Arrange all of the drumsticks in it, cover tightly, and bring the water to a boil over high heat. Steam over moderately high heat for about 20 minutes, until tender and cooked to the bone. Remove the drumsticks and let them cool completely. Reserve the juices for another use.

4. In a medium bowl stir together the cornstarch, flour, and salt; stir in ¾ cup cold water, stirring until smooth. Chill about 30 minutes. Stir in the baking soda.

5. Pour 1 inch vegetable oil into a large skillet or saucepan and place over moderately high heat. When oil is very hot (just below the smoking point, about 375°), dip the drumsticks, one at a time, in the batter to coat and place in the hot oil without crowding the pan. Fry until crisp and golden brown, turning once, 3 to 4 minutes. Drain on paper towels. Serve hot with the dipping sauce and mustard.

Apricot Sauce

MAKES ABOUT ²/₃ CUP

½ cup apricot preserves
1 tablespoon soy sauce
1 tablespoon white vinegar
2 teaspoons oriental sesame oil

1. In a small bowl, mash the apricot preserves with a fork. Stir in the soy sauce, vinegar, and sesame oil. If making ahead, cover and refrigerate.

Spicy Honey Mustard

MAKES ABOUT 1½ CUPS

¾ cups cider vinegar
12 whole black peppercorns
8 whole cloves
8 whole juniper berries
1 bay leaf
1 4-ounce can Colman's powdered mustard
¼ cup honey
2 tablespoons packed dark brown sugar
1 tablespoon vegetable oil
1 tablespoon Worcestershire sauce
½ teaspoon ground ginger
¼ teaspoon ground cumin
¼ teaspoon ground allspice
1 teaspoon salt

1. In a small nonaluminum saucepan combine the vinegar, peppercorns, cloves, juniper berries, and bay leaf. Place over moderate heat and bring to a boil. Lower the heat and simmer for 5 minutes. Let cool to room temperature.

2. In a food processor or blender combine the powdered mustard, honey, brown sugar, vegetable oil, Worcestershire sauce, ginger, cumin, and allspice; strain the cooled vinegar over the ingredients, discarding solids. Blend the mustard mixture to a smooth purée, scraping down the sides once or twice. Cover and chill at least 1 day before serving.

Hakka Salt-baked Drumsticks

Without a doubt, this is my favorite way to cook drumsticks; they are falling-off-the-bones tender, juicy, and *very* tasty. The Hakka people of China traditionally are nomads. Their technique of baking chicken in salt evolved because they had no ovens. They

MAKES 12 (4 SERVINGS)

24 slices fresh ginger, each the size of a quarter
12 medium scallions
12 medium drumsticks (3 pounds)
5 to 6 pounds (2 boxes) kosher salt

Dipping Sauce:

½ cup chicken broth
2 tablespoons orange juice
2 tablespoons soy sauce
1 tablespoon white vinegar
1 tablespoon oriental sesame oil
1 medium scallion, minced
1 tablespoon minced fresh ginger

1. Preheat the oven to 450°. Have ready twelve 8-inch squares of aluminum foil. Place 1 ginger slice on a sheet of foil. Slice the scallions in half lengthwise and put 1 half over the ginger. Add a drumstick, pointing corner to corner; top with a ginger slice and scallion half. Bring the two corners of the foil up over the two ends of the drumstick, then fold up the other two corners and wrap the drumstick in foil, shaping it to conform to the drumstick. Repeat with all 12 drumsticks.

2. Put the salt into a large heavy ovenproof dutch oven or pot and place over high heat for 10 minutes, stirring frequently. Carefully dump out half into a bowl. Spread out the drumsticks in the salt left in the pot and cover completely with the remaining hot salt. Bake 45 minutes. Let stand 10 to 15 minutes. Fish out the packets with a slotted spoon and tongs and shake off the salt. Each diner unwraps his parcels and dips them into the sauce, which you should serve in individual shallow bowls.

3. Make the sauce: In a small bowl stir together the chicken broth, orange juice, soy sauce, vinegar, and sesame oil. Stir in the scallions and ginger. (You can do this a day or two ahead of time.)

dug holes in the ground and covered hot charcoal with salt. Salt is a great conductor of heat. The drumsticks are wrapped in aluminum foil; they do not become salty. You will need a large quantity of inexpensive kosher salt (which can be reused).

Paella

Although often made
with long-grain rice
in this country, true
paella should be made
from the short-grain
rice from Valencia,
Spain. If you can't
find any, use short-
grain Japanese rice
instead.

MAKES 6 SERVINGS

- **3** cups strong Basic Chicken Stock (page 47), or double-strength canned broth
- **1** 8-ounce bottle clam juice
- **1** cup dry white wine
- **1** bay leaf
- **1/2** teaspoon saffron threads
- **3** large red bell peppers (about 1 pound total)
- **4** links Spanish *chorizo* (6 to 8 ounces total)
- **6** tablespoons olive oil
- **12** medium chicken drumsticks (3 pounds), or 6 drumsticks and 6 thighs
- **1** pound marbled pork leg or loin, cut into 1-inch cubes
- **18** jumbo shrimp (1 1/2 pounds), shelled
- **1** large onion, peeled and coarsely chopped
- **2** large garlic cloves, peeled and minced or crushed through a press
- **2** cups (about 1 pound) short-grain Spanish or Japanese rice
- **1/2** pound green beans, trimmed and cut into 2-inch lengths
- **2** tablespoons fresh lemon juice
- **2** teaspoons salt
- **1/4** cup chopped parsley
- **4** medium scallions, thinly sliced

1. In a medium saucepan combine the chicken stock, clam juice, 1/2 cup of the wine, bay leaf, and saffron; bring to a boil over moderate heat. Lower the heat and simmer for 10 minutes; reserve until needed.

2. Roast the red peppers by placing them directly on the burners of a gas stove or as close to the heat source as possible under an electric broiler; turn frequently with tongs until blistered and black all over. Let them cool for a minute and then put them in a plastic bag, twisting the top to enclose. Chill for at least 10 minutes. Cut out the stems and core and scrape the charred skin away. Cut the peppers into 1-inch squares.

3. Prick the *chorizos* several times with a fork and put them in a small saucepan; cover with water and bring to a boil over moderate heat. Simmer for 10 minutes and let stand for 5 minutes. Drain, cool, and cut into ¼-inch slices.

4. Spoon 2 tablespoons of the olive oil into a large heavy paella pan, skillet, or dutch oven and place over moderately high heat. Add half the chicken pieces and brown well, covered with a spatter screen if desired, about 5 minutes. Turn and brown about 3 minutes longer. Remove, and brown the remaining chicken. Return all chicken to the pan and add the remaining ½ cup white wine; cover and bring to a boil. Simmer 5 minutes, then uncover and cook until the wine has evaporated and the chicken is cooked (cut into one drumstick with a knife and check). Transfer chicken to a platter, cover with aluminum foil, and reserve.

5. Add 1 tablespoon of the remaining olive oil to the pan and brown the pork cubes over moderately high heat for 3 to 5 minutes; turn and cook a minute longer. Reserve in a small bowl.

6. With a sharp knife, butterfly the shrimp by slicing each halfway into the outside curved edge. Scrape out any vein if present. Quickly sauté in the pan over high heat, just for a minute, until they turn pink but are not cooked through. Remove and reserve.

7. Spoon 1 tablespoon of the remaining olive oil into the pan and place over moderate heat. Add the onion and sauté to soften and lightly brown, about 5 minutes. Add the garlic and cook a minute longer. Scoop out and reserve on a plate.

8. Preheat the oven to 325°. Spoon the remaining 2 tablespoons olive oil into the pan and place over moderately high heat. Add the unwashed rice grains and sauté until opaque and lightly browned, stirring frequently, about 5 minutes. Measure the broth; pour in 3½ cups. Add the green beans, lemon juice, and salt; bring to a boil over moderate heat. Cook, stirring occasionally, for 10 minutes, until the broth is almost absorbed. Remove from the heat and gently stir in the *chorizo*, red peppers, pork, parsley, and scallions. Bury the shrimp in the rice and top with the drumsticks. Bake, uncovered, 25 minutes, until hot and the broth has been absorbed. Serve hot, with lemon wedges if desired.

Ground Chicken

8

Chicken is lighter and lower in calories and cholesterol than ground beef, but you can do just as much and more with it. Ground chicken has always been popular in China and Japan, where it is favored for various dumplings and fillings, and now it is becoming increasingly popular and available in this country too. If you can't get it in your supermarket, you can make your own in a food processor or meat grinder. The best flavor and texture will be achieved by combining a blend of light and dark meats.

Spaghetti with chicken meatballs, chicken thief shepherd's pie, meatloaf, potato gnocchi with chicken pesto, and sloppy joes with pickles and mustard are fresh and delicious starring in their new chicken roles. You can even make stuffed peppers and stuffed cabbage (both Hungarian and Finnish), and overstuffed burritos like those you might find at a California roadside taco stand.

When you work with ground chicken you don't simply substitute it for ground beef. The flavorings and cooking techniques are best altered to enhance the milder meat; this has all been done for you in the recipes here. And most of them will get you in and out of the kitchen fast.

Chicken Meatloaf
with Pan Gravy

Because chicken breasts are used in place of most of the beef, veal, and pork that a traditional old-fashioned meatloaf requires, there is less fat and calories in this one. It contains just a little beef and pork for flavor and moistness. The loaf is a good slicer and is full of flavor. Preparation will be easiest if you have a food processor for grinding the mushrooms and chicken and for making fresh bread crumbs. If you want to serve the meatloaf with mashed potatoes and gravy, see the note that follows for making gravy from

MAKES 8 SERVINGS

1½ tablespoons butter
2 medium onions, peeled and finely chopped
1 cup finely chopped celery
¼ cup chopped celery leaves
2 large garlic cloves, peeled and minced or crushed through a press
1 teaspoon dried basil
¾ teaspoon dried thyme
½ pound fresh mushrooms, coarsely ground (2½ cups)
1½ teaspoons salt
½ teaspoon black pepper
1 pound skinless boned chicken breasts, or ground chicken (see page 14)
½ pound lean ground beef
½ pound ground pork
1 14½-ounce can stewed tomatoes, drained and chopped
1 cup fresh bread crumbs, made from firm homemade-style white bread or English muffins
2 large eggs, slightly beaten
⅔ cup bottled chili sauce or ketchup
½ cup chopped fresh parsley leaves
4 thin slices smoked bacon, halved crosswise

1. Melt the butter in a large heavy skillet over moderate heat. Add the onions, celery, and celery leaves; sauté to soften, about 5 minutes. Add the garlic, basil, and thyme and cook 1 minute longer. Stir in the mushrooms, salt, and pepper and cook over moderately high heat until the liquid has evaporated, 3 to 5 minutes. Turn into a large mixing bowl and cool to room temperature.

2. Preheat the oven to 350°. Lightly oil a 13-by-9-inch shallow baking dish.

3. Cut the chicken into large chunks and coarsely grind in a food processor or through a meat grinder; crumble over the cooled vegetable mixture. Crumble in the beef and pork. Add the drained stewed tomatoes, the bread crumbs, eggs, ⅓ cup of the chili sauce, and the parsley. Mix with your hands or a big spoon until evenly blended. Plop the mixture into the prepared baking dish and shape into a 10-by-5-inch oval loaf. Spread the top and sides with the remaining ⅓ cup chili sauce and arrange the halved slices of bacon crosswise over the top. Bake in the center of the oven for about 1 hour, until the juices run clear when the center is stuck with a long skewer. Let stand for 10 to 15 minutes before serving. Cut into slices and serve hot. If serving cold, cool to room temperature, cover, and chill for several hours.

NOTE: To make pan gravy, tilt the baking dish and spoon all of the drippings into a cup. When the fat rises to the top, spoon it off and discard it (you will have about ¼ cup degreased pan drippings). Melt 1½ tablespoons butter in a small heavy saucepan over moderate heat. Stir in 3 tablespoons all-purpose flour and cook for a minute, stirring. Pour in 1¾ cup chicken stock or broth, ¼ cup dry white wine (or extra broth), and the drippings. Stirring constantly, bring to a boil over moderate heat, until thickened and smooth. If needed, add a pinch of salt to taste. Makes about 2 cups.

the pan drippings. Green peas make a good, traditional accompaniment.

Stuffed Red and Green Peppers

You can use all red or all green bell peppers to make this recipe, but it's tasty and colorful to offer your guests one of each. It's a good idea to use small peppers for stuffing, otherwise there will be too much filling in proportion to the peppers. Just ½ pound of Italian sausage is enough to flavor 12 stuffed peppers.

MAKES 12 (6 SERVINGS)

- **6** small red bell peppers (1¼ pounds)
- **6** small green bell peppers (1¼ pounds)
- **½** cup long-grain white rice
- **½** pound sweet Italian sausage (2 to 3 links)
- **2** medium onions, peeled and chopped
- **2** large garlic cloves, peeled and minced or crushed through a press
- **½** cup grated Parmesan cheese
- **1** tablespoon dried basil, crumbled
- **1** teaspoon dried oregano, crumbled
- **2** teaspoons salt
- **¼** teaspoon black pepper
- **1** pound skinless boned chicken thighs, ground (see Note)
- **2** large eggs
- **2** 8-ounce cans tomato sauce

1. Bring a large pot of lightly salted water to a boil over high heat. With a paring knife, cut downward around the stem of each pepper to make a 1½- to 2-inch round opening and take off the tops (as opposed to simply slicing off the top, because there would be too much waste). With a small spoon, scoop out the ribs and seeds; invert each pepper and firmly tap to knock out any remaining seeds. Drop 4 to 6 of the peppers into the boiling water; when the boil resumes, boil for 2 minutes. Take out with tongs and drain upside down in a colander. Repeat to blanch all the peppers.

2. Bring 1½ to 2 quarts of water to a boil in a medium saucepan. Gradually add the rice so the boiling doesn't stop, and boil for 10 minutes. Add 1 cup of cold water to stop the cooking, then drain in a strainer. Dump into a large bowl.

3. Adjust an oven shelf to the top third of the oven and pre-heat to 375°.

4. Slit the sausage casings lengthwise and take out the meat; crumble it into a heavy medium skillet and brown over moderate heat until no longer pink; scoop out with a slotted spoon and add to the rice. Spoon out and discard all but 1 tablespoon of the fat in the skillet. Add the onions and sauté over moderate heat to soften and lightly brown, about 5 minutes. Add the garlic and cook a minute longer; scrape the contents of the pan over the rice. Stir into the bowl the Parmesan cheese, basil, oregano, salt, and pepper until evenly mixed. With your hand or a big spoon, mix in the ground chicken, eggs, and 1 can of the tomato sauce.

5. Using about ½ cup of the stuffing for each, stuff the peppers, putting them upright in a shallow 13-by-9-inch baking pan as they are filled (it looks best to alternate the colors). Pour the remaining can of tomato sauce over the peppers and pour ½ cup water in the pan around them. Bake, uncovered, for about 1 hour, until browned on top and cooked throughout. Serve hot or warm.

NOTE: If you are starting with whole thighs, use 2 pounds and remove skin and bones as described on page 13. Put the skinless boned chicken thighs in a food processor and grind fine, or put through the fine blade of a meat grinder.

Hungarian Stuffed Cabbage Rolls with Tomato Sauce

Made with ground chicken, and ground pork for flavor, these tasty treats contain a fraction of the calories of those stuffed with pork and beef. They are best made several hours ahead and then gently reheated, and are a good choice for a big family get-together or a Superbowl party.

MAKES 24 (8 TO 12 SERVINGS)

- **2** medium-large firm solid heads green cabbage (2½ to 3 pounds each)
- **½** cup long-grain white rice
- **2** pounds ground chicken (see page 14)
- **1** pound ground pork
- **2** large eggs
- **1** 8-ounce can tomato sauce
- **1** large onion, peeled and grated or finely chopped
- **1** large garlic clove, peeled and minced or crushed through a press (optional)
- **2** teaspoons paprika
- **2** teaspoons dried basil, crumbled
- **½** teaspoon dried thyme, crumbled
- **1** tablespoon salt
- **½** teaspoon black pepper
- **1** 46-ounce can tomato juice

1. Pour about 2 inches of water into a large heavy pot or dutch oven and bring to a boil over high heat. Meanwhile, use a paring knife to cut the core from each head of cabbage, cutting them out in large cone shapes, and discard. Put one head of cabbage into the boiling water (unless both will fit), cover, and boil, turning once in a while, until the outer leaves are tender and translucent, about 10 minutes. If any outer leaves have fallen off, leave them in the water until tender. To take the cabbage from the water, jab a long fork into the core area and remove; take off the tender leaves and drain in a colander. Return the head of cabbage to the water and cook until more leaves are tender, 3 to 5 minutes. As the cabbage cooks, the outer leaves become tender in progressively less time. Repeat with the second head of cabbage. You will need 24 of the biggest and best leaves for stuffing; coarsely chop the rest and place in a 4- to 5-quart nonaluminum or noncorrosive dutch oven, kettle, or roasting pan.

2. If you wish, slice off the raised portion of the vein on each leaf by slicing flush to the leaf with a paring knife, being careful not to cut clear through.

3. Pour 4 to 6 cups of water into a heavy medium saucepan and bring to a boil over high heat. Slowly add the rice so the boiling doesn't stop. Boil for 5 minutes; add 1 cup cold water to stop the cooking and then drain in a strainer. Dump into a large mixing bowl and let cool to room temperature.

4. Crumble the ground chicken and pork over the rice. Add the eggs, tomato sauce, onion, garlic, paprika, basil, thyme, salt and pepper. Using your hand, mix thoroughly in a circular motion. (Do not taste raw chicken or pork.)

5. Place a leaf, vein side down so leaf is cupped upward, on a plate and scoop about ⅓ cup of the chicken filling into the center; pat the filling into a shape about 2 inches wide and 3 to 4 inches long. Fold the bottom (stem end) up over the filling. Fold the two sides inward and roll up tightly, pushing the ends in with your finger to hold them in place. Arrange rolls seam side down on the bed of chopped cabbage in the pan. When you have made a tight compact layer, prick each cabbage roll twice with a long fork or a skewer. Pour in enough tomato juice to barely cover. Repeat to make more layers, using up all the cabbage, filling, and tomato juice. Cover, place over moderate heat, and bring slowly to a boil. Lower the heat and simmer, covered, over low heat, until very tender, 1¼ to 1½ hours. Let stand at least 45 minutes before serving. Be sure to serve some of the chopped cabbage from the bottom of the pan on each plate with the stuffed cabbage rolls.

Finnish Stuffed Cabbage Rolls

Since I am Finnish-American, stuffed cabbage rolls such as these have been featured at many get-togethers in my family. No two people ever agree as to exactly how they should be made, but usually they are filled with pork, beef, and veal, not chicken. It took quite a bit of experimenting to get them to work properly with ground chicken. The result is light and delicious. Unlike other types of cabbage rolls, which are usually simmered in a sauce, these are topped with bacon, brushed with syrup, and roasted; they develop a cara-

MAKES 12 (6 SERVINGS)

- **2** medium-large firm solid heads green cabbage (2½ to 3 pounds each)
- **¼** cup long-grain white rice
- **¾** cup soft fresh bread crumbs or 1 English muffin
- **1** cup heavy cream
- **1** pound ground chicken (see page 14)
- **½** pound ground pork
- **1** large egg
- **1** large tart green cooking apple, peeled and coarsely grated
- **1** medium onion, peeled and coarsely grated
- **¼** teaspoon ground allspice
- **¼** teaspoon grated nutmeg
- **1½** teaspoons salt
- **¼** teaspoon black pepper
- **½** cup dark corn syrup
- **3** slices smoked bacon, each cut in 4 pieces

1. Pour about 2 inches of water into a large dutch oven or roasting pan and bring to a boil over high heat. Meanwhile, with a sharp knife, cut the core from each head of cabbage, cutting them out in large cone shapes; discard. Put one head (or both if you have used a roasting pan) in the boiling water. Cover and boil, turning once in a while, until the outer leaves are tender and translucent, about 10 minutes. If any outer leaves fall off, leave them in the water until tender. As they become tender and translucent, take them out with tongs and drain them in a colander. To take the whole head of cabbage out, jab the core with a long fork. Then remove the tender outer leaves and return the head to the pan. Cook until more leaves are tender, 3 to 5 minutes. As the cabbage cooks, the cooking times becomes progressively shorter. You will need 24 leaves; divide them into two stacks, large and medium.

2. Pour about 1 quart of water into a medium saucepan and bring to a boil over high heat. Slowly add the rice so the boiling doesn't stop, and boil for 10 minutes, until almost tender. Add a cup of cold water to stop the cooking and drain in a strainer; dump into a large bowl.

3. Preheat the oven to 325°. Put the fresh bread crumbs in a small bowl (if using an English muffin, simply crumble into the bowl) and pour in the heavy cream.

4. Crumble the ground chicken and pork over the rice and add the bread crumbs and cream, the egg, grated apple, grated onion, allspice, nutmeg, salt, and pepper; mix well with your hands, in a circular motion, until blended. (Do not taste raw chicken and pork.)

5. Put one large cabbage leaf, vein side down, in front of you. With a half-cup measure scoop up a scant ½ cup filling (½ cup minus 1 tablespoon). Spread about 2 tablespoons of it near the stem end. Top with a medium leaf, placing it so the vein is just slightly to the right of the one below it. Add the remaining filling from that ½-cup measure and shape into a 2-by-4-inch log near the stem. Fold the 2 stems up over the filling to cover; fold the right and left sides inward to cover the filling, then roll up tightly. Place seam side down in a large shallow baking pan. Repeat. If all 12 stuffed cabbage rolls won't fit in a single layer in one pan, roast in two (such as one 13-by-9 pan and one 8-inch square pan). Pour ¼ cup water into the pan around the rolls. Use half the syrup to brush the tops and put 1 piece of bacon atop each. Cover with aluminum foil and bake for 30 minutes. Uncover and bake about 1½ hours longer, basting oc-

melized glaze. Each has a double leaf for added protection during the long roast. They should be served with lingonberry sauce, but cranberry will do in a pinch. Mashed or boiled potatoes make a classic accompaniment.

casionally with the pan juices and drizzling with the remaining syrup twice during the last 30 minutes. When done, the rolls should be golden brown on top. Let stand 20 minutes and serve hot.

Mexican Meatball Soup

This Mexican classic soup, *sopa de albondigas*, is traditionally made from beef and pork. It is light and satisfying when made with ground chicken, and healthy, too, with all the vegetables. If you use canned or frozen chicken broth, it's a snap to put together.

MAKES 8 SERVINGS

Meatballs:

- ¼ cup long-grain white rice
- 1 pound ground chicken (see page 14)
- ¼ cup chopped fresh cilantro
- ¼ cup grated onion (1 small)
- 2 tablespoons plain dry bread crumbs
- 1 egg yolk
- 1¼ teaspoons salt
- ½ teaspoon ground cumin
- ¼ teaspoon dried oregano, crumbled
- ⅛ teaspoon black pepper

Soup:

- 1 tablespoon butter
- 1 medium onion, peeled and chopped
- 1 medium garlic clove, peeled and minced or crushed through a press
- 8 cups Basic Chicken Stock (page 47) or canned broth
- 1 16-ounce can whole tomatoes, with juice
- 1 medium zucchini, cut into ½-inch slices and quartered

1 cup sliced (1-inch) green beans
2 medium carrots, peeled and thinly sliced
2 tablespoons chopped fresh cilantro

1. Prepare the meatballs: Bring a medium pot of water to a boil over high heat. Slowly add the rice so the boil doesn't stop. Boil 10 minutes until partially cooked. Add 1 cup cold water and then drain in a strainer.

2. Put the rice in a large bowl and let cool slightly. Add the chicken, cilantro, onion, bread crumbs, egg yolk, salt, cumin, oregano, and pepper. Mix well. Cover and place in the refrigerator until needed.

3. Prepare the soup: Melt the butter in a large heavy soup pot or saucepan over moderate heat. Add the onion and sauté to soften, about 5 minutes. Add the garlic and cook a minute longer. Pour in the broth. Add the tomatoes and juice, breaking up the tomatoes with a spoon. Add the zucchini, green beans, and carrots; bring to a boil over moderate heat, then lower the heat so the soup simmers.

4. Using 2 tablespoons of the chicken for each meatball, shape the meatballs. If you have a ⅛-cup measure, dip it in cold water and use it as a measure. Dip your hands in cold water and roll the chicken into balls, dropping them into the simmering soup. Partially cover and simmer for 30 minutes. (If there is a layer of fat on the top surface of the soup, blot with a paper towel.) Add the cilantro and serve hot.

Chinese Chicken Corn Soup

A good sweet-corn flavor enhances ground chicken in this creamy Chinese soup. It's usually made with crabmeat but chicken makes it delicious, less expensive, and more accessible. Little dots of green scallion garnish the milky-yellow soup.

MAKES 6 SERVINGS

2 cups fresh corn kernels, cut from about 3 ears, or frozen, thawed
4 cups Chinese Chicken Broth (page 47) or canned broth
1 tablespoon vegetable oil
1/2 pound ground chicken (see page 14)
1/4 cup plus 1 tablespoon dry sherry
2 teaspoons sugar
5 slices fresh ginger, each the size of a half dollar
2 teaspoons soy sauce
1 teaspoon salt, or more to taste
Pinch black pepper
2 large eggs
1 tablespoon oriental sesame oil
3 tablespoons cornstarch
1 medium scallion, thinly sliced

1. In a blender or food processor combine the corn kernels with 1/2 cup of the chicken stock and blend to a coarse purée.
2. Spoon the vegetable oil into a 3-quart saucepan or soup pot and place over moderately high heat. Add the chicken and cook, breaking it up with a spoon, until lightly browned, 3 to 4 minutes. Add 1/4 cup of the sherry, the puréed corn, the remaining 3 1/2 cups of stock, and the sugar; bring to a boil, then simmer over low heat for 2 to 3 minutes. Add the ginger, soy sauce, salt, and pepper; simmer for 2 to 3 minutes and then reduce the heat slightly to keep at a bare simmer. In a bowl whisk the eggs with the sesame oil; pour in, half at a time, in a big swirl to make petals, and let cook for 30 seconds before stirring.
3. Dissolve the cornstarch in 1/4 cup cold water and pour into

the soup. Simmer, stirring, to thicken. Remove from the heat and stir in the remaining 1 tablespoon sherry. Serve hot, garnished with slices of scallion.

Chicken and Potato Omelet

MAKES 6 SERVINGS

1 pound red-skinned potatoes (3 to 4 medium)
2 teaspoons plus a pinch salt
1 tablespoon olive oil
6 slices bacon (4 to 5 ounces), cut in ½-inch pieces
2 medium onions, peeled and chopped
½ pound ground chicken (see page 14)
¼ cup chopped fresh parsley
¼ teaspoon black pepper
10 large eggs
½ cup light cream or half and half
¼ cup dry white wine
¼ teaspoon paprika

This thick and hearty open-faced omelet is closely related to both the Italian frittata and the Spanish tortilla de papas. Because I find both of those tricky for most people to do on top of the stove (where they are traditionally cooked), I have come up with this foolproof oven version. It's a good choice for entertaining, since there's no last-minute fuss; you can be doing other things during the hour that it bakes and it can remain hot

1. Put the potatoes in a medium pot and cover by 1 inch with cold water. Add a pinch of salt and bring to a boil over high heat. Partially cover and boil over moderately high heat until tender when pierced with a fork, about 30 minutes. Drain and cool. These can be prepared a day ahead.

2. Preheat the oven to 300°. Line an 8- or 9-inch square baking pan with aluminum foil. Lightly coat the foil with olive oil. Choose a larger pan for a hot water bath for it to bake in.

3. Spoon the olive oil into a large heavy skillet. Cut the pota-

for 30 to 60 minutes once it's done. In Spain, this is served cold, cut into cubes, as part of a tapa selection. The smoky bacon complements the ground chicken, while the white wine adds flavor to the eggs.

toes (peeled or unpeeled, as you wish) into ¾-inch cubes and add to the pan. Place over moderately high heat and brown well, about 5 minutes on the first side. Stir and brown about 3 minutes longer. Scoop out and turn into a bowl.

4. Add the bacon to the skillet and cook over moderate heat until crisp and golden, stirring occasionally, about 5 minutes. Spoon off all but 1 tablespoon of the fat. Add the onions and sauté to soften, about 3 minutes. Add the chicken and cook, breaking it up with a spoon, just until done, about 3 minutes. Add the chicken mixture to the potatoes and stir in the parsley, ½ teaspoon salt, and all the pepper. Turn into the prepared pan.

5. In a large bowl, whisk the eggs with the light cream, white wine and remaining 1½ teaspoons salt. Pour over the chicken mixture and sprinkle with the paprika. Put the pan into a larger pan with enough hot tap water to reach halfway up the sides. Bake for about 1 hour, just until the center is set. Remove both pans from the oven but leave the omelet pan in the water bath so it remains hot (unless of course you are serving it cold as a tapa). Cut into squares or rectangles and take out with a spatula.

Quesadillas

These aren't the usual quesadillas of folded flour tortillas. Instead, these are flour tortillas sandwiched with a filling of

MAKES 8

- ½ pound ground chicken (see page 14)
- 1 garlic clove, peeled and minced or crushed through a press
- ½ teaspoon dried oregano, crumbled
- ½ teaspoon ground cumin

½ teaspoon salt
 ¼ teaspoon black pepper
16 7- to 8-inch flour tortillas
 1 cup canned refried beans
 1 cup sliced pitted black olives
 ½ cup sliced scallions
 ½ cup mild to medium-hot taco sauce, plus more for serving
 2 cups (½ pound) shredded Monterey Jack cheese
 ⅓ cup vegetable oil

ground chicken, black olives, scallions, beans, and melted Monterey Jack cheese. They are browned in a skillet and cut into wedges. Perfect with margaritas for a cocktail fiesta.

1. Put the chicken in a heavy medium skillet and place over moderately high heat. Cook, breaking up the meat with a spoon, until lightly browned. Add the garlic, oregano, cumin, salt, and pepper; cook 1 to 2 minutes longer, adding 1 to 2 tablespoons of water if the filling seems dry.

2. Place one tortilla on a plate and spread with 2 tablespoons refried beans. Sprinkle on 2 tablespoons of the chicken filling, 2 tablespoons olives, and 1 tablespoon scallions. Splash on 1 tablespoon taco sauce and top with ¼ cup of the Monterey Jack cheese. Add a second flour tortilla on top to cover the ingredients.

3. Spread 2 teaspoons of the vegetable oil in a heavy medium skillet and place over moderate heat. Slide in the quesadilla and reduce the heat to low. Cook 3 to 4 minutes per side, until golden brown, pressing lightly on top with a spatula as the cheese melts. Turn once or twice as needed, until the cheese is melted and the tortilla golden. Transfer to a board and cut into 4 to 8 wedges. Serve hot. Repeat to make more quesadillas, adding 2 teaspoons of the oil for each.

Vietnamese Chicken Dumplings

This is my idea of a fun cooking project. Not only is the result different and delicious, it is always interesting to work with new or unusual ingredients. You'll need some special ingredients for this recipe, but they are easily obtainable in oriental grocery stores. A tortilla press is the easiest way to flatten the dough but a rolling pin will work as well. After the dumplings are steamed, the tapioca–wheat starch wrappers turn translucent and you can see the filling inside. The sauce is best made a day ahead and the dumplings improve if made several

MAKES 32

Dough

- **1** cup packed wheat starch
- **½** cup packed tapioca starch
- **2** teaspoons vegetable oil, plus additional for brushing

Chicken Filling:

- **7** dried Chinese mushrooms
- **1** tablespoon small dried tree ears
- **1** tablespoon vegetable oil
- **½** pound ground chicken (see page 14)
- **1** large garlic clove, peeled and minced or crushed through a press
- **4** ounces fresh mushrooms, finely diced
- **1** tablespoon tapioca starch
- **1½** tablespoons Vietnamese or Thai fish sauce (*nuoc nam* or *nam pla*)
- **¼** cup chopped fresh cilantro
- **¼** cup minced scallions
- **½** teaspoon sugar

Dipping Sauce:

- **⅓** cup Vietnamese or Thai fish sauce (*nuoc nam* or *nam pla*)
- **¼** cup rice vinegar
- **2** tablespoons sugar
- **1** large garlic clove, peeled and crushed through a press
- **1/16** to ⅛ teaspoon cayenne pepper
- **1** small carrot, peeled and cut into very fine shreds about ½ inch long

1. Make the dough: Stir together the wheat starch, tapioca starch, and salt in a large bowl. Add the oil. Bring a pot of water to a full boil and immediately pour 1 cup of it into the starch mixture; stir with a chopstick to make a sticky dough. It is important that the water be boiling hot. Cover until just cool enough to handle and then knead until smooth, 2 to 3 minutes. Divide into 4 equal portions, shaping into 6-inch ropes; cover and set aside at room temperature until needed.

2. Make the filling: Put the dried mushrooms and the tree ears in separate small bowls. Pour 1/2 cup boiling water over each and let soften for about 30 minutes. Drain, reserving 1/4 cup of the mushroom liquid and discarding the rest. Slice off the stems from the mushrooms and chop the caps. Slice away and discard any hard parts of the tree ears and mince the rest.

3. Spoon the vegetable oil into a heavy medium skillet and place over moderately high heat. Add the chicken and garlic and cook until lightly browned, breaking up with a spoon, 3 to 4 minutes. Add the fresh mushrooms, soaked mushrooms, and tree ears; cook 1 to 2 minutes. Dissolve the 1 tablespoon tapioca starch in the 1/4 cup reserved mushroom liquid and add to the pan. Stir in the fish sauce and cook until slightly thickened, about 1 minute. Remove from the heat and stir in the cilantro, scallions, and sugar. Let cool to room temperature.

4. Make the dipping sauce: In a small bowl stir together the fish sauce, rice vinegar, sugar, garlic, cayenne, and carrot. Cover and chill if making ahead. Otherwise, serve at room temperature.

5. Shape the dumplings: Cut thirty-two 3-inch squares of aluminum foil and brush lightly with vegetable oil. You'll need a large steamer, which can be a rack over a large roasting pan with a baking sheet for a lid.

6. Cut 1 rope (a quarter) of the dough into 8 equal slices. If using a tortilla press to flatten, dip your fingers in vegetable oil and lightly coat the slices. (If using a rolling pin, lightly dust

hours ahead and then resteamed.

with all-purpose flour.) If using a tortilla press, lightly coat with oil the inside of a folded sheet of plastic wrap that lines the press. Press or roll a piece of dough into a 3½-inch round. Add 1 tablespoon filling and fold the dough over to make a half round, taking care not to press the top of the filling or it might tear. Place on a square of oiled foil and repeat. If only 8 will fit in your steamer, steam them now, for 5 minutes over moderately high heat. If more will fit, shape 8 more, and so on. Steam for 5 minutes. After cooling steam, covered, for 3 to 4 minutes to reheat. Serve hot with the dipping sauce.

Chicken and Prickly Rice Dumplings

These luscious little Japanese dumplings with their rice grains sticking out in every direction look like sea urchins. They are especially good served warm with the dipping sauce and make a great hors d'oeuvre.

MAKES 3 DOZEN

Dumplings

1 cup long-grain white rice
1 pound ground chicken (see page 14)
1 cup finely chopped fresh mushrooms
1 small onion, peeled and finely chopped
2 medium scallions, finely chopped
3 tablespoons soy sauce
2 tablespoons sugar
2 tablespoons cornstarch
¼ teaspoon salt

Dipping Sauce:

- ¼ cup soy sauce
- 1 tablespoon lemon juice
- 2 teaspoons sugar
- 1 small garlic clove, peeled and minced or crushed through a press

1. Put the rice in a large bowl and add 3 to 4 cups of cold water. Let soak 1 hour; rinse and drain in a strainer. Put the rice on a plate.

2. In a large bowl combine the ground chicken, mushrooms, onion, scallions, soy sauce, sugar, cornstarch, and salt; mix well with your hands until blended. If you must taste for seasoning, cook a dab and then taste.

3. Using a mounded tablespoonful for each dumpling, roll between the palms of your hands into balls about 1¼ inches in diameter. Roll in the rice grains to coat completely and set aside on a heatproof plate. Continue making the dumplings and arrange them ½ inch apart (two plates will be needed).

4. Rig up a makeshift steamer by placing trivets or small cans (such as tuna cans open at both ends) in a dutch oven. Pour in about 1 inch of water and bring to a boil over high heat. Add a plate of dumplings, cover, and steam over moderately high heat for 20 minutes. Remove and cover with plastic until serving time. Repeat with the remaining dumplings. Serve hot; if necessary, resteam for 3 to 4 minutes.

5. Prepare the dipping sauce: In a small bowl stir together the soy sauce, lemon juice, sugar, garlic, and ¼ cup cold water. Serve in small dishes with the dumplings.

Sake-braised Chicken Dumplings

It's difficult to eat just one or two of these tasty little meatballs. Although they make a perfect hors d'oeuvre, they can also be served as a main course with sticky rice and stir-fried broccoli.

MAKES 36

Dumplings:
1 pound ground chicken (see page 14)
¼ cup minced scallion, including green parts
1 egg yolk
1 tablespoon all-purpose flour
1 tablespoon soy sauce
2 teaspoons grated fresh ginger
¼ teaspoon salt

Sake Broth:
1½ cups Basic Chicken Stock (page 47) or canned broth
½ cup sake
3 slices fresh ginger, each the size of a quarter
2 tablespoons sugar
1 tablespoon soy sauce
1 teaspoon white vinegar
1 tablespoon cornstarch

1. Prepare the dumplings: In a large mixing bowl combine the chicken, scallion, egg yolk, flour, soy sauce, ginger, and salt; mix well to blend. If making ahead, reserve in the refrigerator.

2. Prepare the sake broth: In a 10-inch nonaluminum skillet combine the chicken stock, sake, ginger, sugar, and soy sauce; bring to a boil over moderate heat. Lower the heat and keep at a simmer.

3. Dip your hands into cold water and shape the dumplings, using about 1 tablespoon for each and rolling them into 1-inch balls; drop them into the simmering broth. Poach 5 to 6 minutes, until cooked. Stir in the vinegar.

4. In a cup dissolve the cornstarch in 1 tablespoon cold water. Stir into the broth and simmer for a minute or two to thicken slightly. Let stand at least 10 minutes before serving. Discard the ginger slices and serve hot.

Crisp Chicken-Cheese Tacos

MAKES 12

Filling:

2 tablespoons vegetable oil

2 medium red-skinned potatoes (12 ounces total)

1 pound ground chicken (see page 14)

2 medium garlic cloves, peeled and minced or crushed through a press

1 teaspoon ground cumin

½ teaspoon dried oregano, crumbled

½ teaspoon salt

¼ teaspoon black pepper

1 6-ounce can pitted black olives, drained and finely chopped

¾ cup (3 ounces) shredded medium Cheddar cheese

¾ cup (3 ounces) shredded Monterey Jack cheese

The secret to the success of these crunchy tacos is in the initial browning of the shredded potato in the filling. Cheese is stirred into the filling to add flavor and hold it together. These are not authentic Mexican tacos, but rather a variation on some that are popular in California. You don't need grated cheese in the tacos because there is plenty in the filling.

Tacos:

Vegetable oil

12 6-inch corn tortillas

1½ cups diced (½-inch) tomato

1½ cups shredded romaine lettuce heart or iceberg lettuce

¼ cup hot taco sauce

Salt

1. Make the filling: Spoon the vegetable oil into a large heavy skillet and place over moderately high heat. Peel the potatoes and shred them through the coarse side of a cheese grater. Scatter them in an even layer in the hot oil and poke 5 or 6 holes in the layer with a spoon (for steam to escape); brown very well without disturbing, 5 to 8 minutes; loosen the pancake, turn with a spatula, and brown the other side 2 to 3 minutes longer.

2. Add the chicken, garlic, cumin, oregano, salt, and pepper; push the chicken into the potato with a large spoon, cooking it and stirring it to blend, 3 to 4 minutes. Stir in the olives and both cheeses. Cook until the cheese melts and stir in 2 tablespoons of water. Remove from the heat. Transfer to a bowl and let cool to room temperature.

3. Make the tacos: Pour ⅛ inch of vegetable oil into a heavy medium skillet and place over moderately high heat. Spoon ¼ cup of the taco filling in a line across the center of a corn tortilla. Fold the tortilla, taco-style, and lower the fold into the hot oil (it should be kept at just below the smoking point) and swish back and forth for a few seconds to set the fold. Lay the taco on one side and fry until crisp and deep golden brown while you assemble another and add it to the skillet. The tacos should fry about 2 minutes per side. As they are done, drain upside down in a colander lined with paper towels. Repeat to make 12 tacos.

4. To assemble tacos, gently open each one and add 2 tablespoons each of diced tomato and shredded lettuce. Add 1 teaspoon taco sauce (or more to taste) and sprinkle lightly with salt. Serve hot.

"Zappo" Chicken Burgers

MAKES 6

Chicken Burgers:

- **1** pound ground chicken (see page 14)
- **½** cup sour cream
- **1** medium scallion, finely chopped
- **½** teaspoon salt
- **⅛** teaspoon black pepper
- Paprika
- **6** hamburger buns, split and toasted

Dressing:

- **¼** cup Mayonnaise (page 383)
- **2** tablespoons ketchup
- **2** tablespoons sweet pickle relish or minced sweet pickle
- **1** tablespoon minced dill pickle
- **2** teaspoons mustard (any kind)

Nothing could be easier than this fresh recipe. Juicy chicken burgers cook in the microwave in 2 to 3 minutes! If you wish, eliminate the hamburger rolls and dressing and serve the burgers on plates with potatoes and vegetables.

1. Make the chicken burgers: In a mixing bowl stir together the ground chicken, sour cream, scallion, salt, pepper, and 2 tablespoons water until blended. Shape and cook 1, 2, or 3 at a time: Lightly oil a flat round microwave dish or glass pie pan. Using a ⅓-cup measure, scoop out the chicken mixture and plop it out onto the dish (if making one burger, center; evenly space if making two or three). Pat into a 3-inch patty. Cover with waxed paper or microwave plastic wrap and slit once over each. Sprinkle lightly with paprika. The cooking time for these burgers was tested in a 700-watt microwave oven at full power (adjust accordingly depending on the size of your oven): Cook 1 burger for 2 minutes or cook 2 to 3 burgers for 3 minutes. Let stand for 1 minute before serving. Uncover and serve with the dressing, on toasted buns.

2. Make the dressing: In a small bowl stir together the mayonnaise, ketchup, relish, dill pickle, and mustard. Cover and chill if making ahead.

Sloppy Joes with Pickles and Mustard

Here's that favorite 1950s sandwich freshened up with ground chicken and fragrant seasonings. The crunchy dill pickle slices and tangy mustard start the mouth watering before you bite into one. It's easy to polish off two of these at one sitting.

MAKES 12

2 tablespoons olive oil
2 cups finely diced celery (4 to 5 medium ribs)
2 medium onions, peeled and chopped
2 large garlic cloves, peeled and minced or crushed through a press
1 tablespoon chili powder
1 tablespoon dried basil, crumbled
1 teaspoon dried oregano, crumbled
1/2 teaspoon dried thyme, crumbled
1/2 teaspoon ground cumin
1 1/2 pounds ground chicken (see page 14)
1 tablespoon sugar

1 teaspoon celery salt
1 teaspoon salt
¼ teaspoon black pepper
½ cup dry white wine
3 8-ounce cans tomato sauce
2 tablespoons cider vinegar
½ cup mustard, brown, golden, or yellow
12 hamburger buns with sesame seeds
36 thin dill pickle slices

1. Spoon the olive oil into a large heavy nonaluminum sauce-pan and place over moderate heat. Add the celery and onions; sauté to soften and lightly brown, 5 to 7 minutes. Stir in the garlic, chili powder, basil, oregano, thyme, and cumin; cook 1 minute longer.
2. Add the chicken and cook, breaking up the meat with a spoon, until lightly browned, 3 to 4 minutes over moderately high heat. Add the sugar, celery salt, salt, pepper, and white wine; bring to a boil over moderate heat; add the tomato sauce and vinegar. Simmer, stirring frequently, until very thick and reduced to 6 cups, 40 to 50 minutes. Watch very carefully during the last 10 to 15 minutes, as it thickens, and do not let it scorch.
3. Spread 1 teaspoon mustard over each cut side of each bun. Put 3 pickle slices on the bottom half of each and add ½ cup of the filling; top with remaining bun halves. Serve hot.

Jumbo Pizza Loaves

These can be a sand-
wich supper or hot
lunch when cut into
wedges; thinly sliced
they can be a tasty
treat with cocktails,
beer, or wine. You can
substitute cooked,
sliced Italian sausage
for the pepperoni and
add sliced black
olives if you like.

MAKES 4 SERVINGS

- **1** tablespoon olive oil
- **1/2** pound ground chicken (see page 14)
- **4** ounces (4 large) fresh mushrooms, thinly sliced
- **1** large garlic clove, peeled and minced or crushed through a press
- **1/2** teaspoon dried oregano, crumbled
- **1/2** teaspoon dried basil, crumbled
- **1/2** teaspoon salt
- **1/4** teaspoon black pepper
- **1/2** cup finely chopped pepperoni
- **3/4** to 1 cup fresh or bottled spaghetti sauce
- **1** 14- to 16-inch loaf crusty Italian bread, sliced in half horizontally
- **1/2** pound whole-milk mozzarella cheese, coarsely shredded
- **2** tablespoons grated Parmesan cheese

1. Preheat the oven to 400°. Spoon the olive oil into a large heavy skillet and place over moderate heat. Add the chicken and brown well, stirring to break up the pieces. Add the mushrooms, garlic, oregano, basil, salt, and pepper; stir to cook the mushrooms, 2 to 3 minutes. Add the pepperoni and cook a minute longer. Stir in 1/2 cup of the spaghetti sauce.

2. Using your fingers, pull out some of the soft bread from the centers of each half of the bread to make a slightly concave shell. Place the bread shells on a baking sheet and spread with 1/4 to 1/2 cup spaghetti sauce, depending on the dryness of the bread. Toss all but 1/2 cup of the mozzarella with the filling and mound on the bread halves. Sprinkle tops with the remaining 1/2 cup mozzarella and the Parmesan cheese. Bake until hot and lightly browned, about 12 minutes. Cut each half on the diagonal into 8 slices. Serve hot. If using as an hors d'oeuvre, cut each half into 16 slices.

California Burritos

MAKES 8

1 tablespoon vegetable oil
1 medium onion, peeled and finely chopped
1 large garlic clove, peeled and minced or crushed through a press
1 pound ground chicken (see page 14)
1 tablespoon chili powder
2 teaspoons all-purpose flour
½ teaspoon ground cumin
½ teaspoon dried oregano, crumbled
1 teaspoon salt
¼ teaspoon pepper
1 16-ounce can refried beans
3 cups (12 ounces) coarsely shredded mild Cheddar, such as longhorn
1 8-ounce can tomato sauce
1 to 2 tablespoons hot chili sauce or taco sauce
8 8-inch flour tortillas

This quick and easy throw-together dish tastes like the burritos served at taco stands in California. The creamy beans are spread over a soft flour tortilla and the filling is spooned across the center with cheese and a simple sauce. If you can find *salsa de chile chipotle* (my favorite) the burritos will be a bit smoky; if not, any taco sauce or chile sauce will work well. For burritos made with shredded chicken, see page 76.

1. Spoon the vegetable oil into a large heavy skillet and place over moderate heat. Add the onion and sauté to soften and lightly brown, about 5 minutes. Add the garlic and cook a minute longer. Add the chicken, increase the heat to moderately high, and cook, breaking up the meat with a spoon, until lightly browned, 3 to 4 minutes. Add the chili powder, flour, cumin, oregano, salt, and pepper; cook for 1 to 2 minutes. Pour in ¼ cup water and cook until thickened, 1 to 2 minutes longer.

2. Spoon the refried beans into a medium pot; add about ¼ cup water (or just enough to make a good spreading consistency) and heat over moderate heat until hot; stir in 1 cup cheese until melted. If desired, add salt to taste.

3. In a small bowl stir the tomato sauce with 1 tablespoon of the chili sauce; taste for hotness and add more if desired.

4. Place a dry skillet or griddle over moderate heat. Place one tortilla on the hot surface; turn several times until hot and supple, 10 to 15 seconds. Transfer to a plate and spread with about ¼ cup of the refried beans, covering the entire tortilla. Spoon a generous ¼ cup of the chicken filling in a line across the lower third and top with ¼ cup of the remaining cheese. Spoon on 1 to 2 tablespoons of the sauce. Fold one third of the tortilla up over the filling; then fold the ends inward and roll up. Place seam side down on a platter and repeat with the remaining ingredients to make more burritos. Serve hot.

Old Pockmarked Mrs. Chen's Bean Curd with Chicken Sauce

I didn't make up this title. It's a classic Szechuan dish dating back to the Manchu

MAKES 2 TO 4 SERVINGS (5 CUPS)

7 dried Chinese mushrooms
3 tablespoons cornstarch
2 tablespoons Chinese rice wine or dry sherry

1 tablespoon soy sauce
2 tablespoons peanut oil
2 tablespoons minced fresh ginger
1 large garlic clove, peeled and minced or crushed through a press
½ pound ground chicken (see page 14)
2 tablespoons Szechuan hot bean sauce
½ cup thinly sliced scallions, including green parts
¾ cup chicken stock or canned broth
4 cups diced (½-inch) fresh firm bean curd (1 pound)
1 tablespoon oriental sesame oil
¼ teaspoon finely ground toasted Szechuan pepper or other black pepper

1. Put the Chinese mushrooms in a small bowl; add ½ cup boiling water and let soften for 30 minutes. Drain, reserving ¼ cup of the soaking liquid for the sauce. Slice off the stems from the mushrooms and discard. Chop the caps.

2. In a medium bowl dissolve the cornstarch in ¼ cup cold water; stir in the rice wine, soy sauce, and mushroom soaking liquid; reserve.

3. Place a large heavy wok or dutch oven over high heat. Add the peanut oil, swirling the pan to coat. Add the ginger and garlic; cook for 10 seconds. Add the chicken and stir-fry, breaking up the meat, until cooked, 1 to 2 minutes. Add the hot bean sauce and stir for a minute. Add all but 2 tablespoons of the scallions and all of the reserved chopped mushrooms; cook for 30 seconds. Add the chicken broth and bean curd; bring to a boil. Stir the sauce and add it; cook until thick and bubbling. Stir in the sesame oil and pepper. Serve hot, topped with the reserved scallions.

Dynasty (1862–75), though I have adapted it to use ground chicken instead of the traditional pork. It is spicy Chinese comfort food at its best, hot and highly flavored. There are several levels of heat and spiciness from the pepper and the hot bean sauce. The smooth custardy curd flecked with chicken and scallions has a deep exotic flavor, contributed by the fermented soy beans in the hot bean sauce. It's a powerful dish and best served with noodles and bok choy or another green vegetable such as asparagus or green beans. You will need a few special Chinese ingredients.

Chicken Chili and Beans

This rustic Southwestern-style chili is delicious right after cooking, but the flavors intensify when it is cooled to room temperature and later reheated. If you buy chicken hot dogs you can make unbelievably tasty double-chicken chili dogs.

MAKES 10 CUPS

- ¼ cup bacon fat or vegetable oil
- 4 medium onions, peeled and chopped
- 3 large garlic cloves, peeled and minced or crushed through a press
- 2 pounds ground chicken (see page 14)
- ⅓ cup chili powder
- 1 tablespoon salt
- 1 tablespoon unsweetened cocoa powder
- 2 teaspoons whole fennel seeds
- 2 teaspoons dried oregano, crumbled
- 2 teaspoons ground cumin
- 2 bay leaves
- ½ teaspoon cayenne pepper (optional)
- 1 28-ounce can whole tomatoes, with juice
- 1 8-ounce can tomato sauce
- 1 12-ounce bottle dark beer, preferably Mexican
- 3 16-ounce cans small pink or red beans, rinsed and drained

1. Spoon 2 tablespoons of the bacon fat into a 4-quart heavy nonaluminum ovenproof saucepan or dutch oven and place over moderate heat. Add the onions and sauté to soften and lightly brown, 5 to 7 minutes. Add the garlic and cook a minute longer. Scoop out, transfer to a bowl, and reserve.

2. Melt the remaining 2 tablespoons bacon fat in the pan and place over moderately high heat. Add the chicken and break up with a spoon as it browns. Stir in the chili powder, salt, cocoa, fennel seeds, oregano, cumin, bay leaves, cayenne, and whole tomatoes with juice. Break up the tomatoes with a spoon.

Return the onions to the pot and add the tomato sauce and beer. Bring to a boil over moderate heat. Lower the heat and simmer, uncovered, for 30 minutes, stirring occasionally.

3. Preheat the oven to 325°. Stir the beans into the pot. Bake, uncovered, 1 hour, stirring gently once in a while and adding ½ cup water after 30 minutes. Serve hot; see reheating note below for the best chili.

NOTE: To reheat chili, stir in 1 teaspoon each cocoa and chili powder along with ¼ teaspoon each oregano and cumin. If thick, add ½ cup water. Bake at 325° about 1 hour, stirring gently once or twice.

Eggplant Parmigiana

MAKES 8 SERVINGS

Sauce:

  2 tablespoons olive oil
  1 large onion, peeled and chopped
  1 large garlic clove, peeled and minced or crushed
       through a press
1½ teaspoons dried basil, crumbled
  1 teaspoon dried oregano, crumbled
  1 8-ounce can tomato sauce
  1 16-ounce can whole tomatoes in juice
  1 teaspoon salt
  ¼ teaspoon black pepper

There are many variations on this theme. I like the simple fresh flavor of this version because it takes advantage of vine-ripened summer tomatoes. It is not as highly seasoned as some of my dishes and that's the way I want it to be. If I am in the mood for a more powerful wallop I will spread the first layer of eggplant with ½ cup of pesto. This is excellent when made several hours or even a day ahead.

Filling and Topping:

2 pounds (4 large) ripe tomatoes
1½ pounds ground chicken (see page 14)
1 large firm eggplant (slender but heavy for its size)
3 large eggs
¾ cup all-purpose flour
2 tablespoons olive oil
1 pound whole-milk mozzarella cheese, coarsely grated
1 cup grated Parmesan cheese

1. Make the sauce: Spoon 1 tablespoon of the olive oil into a heavy medium saucepan and place over moderate heat. Add the onion and sauté to soften, about 5 minutes. Add the garlic, basil, and oregano and cook a minute longer. Add the tomato sauce and tomatoes with juice, breaking up the tomatoes with a spoon. Bring to a boil over moderate heat. Lower the heat and simmer until thick, 20 to 30 minutes. Stir in the salt and pepper.

2. Make the filling: There are two easy ways to peel tomatoes: If you have a gas flame, secure one tomato through the stem end onto a long fork and turn it slowly in the flame so it blisters all over. Repeat with the others. Otherwise, drop the tomatoes into a large pot of boiling water for 10 to 15 seconds and refresh them under cold water. Peel with a paring knife. Cut out the cores but do not squeeze out the seeds and juice. Reserve.

3. Spoon the remaining 1 tablespoon olive oil into a large heavy skillet and place over moderately high heat. Add the chicken and cook, breaking up the meat with a spoon, until lightly browned, 3 to 5 minutes. Add a little salt and pepper to taste.

4. Cut the eggplant crosswise into thin ⅛- to ¼-inch slices. Whisk the eggs in a shallow dish or pie pan with 2 tablespoons cold water. Dump the flour into another shallow dish or pie pan. Adjust a shelf to the upper third of the oven and preheat to 400°.

5. Pour ⅛ inch of the olive oil into a large heavy skillet and place over moderately high heat until just beginning to smoke. Adjust the heat as needed while you brown the eggplant but keep it fairly high so the coating on the eggplant will brown. One at a time, dip the eggplant slices first in flour; shake off the excess and then dip into egg to coat and carefully place in the hot oil. Repeat until you have a full single layer. Brown well, 3 to 4 minutes; turn and brown the other side 1 to 2 minutes longer. Drain on paper towels. Repeat, using ⅛ inch olive oil for each batch.

6. Assemble the casserole: Arrange half of the eggplant slices in a 13-by-9-by-2-inch baking pan or shallow casserole. The slices should overlap slightly and cover the bottom. Thinly slice half of the peeled tomatoes and arrange them over the eggplant. Sprinkle lightly with salt. Add all of the ground chicken and half of the grated mozzarella. Spread with half the tomato sauce and half the Parmesan cheese. Top with the remaining eggplant, sliced tomatoes (again lightly salted), tomato sauce, mozzarella, and Parmesan cheese. Bake until golden brown and bubbly, 25 to 30 minutes. Serve hot, or cool slightly and serve.

Creamy Chicken Spaghetti Sauce

This creamier, lighter version of Bolognese sauce is thick, rich, and addictively delicious. It is good with spaghetti, linguine, fettuccine, and tortellini.

MAKES 12 CUPS

- **3** tablespoons olive oil
- **2** medium onions, peeled and finely chopped
- **2** medium carrots, peeled and finely chopped
- **2** medium ribs celery, finely chopped
- **3** large garlic cloves, peeled and minced or crushed through a press
- **2** pounds ground chicken (see page 14)
- **1** tablespoon salt
- **1½** cups dry white wine
- **1½** cups half and half or whole milk
- **1** tablespoon plus ½ teaspoon dried basil, crumbled
- **2½** teaspoons dried oregano, crumbled
- **1½** teaspoons whole fennel seeds
- **1** teaspoon dried rosemary, crumbled
- **½** teaspoon grated nutmeg
- **1** 28-ounce can whole tomatoes, with juice
- **1** 28-ounce can tomato purée

1. Spoon the olive oil into a heavy 4-quart nonaluminum saucepan or dutch oven and place over moderate heat. Add the onions, carrots, and celery; sauté to soften and lightly brown, 5 to 7 minutes. Add the garlic and cook a minute longer. Add the chicken and salt; break up the meat with a spoon and brown over moderately high heat. Pour in the wine and boil until almost completely evaporated, 10 to 12 minutes. Add the half and half, 1 tablespoon of the basil, 2 teaspoons of the oregano, the fennel seeds, rosemary, and nutmeg; boil gently over moderate to moderately low heat until thick and creamy and the oil begins to separate from the half and half, about 10 minutes.

2. Add the tomatoes and juice, breaking the tomatoes up with a spoon, and the tomato purée. Bring to a boil over moderate heat and simmer over low heat until thick and rich, about 1 hour. Add the remaining ½ teaspoon each basil and oregano and simmer 10 minutes longer. If needed, add a pinch more salt.

NOTE: To serve, boil pasta al dente; drain well and toss with about 1 tablespoon olive oil per pound. Then toss with a little of the sauce; top with more and serve additional sauce on the side. Of course Parmesan cheese is the perfect topping.

Spanish Spaghetti

This simple dish is modeled after one that I used to enjoy at a little Spanish grocery store in the Chelsea district of Manhattan. The owner was a great cook and he had card tables and folding chairs set up in the back so you could have lunch there while you shopped. It's the kind of dish that can be made hours ahead, or at the last moment. The obvious Spanish additions are the olives, olive oil, and capers.

MAKES 3 OR 4 SERVINGS

- **2** tablespoons olive oil
- **1** large onion, peeled and chopped
- **1** large garlic clove, peeled and minced or crushed through a press
- **1/2** cup chopped parsley
- **1** teaspoon dried basil, crumbled
- **1** teaspoon dried oregano, crumbled
- **1** teaspoon celery salt
- **1/2** teaspoon salt
- **1/4** teaspoon black pepper
- **1/4** to 1/2 teaspoon dried hot red pepper flakes
- **3/4** pound ground chicken (see page 14)
- **1/2** cup sliced small pimiento-stuffed green olives
- **1** tablespoon small capers
- **1** 16-ounce can whole tomatoes, with juice
- **1** 8-ounce can tomato sauce
- **1/2** cup dry white wine
- **1** bay leaf
- **1/2** pound thin spaghetti
- **3/4** cup grated Parmesan cheese

1. Spoon the olive oil into a heavy medium-sized nonaluminum saucepan and place over moderate heat. Add the onion and sauté to soften, 3 to 5 minutes. Add the garlic and 1/4 cup of the parsley; cook a minute longer, then stir in the basil, oregano, celery salt, salt, pepper, and hot red pepper flakes. Add the ground chicken and break it up with a spoon as you brown it over moderate heat.

2. Stir in the olives, capers, tomatoes (breaking them up with a spoon), tomato sauce, white wine, bay leaf, and ½ cup water. Bring to a boil; lower the heat and simmer, stirring occasionally, for about 30 minutes. The sauce will be soupy.

3. Meanwhile, bring a large pot of lightly salted water to a boil over high heat. Drop in the spaghetti and, stirring constantly, return to a full boil. Stir frequently as it boils and cook it until tender but firm to the bite; the sauce will soften the pasta further so do not overcook. Drain in a colander and add the sauce along with ½ cup of the Parmesan cheese. Stir once or twice and let stand, partially covered, for 10 to 15 minutes. Serve hot, topped with the remaining Parmesan and parsley.

Spinach and Chicken Lasagne

MAKES 12 SERVINGS

Chicken-Tomato Sauce (recipe follows)

- **2** pounds fresh spinach or two 10-ounce packages frozen leaf spinach, thawed
- **2** tablespoons olive oil
- **1½** pounds ground chicken (see page 14)
- **2** large garlic cloves, peeled and minced or crushed through a press
- **½** cup dry white wine
- **2** pounds whole-milk ricotta cheese
- **1** pound whole-milk mozzarella cheese, coarsely shredded to make 4 cups
- **1** cup grated Parmesan cheese
- **½** teaspoon grated nutmeg
- **2** teaspoons salt
- **½** teaspoon black pepper
- **1** pound curly-edged lasagne noodles

This big thick lasagne is best made with fresh spinach, but frozen will do in a pinch. It reheats well and can be frozen. The sautéed ground chicken is stirred into the rich cheese filling and there is even more ground chicken in the tomato sauce. You will need a large lasagne pan, about 15 by 10 by 2½ inches.

1. Prepare the recipe for the chicken-tomato sauce up to 3 days ahead. If making ahead, cool, cover, and chill. Preheat the oven to 375°.

2. If using fresh spinach, rinse in cool water; pull off and discard just the thickest tough stems. Put the wet leaves in a large heavy nonaluminum pot such as a dutch oven. Cover tightly and place over high heat. Cook, stirring once or twice, until wilted down. Drain in a strainer over a bowl and let cool. Press with a spoon to extract the liquid. Reserve the liquid for another use, such as soup. Coarsely chop the spinach. If using frozen spinach, drain well and chop.

3. Spoon the olive oil into a large heavy skillet; add the ground chicken and cook over moderately high heat, breaking up the chicken with a spoon, until no longer pink, about 3 minutes. Add the garlic and cook a minute longer. Pour in the wine and boil until completely evaporated, about 5 minutes. Remove from the heat and stir in the spinach.

4. In a large bowl stir together the ricotta cheese, 3 cups of the mozzarella, ¾ cup of the Parmesan, the nutmeg, salt, and pepper; stir in the chicken-spinach mixture. Taste for salt and add a bit more if necessary.

5. Bring a large pot of lightly salted water to a boil over high heat. Add the lasagne noodles, one at a time, and return to a boil, moving them gently with a wooden spoon so that they do not stick together. Boil, stirring occasionally, until they are tender but firm to the bite, 9 to 10 minutes. Drain in a colander and reserve in a large bowl or pot of cold water.

6. Spread ¾ cup of the chicken-tomato sauce in the bottom of a 15-by-10-by-2½-inch baking pan. Drain one-fifth of the noodles on paper towels and slightly overlap them (trimming to fit if necessary) in the pan. Spread with ¾ cup of the chicken-tomato sauce and spoon a quarter of the chicken-cheese-spinach filling over the sauce; top the filling with ¾ cup sauce. Repeat three more times; spread the top with the remaining sauce and sprinkle with the remaining mozzarella and Parmesan. Cover with lightly oiled aluminum foil and bake until hot and bubbly, about 1 hour. Cool on a rack for at least 20 minutes before serving. Cut the lasagne into squares and serve hot.

Chicken-Tomato Sauce

MAKES ABOUT 8 CUPS

2 tablespoons olive oil
1 large onion, peeled and finely chopped
2 large garlic cloves, peeled and minced or crushed through a press
1½ pounds ground chicken (see page 14)
1 tablespoon dried basil, crumbled
2 teaspoons dried oregano, crumbled
1 28-ounce can whole Italian tomatoes, with juice
1 8-ounce can tomato sauce
1 6-ounce can tomato paste
2 cups dry white wine
1½ teaspoons salt
¼ teaspoon black pepper

1. Spoon the olive oil into a large heavy nonaluminum sauce-pan. Add the onion and cook over moderate heat to soften, about 5 minutes. Add the garlic and cook a minute longer. Add the chicken and cook, breaking up with a spoon, until no longer pink, about 3 minutes. Stir in the basil and oregano; cook a minute longer, then stir in the whole tomatoes and juice (breaking up the tomatoes with a spoon), tomato sauce, and tomato paste. Pour in the wine and add the salt and pepper. Bring to a boil over moderate heat. Reduce the heat to low and simmer gently for 45 minutes to an hour, stirring occasionally, until reduced to 8 cups. The sauce should not be very thick. If making ahead, cool to room temperature; cover and store in the refrigerator or freezer.

Spaghetti and Chicken Meatballs with Garlic Toast

These meatballs won't be perfectly round but it doesn't matter. I have simplified the cooking technique; all you do is shape them and bake them in a hot oven instead of browning them in a skillet.

MAKES 6 MAIN-COURSE SERVINGS

Chicken Meatballs:

- **1** English muffin
- **¼** cup milk
- **1½** pounds ground chicken (see page 14)
- **½** cup grated Parmesan cheese
- **1** large egg
- **¼** cup canned tomato sauce
- **¼** cup chopped fresh parsley leaves
- **1** teaspoon salt
- **½** teaspoon dried basil, crumbled
- **½** teaspoon dried oregano, crumbled
- **¼** teaspoon grated nutmeg
- **¼** teaspoon black pepper
- **1** tablespoon olive oil

Tomato Sauce:

- **3** tablespoons olive oil
- **2** medium onions, peeled and chopped
- **2** large garlic cloves, peeled and minced or crushed through a press

1 tablespoon dried basil, crumbled
2 teaspoons dried oregano, crumbled
1 teaspoon whole fennel seeds
½ teaspoon dried rosemary, crumbled
1½ cups dry white wine
2 35-ounce cans whole Italian tomatoes, with juice
3 tablespoons tomato paste
1 tablespoon sugar
2 teaspoons salt
¼ teaspoon hot red pepper flakes
¼ teaspoon black pepper
1 tablespoon butter
1½ pounds spaghetti
½ cup grated Parmesan cheese
Garlic Toast (recipe follows)

1. Prepare the chicken meatballs: Position a shelf in the top third of the oven and preheat to 400°. Lightly oil a 13-by-9-by-2-inch baking pan.

2. Crumble the English muffin into a large bowl; add the milk and let muffin soften 10 minutes. Add the ground chicken, Parmesan, egg, tomato sauce, parsley, salt, basil, oregano, nutmeg, and pepper. Using one hand, mix in a swift circular motion until blended. The mixture will be soft.

3. Dipping your hands in cold water as you work, shape the mixture into 18 meatballs (to judge, use a quarter-cup measure rinsed in cold water for the first one, but don't fill it quite full; plop out and roll into a ball in your hands). Put balls close together in the oiled pan. After all are shaped lightly brush the tops with olive oil. Bake uncovered 25 to 30 minutes, until lightly browned and cooked through.

4. Prepare the tomato sauce: Spoon 1½ tablespoons of the olive oil into a 4-quart heavy nonaluminum saucepan or dutch oven and place over moderate heat. Add the onions and sauté to soften, about 5 minutes. Add the garlic, basil, oregano, fennel, and rosemary; sauté 1 minute. Pour in the wine and bring to a boil. Lower the heat and keep at a simmer.

5. Place a sieve over a bowl and add 1 can of the tomatoes; force through with a spoon or a stiff whisk; discard the seeds and add the purée to the pan. Repeat with the second can of tomatoes. Stir in the tomato paste, sugar, salt, hot pepper flakes, and black pepper. Add the meatballs, including the brown bits in the pan. Bring to a boil over moderate heat. Simmer over low heat 1 hour and 15 minutes to 1 hour and 30 minutes. Stir in the butter. Scoop out the meatballs with a slotted spoon and put them in a serving dish, topping them with 1 cup of the sauce to keep them moist.

6. Bring a very large pot of lightly salted water to a boil over high heat. Drop in the spaghetti and, stirring constantly, bring the water back to a full boil. Stirring occasionally, cook until tender but firm to the bite, 8 to 10 minutes. Drain in a colander. In a large bowl, toss with the remaining 1½ tablespoons olive oil. Serve hot with the sauce and meatballs, Parmesan cheese, and garlic toast.

Garlic Toast

MAKES 6 SERVINGS

- **3** tablespoons olive oil
- **3** tablespoons butter
- **2** large garlic cloves, peeled and minced or crushed through a press
- **¼** teaspoon salt
- **1** 14- to 16-inch loaf crusty Italian bread with or without sesame seeds, split horizontally
- **3** tablespoons grated Parmesan cheese
- **½** teaspoon paprika

1. Preheat the broiler. Spoon the olive oil into a small heavy skillet; add the butter and garlic and place over low heat. Sizzle for 1 to 2 minutes without letting the garlic brown. Add the salt.

2. Partially slice through the bread halves at a 45-degree angle every 2 inches (cut halfway down through the bread) and place on a broiler pan. Drizzle the garlic butter over them and sprinkle with the Parmesan and paprika. Broil until toasted and golden, about 2 minutes. Serve hot.

Here is a good toasty-crisp, crusty garlic bread, not the soggy-moist kind (if you want a soft loaf, wrap in foil and bake instead of broiling). The bread can be prepared well ahead but be sure to broil just before serving.

Spinach Tortellini with Creamy Chicken Sauce

Rosy pink flecks of smoked ham show off the jade green spinach pasta in this creamy dish. Bits of chicken catch in the curls of the tortellini and it's the texture of the folds, pleats, and layers of pasta around the filling that makes the chewing so appealing. Very simple.

MAKES 4 MAIN-COURSE SERVINGS OR 6 PASTA-COURSE SERVINGS

2 tablespoons olive oil
1 medium onion, peeled and chopped
1 large garlic clove, peeled and minced or crushed through a press
2 teaspoons dried basil, crumbled
1/2 pound ground chicken (see page 14)
2 teaspoons all-purpose flour
1/2 cup dry white wine
1 cup light cream
1 teaspoon salt
1/4 teaspoon black pepper
1/4 teaspoon grated nutmeg
1/2 cup finely diced smoked ham (about 3 ounces)
3/4 cup grated Parmesan cheese
1 pound cheese-filled spinach tortellini, fresh or frozen

1. Spoon the olive oil into a heavy medium nonaluminum saucepan and place over moderate heat. Add the onion and sauté to soften, 3 to 5 minutes. Add the garlic and basil; cook a minute longer. Add the ground chicken and cook, breaking up with a spoon, until lightly browned. Stir in the flour to moisten it. Pour in the wine and boil until reduced by half, 2 minutes over moderately high heat. Add the cream, salt, pepper, and nutmeg. Simmer, stirring frequently, for 2 or 3 minutes. Remove from the heat and stir in the ham and 1/2 cup of the Parmesan cheese.

2. Bring a large pot of lightly salted water to a boil over high heat. Add the tortellini and boil, stirring constantly until the boil resumes and frequently thereafter, until tender but firm to the bite. Drain and toss with the sauce. Serve topped with the remaining ¼ cup Parmesan cheese.

Potato Gnocchi with Chicken Pesto Sauce

MAKES 6 TO 8 SERVINGS

Potato Gnocchi:

2 pounds red-skinned potatoes (4 large)
2 teaspoons salt
1½ cups all-purpose flour, plus additional for shaping

Chicken Pesto:

3 tablespoons olive oil
2 medium onions, peeled and chopped
2 large garlic cloves, peeled and minced or crushed through a press
1 pound ground chicken (see page 14)
1 tablespoon all-purpose flour
2 teaspoons salt
1 cup dry white wine
1 cup heavy cream
2 cups fresh basil leaves, lightly packed
¾ cup grated Parmesan cheese
½ cup (2 ounces) walnut pieces

The famous Italian potato dumplings are light and tender when no egg is added to them. They are time-consuming to shape until you get the knack of it, and then they are a breeze. The chicken pesto is light, fragrant, and flavorful.

1. Prepare the potato gnocchi: Put the potatoes in a large heavy pot and add a pinch of salt and cold water to cover by 1 inch. Bring to a boil, partially cover, and cook over moderately high heat until tender when pierced with a fork, 35 to 45 minutes (do not pierce before 35 minutes or potatoes will become soggy). Drain and set aside until cool enough to handle but still warm, about 30 minutes. Peel and dice into a large bowl. With an electric mixer or a potato masher, mash the potatoes. You should have $3\frac{1}{2}$ cups, packed.

2. Add the $1\frac{1}{2}$ cups flour and the salt; work in with your hands to make a soft, slightly sticky dough. Dust well with additional flour. Divide into 8 pieces and dust again with flour. One at a time, roll each piece into a rope about $\frac{3}{4}$ inch thick. Cut into $\frac{3}{4}$-inch lengths. Dust a baking sheet or tray with flour. Pick up one small piece of dough and with your index finger press it against the tines of a dinner fork to flatten and make a grooved impression. Without letting go, roll it toward you (see illustration), lightly pressing against the tines. You are actually dragging the dough toward you to force a slightly curved and concave shape. As it is formed, let it drop onto the floured sheet. Repeat with all the dough. Cover with waxed paper until ready to cook. Gnocchi can be shaped 2 or 3 hours ahead of time but should be cooked after the sauce is made.

3. Prepare the chicken pesto: Spoon 2 tablespoons of the olive oil into a heavy medium nonaluminum saucepan and place over moderate heat. Add the onions and sauté to soften, about 5 minutes. Add the garlic and cook a minute longer. Add the chicken, break up with a fork, and sauté until lightly browned. Spoon in the flour and salt and cook for a minute. Pour in the wine; bring to a boil and cook for 3 minutes to thicken slightly. Pour in the heavy cream and boil 2 minutes longer. Remove from the heat.

4. Rinse the basil leaves and put them in a food processor or blender with just the water clinging to the leaves. Add $\frac{1}{2}$ cup of the Parmesan, the walnuts, the remaining 1 tablespoon olive oil, and 1 tablespoon cold water. Process to a purée. Stir into the sauce.

5. Bring a large pot of lightly salted water to a boil over high heat. One at a time, quickly drop in a quarter of the gnocchi. After they rise to the surface, boil 30 seconds longer, then scoop out with a slotted spoon and add to the sauce. Cook the remaining gnocchi, adding each batch to the sauce as they are done. Serve hot with the remaining 1/4 cup Parmesan sprinkled over the top.

Flaky Chicken and Goat Cheese Pastries

MAKES 60 TO 70

Filling:

- **1** tablespoon olive oil
- **1** medium onion, peeled and finely chopped
- **2** garlic cloves, peeled and minced or crushed through a press
- **1** teaspoon dried tarragon, crumbled
- **1** pound ground chicken (see page 14)
- **1** teaspoon salt
- **1/4** teaspoon black pepper
- **2** tablespoons all-purpose flour
- **1/3** cup dry white wine
- **1** tablespoon lemon juice or vinegar
- **1/2** cup sliced scallions
- **6** ounces mild goat cheese such as Montrachet, coarsely grated

If you have never worked with frozen phyllo pastry sheets, be sure to try this. You'll discover just what a miracle they are. If you had to make parchment-paper-thin sheets of pastry yourself you'd be in the kitchen all day, and just imagine the mess! Pre-rolled sheets are available in most large grocery stores these days. And if you've never sampled goat cheese, here is a perfect showplace for it as well. You can shape the hors d'oeuvres well ahead of time and chill them or even freeze them. They bake up into flaky lightness in just 10 or 12 minutes.

Assembly:

8 tablespoons (1 stick) butter, melted
1/4 cup olive oil
1 pound package phyllo pastry, thawed if frozen
2 egg yolks
2 tablespoons sesame seeds

1. Make the filling: Spoon the olive oil into a large heavy skillet and place over moderate heat. Add the onion and sauté until soft and translucent, 3 to 5 minutes. Add the garlic and tarragon and cook a minute longer. Add the chicken, salt, and pepper; cook, breaking up the chicken with a spoon, until lightly browned, about 3 minutes over moderately high heat.

2. Stir in the flour and cook for 1 minute. Pour in the wine and boil for 2 to 3 minutes, until very thick. Remove from the heat and cool to room temperature. Stir in the lemon juice, scallions, and goat cheese. Set aside.

3. Assemble the pastries: Combine the butter and olive oil in a small saucepan and melt over low heat. Unroll the phyllo and cut it lengthwise into 4 equal strips, cutting directly through the stack with a sharp knife. Stack them on a sheet of plastic wrap directly in front of you on a work surface and cover with the plastic wrap. Phyllo dries very quickly and should be uncovered only as you remove some.

4. Remove 1 strip of phyllo; using a pastry brush, dab all over with melted butter (but don't brush to cover completely). Top with a second strip of phyllo and dab with butter. Put about 2 teaspoons of the chicken filling at one end of the strip and fold up one corner of the phyllo to begin forming a triangle. Continue folding it, flag-style, to make a multilayered triangle that encloses the filling. Lightly brush the top with a bit of butter and put on a baking sheet. Repeat to shape all the pastries, arranging them 1/2 inch apart on baking sheets.

5. In a cup stir the egg yolks with 1 tablespoon cold water. Lightly brush the tops of the pastries with egg glaze and sprinkle with a pinch of the sesame seeds. Cover and chill or freeze, or bake right away.

6. Preheat the oven to 400°. Bake the pastries until flaky and golden brown, 10 to 12 minutes. Serve hot.

Cocks' Combs

MAKES 12

Filling:

- **1** tablespoon olive oil
- **1** large garlic clove, peeled and minced or crushed through a press
- **½** pound ground chicken (see page 14)
- **½** cup dry white wine
- **1** teaspoon dried basil, crumbled
- **½** teaspoon dried oregano, crumbled
- **½** cup ricotta cheese
- **¼** cup grated Parmesan cheese
- **2** tablespoons tomato paste
- **1** egg yolk
- **½** teaspoon salt
- **¼** teaspoon black pepper

This is a quick and easy savory version of the classic cocks' combs usually made from Danish pastry and a sweet filling. In this recipe a tender-flaky biscuit dough is shaped around chicken and cheese filling. They are best hot and fresh, of course, like any biscuit, and are a good companion to a soup lunch. They can be reheated in the microwave. For the best flavor, make the filling a day ahead and chill it, then return it to room temperature before assembling.

Biscuit Dough:

2 tablespoons butter, at room temperature
3½ cups all-purpose flour
1½ tablespoons baking powder
¼ teaspoon salt
½ cup white vegetable shortening
4 tablespoons (½ stick) cold butter
1 cup cold milk

Topping:

1 egg yolk, slightly beaten
2 tablespoons grated Parmesan cheese

1. Make the filling: Spoon the olive oil into a heavy medium nonaluminum skillet and place over moderate heat. Add the garlic and let sizzle without browning for a minute. Add the ground chicken. Break it up with a spoon and brown over moderately high heat for 2 to 3 minutes. Pour in the wine. Add the basil and oregano; cook until the wine completely evaporates, 3 to 5 minutes. When that happens the chicken will begin to sizzle.

2. Turn the filling into a bowl and stir in the ricotta cheese, Parmesan, tomato paste, egg yolk, salt, and pepper. Cool to room temperature. If making ahead, cover and chill. Return to room temperature before using.

3. Make the biscuit dough: Evenly space two shelves in the oven and preheat to 400°. Lightly grease two baking sheets. Stir the soft butter in a cup so it is smooth and spreadable.

4. In a large bowl stir together the flour, baking powder, and salt. Add the shortening, spooning it into bits; thinly slice the cold butter and add it to the flour. Using a pastry blender or two knives, cut the shortening and butter into the flour until it resembles petals about the size of cornflakes. Pour in the milk all at once and stir quickly with a fork to make a soft dough. Knead it on a floured surface (a board or a piece of waxed paper) 4 or 5 times. Pat the dough into a 9-by-12-inch rectangle. Spread with the soft butter. Fold in thirds, letter-style. Dust with flour and quickly roll on a generously floured surface into a 12-inch square.

5. Spoon half of the chicken filling across the center of the dough and pat into a 4-inch band. Fold one end of the dough up over it to cover. Spread the remaining filling on top of the folded dough and then fold the remaining end of the dough up over the filling to cover completely (illustration A). Pinch the seam to enclose and dust with flour.

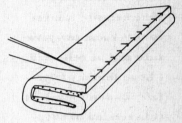

A.

6. Cut the flattened roll into 12 equal slices, using a floured sharp knife. Take one piece, flatten it slightly with your hand, and with a paring knife make 3 evenly spaced cuts halfway through one side. Pick up the piece and place it on a baking sheet, fanning it so the cuts open to resemble a cock's comb (illustration B). Repeat, putting 6 on each sheet.

B.

7. Topping: Using a pastry brush, paint the tops of the cocks' combs with egg yolk to glaze. Sprinkle each with ½ teaspoon of the Parmesan. Bake 15 to 17 minutes, reversing the sheets after 10 minutes, until golden brown. Serve hot.

N O T E : Cold leftover cocks' combs can be heated on a paper towel in the microwave for 20 seconds on full power.

Chicken Thief Shepherd's Pie

There's no getting around it, you'll have to make this ahead of time because it must cool to room temperature and be reheated. I hope that my Irish friends don't cluck at this version of shepherd's pie. It is modeled after one that was served at Center School when I worked in the cafeteria during fifth grade. If you want to pipe decorative potato designs on top, start with 4 pounds of potatoes and use an extra tablespoon of butter when you mash them.

MAKES 8 SERVINGS

Filling:

1½ tablespoons butter
2 medium onions, peeled and chopped
2 large garlic cloves, peeled and minced or crushed through a press
1½ pounds ground chicken (see page 14)
1 tablespoon dried basil, crumbled
1 teaspoon dried oregano, crumbled
1 teaspoon ground cumin
⅛ teaspoon cayenne pepper (optional)
1 cup dry white wine
½ cup all-purpose flour
1 28-ounce can whole tomatoes, with juice
½ cup chicken stock or broth
2 teaspoons salt
¼ teaspoon black pepper

Potato Topping:

3 pounds (6 to 8 large) Idaho baking potatoes
¾ to 1 cup half and half or milk
4 tablespoons (½ stick) butter
2 teaspoons salt
½ teaspoon grated nutmeg
¼ teaspoon black pepper
¼ cup grated Parmesan cheese
½ teaspoon paprika

1. Prepare the filling: Melt the butter in a large heavy nonaluminum skillet over moderate heat. Add the onions and sauté to soften, about 5 minutes. Add the garlic and cook a minute longer. Add the chicken, increase the heat to moderately high, and cook until browned, breaking up the meat with a spoon, 3 to 4 minutes. Add the basil, oregano, cumin, and cayenne pepper; pour in ½ cup of the wine and boil until completely evaporated, about 5 minutes.

2. Sprinkle with the flour and stir to moisten; cook for a minute. Pour in the tomatoes and juice, breaking up the tomatoes with a spoon; add the broth and the remaining ½ cup wine. Stirring constantly, bring to a boil. Lower the heat and simmer, stirring occasionally, about 5 minutes, until thickened. Stir in the salt and pepper. Turn into a 13-by-9-by-2-inch baking pan.

3. Prepare the potato topping: Adjust an oven shelf to the top third of the oven and preheat to 375°. Peel the potatoes and cut them into 1-inch chunks. As they are cut, drop them into a large pot of cold water. Add a little salt and place over high heat. Partially cover and bring to a boil. Boil until very tender, about 20 minutes. Drain in a colander. Pour ¾ cup of the half and half into the pot and add 3 tablespoons of the butter; bring to a boil. Remove from the heat. Return the potatoes and add the salt, nutmeg, and pepper; beat with an electric handheld mixer until fluffy, beating in a little more half and half if potatoes seem dry.

4. Spread the potato topping evenly over the filling, working around the outside edge first and using a spatula. Use the tines of a fork dipped in cold water to make decorative designs, or use some extra mashed potatoes to pipe designs from a pastry bag fitted with a ¾-inch star tip. Dot with the remaining 1 tablespoon butter. Sprinkle with the Parmesan cheese and paprika. Bake 35 to 40 minutes, until golden brown. Let cool completely.

5. To reheat, bake in a 350° oven for 20 to 30 minutes. Or cut individual portions and heat them in a microwave at high power for 2 to 3 minutes. Serve hot.

9 Dishes Using Cooked Chicken

You don't have to bother with cooking a chicken to create a chicken dinner. Many exciting chicken recipes can be put together from fully cooked chickens that you buy in the supermarket or delicatessen. Granted, you will pay a little more for the privilege, but you won't have to fuss. You can get to the fun part *fast*. And no one will notice any difference in the result because these recipes are *designed* to utilize cooked chicken.

Certainly you can save money and cook the bird yourself at home ahead of time, or use leftover cooked chicken that you might have on hand. Either way, the result will be the same. I once made a sensational chicken salad from cold leftover fried chicken that I simply cut up into cubes and tossed with a zesty dressing.

Some of the dishes given here may sound familiar, such as the classic club sandwich, chicken croquettes, and chicken à la king, but all sorts of new chicken creations are possible too— from barbecued chicken quiche in pepper pastry to smoked chicken in buckwheat blini.

When chickens are on sale it's a good idea to buy a couple to make stock, then lift off the breast and thigh meat as soon as they are cooked. That way you will have chicken for recipes in this chapter, and broth to boot.

Other recipes in this book that can be made with cooked chicken:

Chicken Tonnato

Here is a cold, refreshing chicken version of the classic Italian veal with tuna mayonnaise sauce. It's a great dish for entertaining in hot weather because you make it ahead and keep it in the refrigerator. Traditionally it is made with twice as much mayonnaise and olive oil, but this less rich version is terrific, and better for you. Since you need a cooked chicken, buy one at a deli or follow the recipe for the white-cut chicken on page 44.

MAKES 6 SERVINGS

1 4-pound cooked chicken, cooled
1 6- to 7-ounce can solid white tuna packed in oil, drained
3/4 cup Mayonnaise (page 383)
1/2 cup sour cream
4 flat anchovy fillets (half a 2-ounce can)
2 tablespoons lemon juice
2 tablespoons capers
2 teaspoons Dijon or golden mustard
1/2 teaspoon dried oregano, crumbled
1/4 teaspoon salt
1/4 teaspoon black pepper
1/4 cup olive oil

Optional Toppings:

Sliced hard-cooked eggs (see page 352)
Black olives
Capers
Flat-leaf parsley sprigs
Cracked black pepper

1. Pull the skin from the chicken and discard it. Pull the meat from the bones in large pieces, keeping the breast halves whole. Discard the bones. Cut the chicken across the grain into slices about 1/4 inch thick.
2. In the container of a food processor or blender, combine the tuna, mayonnaise, sour cream, anchovies, lemon juice, capers, mustard, oregano, salt, and pepper; blend to a purée. Gradually blend in the olive oil.

3. Spread ½ cup of the tuna sauce in a 12-by-9-inch deep porcelain platter or serving dish. Arrange half of the chicken slices in the dish, saving the best slices for the top. Spread with half the remaining tuna sauce. Arrange the rest of the chicken in the dish and spread with the remaining sauce. Cover with plastic wrap and chill for at least 24 hours.

4. Uncover the chicken *tonnato* and decorate the top with sliced hard-cooked eggs, black olives, capers, and parsley sprigs. Crack black pepper over the top and serve cold.

Chicken Grilled Cheese Sandwich

MAKES 1 SANDWICH

2 slices white or whole wheat bread
2 teaspoons Mayonnaise (page 383) or mustard
2 slices Cheddar, Swiss, provolone, mozzarella, or American cheese, trimmed to fit the bread
2 thin slices roasted chicken breast
2 thin slices tomato (optional)
Salt and pepper
2 teaspoons butter, softened

1. Place a heavy skillet or griddle over moderate heat.

2. Place the slices of bread side by side. Spread each with 1 teaspoon mayonnaise or mustard (or ½ teaspoon of each). Put 1 slice of cheese over each. Add the chicken and optional tomato to one and sprinkle lightly with salt and pepper. Invert one over the other to make a sandwich.

3. Butter the top and place buttered side down in the hot skil-

This is so simple and so good; I usually make it when there is leftover chicken from a deli-purchased rotisserie chicken. Be flexible when it comes to making it; I like a combination of provolone and mozzarella with sliced tomato, but sometimes I prefer Cheddar. For a variation, add crisp bacon or sliced green

olives instead of
tomato.

let. Grill for 3 to 4 minutes, until golden brown. Spread top with remaining butter, turn, and grill until toasted golden brown; when done the cheese inside should be melted. Serve hot.

NOTE: If you are grilling 3 sandwiches at a time you can melt 1 tablespoon butter in the pan before putting the sandwiches in; then add another tablespoon butter and turn them.

Classic Club Sandwich

Although often made with turkey, the original club sandwich was created with chicken and two slices of bread. Today it's a three-layer marvel of a sandwich, very good with potato chips or potato salad and pickles and olives.

MAKES 1 SANDWICH

2 slices smoked bacon
3 slices white or whole wheat bread, or a combination
4 teaspoons Mayonnaise (page 383)
2 thin slices tomato
Salt and pepper
2 thin slices roasted chicken breast
1 leaf crisp romaine or iceberg lettuce
2 pimiento-stuffed green olives
2 pitted black olives

1. In a heavy skillet (or microwave oven), fry the bacon crisp and golden brown. Drain on paper towels.
2. Stack the bread and slice off the crusts with a serrated knife. Toast the bread.
3. Place one slice of toast on a cutting board. Spread with 1 teaspoon of mayonnaise; add 1 slice of tomato and sprinkle lightly with salt and pepper. Top with the 2 slices of chicken. Spread a slice of toast with 1 teaspoon mayonnaise and invert

over chicken. Spread other side with 1 teaspoon mayonnaise and add the remaining tomato slice. Sprinkle with salt and pepper. Break the bacon slices in half and put all 4 pieces atop the tomato. Add the lettuce. Spread the remaining teaspoon mayonnaise on one side of the last slice of toast and invert over the lettuce. Holding and pressing firmly on top, use a serrated knife to slice the club sandwich into quarters. Secure each quarter with a toothpick and attach an olive to the top of each. Arrange on a plate and serve.

Mexican Club Sandwich

MAKES 1 SANDWICH

4 thin slices white bread
2 tablespoons (6 teaspoons) Mayonnaise (see page 383)
1 slice American cheese (or Swiss, for a variation)
3 thin slices tomato
Salt
1 thin slice raw onion
2 slices roasted chicken breast
1 to 2 thin slices ham, trimmed to fit the bread.
4 thin slices pickled jalapeño

1. Stack the bread and slice off the crusts with a serrated knife. Toast the bread (in Mexico this is done on a grill with ridges so the toasted lines are decorative).
2. Put one slice of toast on a cutting board; spread with 1 teaspoon mayonnaise and top with the slice of cheese and a tomato slice. Lightly sprinkle with salt and add the onion slice. Spread

Although similar sandwiches are served all over Mexico, this version is especially popular around the square at the sidewalk cafes in Oaxaca. My favorite is served at the Bar del Jardin and I have modeled this recipe after the ones I've eaten there for so many years. Yes, even though there are so many

1 teaspoon mayonnaise over a slice of toast and invert over the onion. Spread with 1 teaspoon mayonnaise and add the chicken slices. Top with a tomato slice and sprinkle with salt. Spread a slice of toast with 1 teaspoon mayonnaise and invert over the tomato. Spread with 1 teaspoon mayonnaise and add the ham. Top with the sliced jalapeño and finally the last slice of tomato. Spread the remaining 1 teaspoon mayonnaise over the last slice of toast and invert to make the club sandwich. Press firmly and cut into quarters with a serrated knife. Secure each quarter with a toothpick. Arrange on a plate and serve.

Italian Chicken Salad Sandwiches with Anchovies and Eggs

I first tasted sand-
wiches like these at
Harry's Bar in Venice.
For those who sit at
the bar, the kitchen
offers a dazzling se-
lection of cool sand-
wiches to tide them
over until the big meal
of the day. Even people
who say they don't like
anchovies dig into
these with gusto.

MAKES 10 SMALL SANDWICHES

1 cup finely chopped cooked chicken breast
4 hard-cooked eggs, finely chopped
1 2-ounce can flat anchovy fillets, drained and chopped
1 small onion, grated
⅓ cup Mayonnaise (page 383)
¼ teaspoon black pepper
Salt to taste (optional)
20 thin slices firm white or whole wheat bread
8 tablespoons (1 stick) unsalted butter, softened
¼ cup finely chopped parsley or black olives

1. In a medium bowl combine the chicken, eggs, anchovies, onion, and pepper. Stir in the mayonnaise. Taste for salt and add a pinch if necessary, though the saltiness of the anchovies should be enough.

2. Spread each slice of bread with about 1 teaspoon of the butter. Then spread 3 tablespoons of the chicken filling evenly over 10 slices of the bread. Mound about 1 teaspoon of the chopped parsley or black olives over the center of the chicken filling. Place the remaining 10 bread slices, buttered side down, over the filling. With a serrated knife, trim off about ¼ inch (the crust) from each side. Cut the sandwiches diagonally in half.

3. Dip a clean kitchen towel or several layers of paper towels in cold water and wring out. Stack the sandwiches and wrap them tightly in the damp cloth. Refrigerate until serving time, and serve cold. These sandwiches can be made up to 6 hours ahead of time and kept this way; if making farther ahead, wrap the sandwiches in plastic wrap.

Chicken and Spinach Cannelloni

Rich and creamy with two sauces and home-made pasta, this is a good dish to make ahead of time. It's a lot of work, just the kind of cooking project I love for a Sunday afternoon. You can save time and buy sheets of store-bought pasta if you know where to find them. This dish can also be served in individual gratin dishes. If it's to be a pasta course rather than a main course, consider serving roast leg of lamb and asparagus, or roast beef and carrots. You will need leftover cooked chicken or a deli-roasted chicken for the filling.

MAKES 32

Pasta:

1½ cups all-purpose flour
  2 large eggs

Filling:

  1 pound fresh spinach or one 10-ounce package frozen leaf spinach, thawed
  2 tablespoons olive oil
  1 medium onion, peeled and finely chopped
  1 large garlic clove, peeled and minced or crushed through a press
1½ cups packed finely diced (¼-inch) cooked chicken breast and thigh
  1 cup ricotta cheese
  1 cup grated Parmesan cheese
⅓ cup heavy cream
  2 egg yolks
½ teaspoon grated nutmeg
½ teaspoon dried oregano, crumbled
  1 teaspoon salt
⅛ teaspoon black pepper

Tomato Sauce:

  2 tablespoons olive oil
  1 medium onion, peeled and finely chopped
  1 large garlic clove, peeled and minced or crushed through a press
  1 16-ounce can whole tomatoes, with juice
¼ cup dry white wine
  2 tablespoons tomato paste

2 teaspoons dried basil, crumbled
1 teaspoon sugar
½ teaspoon salt
⅛ teaspoon black pepper

Cream Sauce:

3 tablespoons butter
¼ cup all-purpose flour
1 cup light cream
½ cup milk
¼ cup white wine
½ teaspoon salt
⅛ teaspoon cayenne pepper

Topping:

2 tablespoons butter, cut into bits
¼ cup grated Parmesan cheese

1. Make the pasta: Place the flour in a large shallow bowl and make a well in the center. Add the eggs. Using a fork, beat the eggs together in a circle. As you stir, gradually incorporate the flour from around the sides of the well into the eggs. Continue stirring until the dough becomes too thick to stir. Then, with floured fingers, incorporate enough of the remaining flour to make a stiff but not dry dough. Remove from the bowl and knead, adding a bit more flour if needed to prevent sticking, for 10 minutes, to make a satin-smooth dough that is neither sticky nor dry. The kneading can be done on a lightly floured board or with the dough held in both hands (which I find easier) while pinching and folding it this way and that. Cover and let rest for 1 hour; if making further ahead, wrap in plastic and chill.
2. Make the filling: Rinse the spinach in a sinkful of cool water and pull off and discard just the thick tough stems. Put

the wet leaves into a large heavy nonaluminum pot; cover and place over high heat and cook, stirring once or twice, until wilted down, 2 to 3 minutes. Drain well in a strainer placed over a bowl. When cool, press to squeeze out a little more of the remaining liquid. (Reserve the liquid for another use, such as a soup.) Finely chop the spinach; you should have 1 cup. If using frozen, simply drain and chop.

3. Spoon the olive oil into a heavy medium skillet and place over moderate heat. Add the onion and sauté to soften, about 5 minutes. Add the garlic and cook a minute longer. Add the spinach; increase the heat to high and cook for 1 minute. Remove from the heat and scrape into a large bowl. Stir the chicken into the bowl and let the mixture cool to room temperature. Stir in the ricotta cheese, Parmesan cheese, heavy cream, egg yolks, nutmeg, oregano, salt, and pepper. Set aside. (Chill if you made this a few hours ahead.)

4. Make the tomato sauce: Spoon the olive oil into a heavy medium nonaluminum saucepan and place over moderate heat; add the onion and sauté to soften, 3 to 5 minutes. Add the garlic and cook a minute longer. Add the tomatoes and juice, breaking up the tomatoes with a spoon. Stir in the white wine, tomato paste, basil, sugar, salt, and pepper. Bring to a boil over moderate heat. Simmer over low heat until thick and reduced to 2 cups, 20 to 25 minutes.

5. Roll the pasta: Knead the pasta briefly on a floured surface and divide into 4 equal pieces; pat each into a 3-inch square. Dust them with flour. Using a pasta machine (either hand-cranked or one with electric rollers) and working on a floured surface, one at a time pass the pieces of pasta through the widest setting three times. Continue passing them through, reducing the space between the rollers each time, until the pasta is very thin (each strip should measure about 4 by 24 inches). Cut each piece into eight 3-by-4-inch rectangles.

6. Meanwhile, bring a large pot of lightly salted water to a boil over high heat. Drop in 4 to 6 pieces of pasta and leave in 10 seconds. Quickly scoop out with a slotted spoon and tongs and drop into a large bowl of cold water. Continue cooking the pasta in batches. As soon as it is cool, arrange it on paper towels so the noodles do not touch each other.

7. Assemble the cannelloni: Adjust a shelf to the top third of the oven and preheat to 400°. Spread ½ cup of the tomato sauce in a 15-by-10-by-1-inch jelly roll pan or large shallow baking dish.

8. Working on a plate or a board, assemble one cannelloni at a time. Take one piece of drained pasta and spread it with about 2 tablespoons of the chicken filling. Starting at one short end, loosely roll up and place in the prepared pan. Continue assembling the rolls, arranging them close together in the pan. Spread all of the tomato sauce over them.

9. Make the cream sauce: Melt the butter in a heavy medium saucepan over moderate heat. Add the flour and cook for 2 to 3 minutes, stirring. Pour in the cream and milk; stirring constantly, bring to a boil. Pour in the wine and add salt and cayenne pepper. Stirring constantly, simmer for 3 to 4 minutes, until thick. Spread over the tomato sauce.

10. Complete the topping: Dot the top with the butter and sprinkle with the Parmesan cheese. Bake until golden brown and bubbly, 15 to 20 minutes. Let stand 10 minutes before serving.

Chicken Egg Fu Yung

Here you'll need both chicken and eggs. The browned onions and eggs with crisp bean sprouts add all the right textures and flavors. The initial browning of the onions is the key to success here. I prefer these without any sauce, as they are eaten in China, but a sauce recipe is included since most Americans are accustomed to eating egg fu yung with gravy. In a sense these are omelets, and they make a good brunch dish.

MAKES 6 (2 TO 3 SERVINGS)

6 dried Chinese mushrooms
3 tablespoons vegetable oil
2 medium onions, peeled and cut lengthwise into ¼-inch slivers
5 large eggs
1 tablespoon oriental sesame oil
1 cup diced (½-inch) cooked chicken breast and/or thigh
1 cup fresh bean sprouts
½ teaspoon salt
⅛ teaspoon black pepper

Sauce:

1 cup Basic Chicken Stock (page 47) or canned broth
2 tablespoons Chinese oyster sauce
2 tablespoons dry sherry
1 tablespoon black soy sauce
1 tablespoon cornstarch
1 teaspoon sugar
1 teaspoon oriental sesame oil
3 slices fresh ginger
1 garlic clove, peeled and sliced

1. Place the mushrooms in a small bowl and add ½ cup boiling water. Let soak about 30 minutes to soften. Drain, reserving ¼ cup of the soaking liquid. Slice off the mushroom stems and discard. Chop the caps.

2. Spoon 1 tablespoon of the vegetable oil into a heavy medium skillet and place over moderately high heat; add the onions and cook until browned and softened, 3 to 5 minutes, stirring frequently. Transfer to a plate and let cool.

3. Crack the eggs into a large bowl. Add the sesame oil and whisk until blended. Stir in the chicken, bean sprouts, salt, pepper, and reserved mushrooms, soaking liquid, and onions.

4. Spoon 1 tablespoon of the remaining oil into a large heavy skillet and place over moderate heat. When very hot, ladle in 3 pancakes, using ½ cup for each and stirring the mixture each time before measuring. Brown well over moderately high heat for 1 to 2 minutes; turn with a spatula and brown the remaining side about 1 minute longer, until cooked. Repeat, using the remaining 1 tablespoon oil. Transfer to a hot platter.

5. Make the sauce: In a small heavy saucepan stir together the chicken stock, oyster sauce, sherry, soy sauce, and cornstarch until smooth; stir in the sugar, ginger, and garlic; and place over moderate heat. Stirring constantly, bring to a boil to thicken. Remove the ginger and garlic and pour the hot sauce over the egg fu yung.

Chicken à la King

So many old recipes for this 1950s favorite turn out just plain awful. This is my way to make it and I like to serve it in bread croustades (toast cases), but you can also serve it over biscuits or even over noodles or in puff pastry patty shells. You can buy a cooked chicken from a deli or cook one yourself. Make the croustades or biscuits first.

MAKES 6 SERVINGS

- **1** large bell pepper, or one 4-ounce jar pimientos
- **6** tablespoons (¾ stick) butter
- **½** pound fresh mushrooms, thinly sliced
- **¼** cup chopped green bell pepper
- **¼** cup minced white of scallion, or shallots
- **½** cup all-purpose flour
- **2½** cups Basic Chicken Stock (page 47) or canned broth
- **1** cup heavy or light cream
- **½** cup dry sherry
- **¼** teaspoon grated nutmeg
- **1½** teaspoons salt
- **⅛** teaspoon black pepper
- **3** egg yolks
- **4** cups diced (½- to ¾-inch) cooked chicken
- **6** Croustades (page 372) or Beautiful Biscuits (page 371)
- **¼** cup chopped fresh parsley leaves
- **6** parsley sprigs, for garnish

1. Roast the pepper by placing it directly on the burner of a gas stove with the flame turned to high, or as close as possible to the heat source of an electric broiler. Turn frequently with tongs until blistered and black all over. Let cool for a minute, then place in a plastic bag and chill for 10 minutes. Cut out the stem and core, remove all seeds, and scrape away the blackened skin. Cut the pepper into ½-inch squares. If using pimientos, simply drain and cut into squares.

2. Melt the butter in a large heavy saucepan over moderate heat. Add the mushrooms, green bell pepper, and scallion; sauté to brown the mushrooms lightly, about 3 minutes. Stir in the flour and cook for 1 minute. The mixture will be dry. Pour in the chicken stock, cream, and sherry; stirring constantly, bring to a boil. Add the nutmeg, salt, and pepper; simmer, stirring frequently, 2 to 3 minutes. The sauce will taste salty but will balance when the chicken is added.

3. In a large bowl whisk the egg yolks. Gradually whisk in about 2 cups of the hot thickened sauce; pour everything back into the pot, stirring, and cook gently 2 to 3 minutes to thicken. Stir in the roasted pepper, chicken, and parsley and heat over low for about 2 minutes.

4. If using croustades, put a warm croustade on a dinner plate and fill with a generous cup of the filling, letting it spill over onto the plate. Garnish the plate with a sprig of parsley and serve hot. Or pour the chicken mixture over split hot biscuits.

Chicken Croquettes

MAKES 24 STICKS OR 48 BALLS

Croquette Mixture:

1 cup cold milk
½ cup chicken stock or canned broth
¾ cup all-purpose flour
2 tablespoons butter
¼ cup dry white wine
1 tablespoon onion juice (see Note)
1 tablespoon lemon juice
2 teaspoons salt
¼ teaspoon grated nutmeg
⅛ teaspoon black pepper
2½ cups lightly packed finely chopped cooked chicken

These tasty old-fashioned morsels are perfect for a Spanish tapa party or a cocktail party. You start with cooked chicken so that means you can buy a deli-roasted bird and save time. Most recipes for croquettes call for quite a lot of butter, but I have devised a way to dissolve the flour in milk rather than fat, so only 2 tablespoons of butter are required. Make the base a day ahead and coat the croquettes well in advance. They are crunchy on the outside and creamy within, and are good at room temperature. Frying is best done in an electric deep-fryer.

Coating, Cooking, and Serving:

½ cup all-purpose flour
1½ cups plain dry bread crumbs
3 large eggs
Vegetable oil
Salt
Lemon wedges

1. Combine the milk and broth in a large shallow bowl. Place a sieve over a sheet of paper and add all of the flour to it. Holding the sieve carefully over the milk mixture (and returning any flour that sifted through onto the paper back to the sieve), gradually sift flour over the surface of the liquid, whisking it in each time a light film forms on top.

2. Transfer mixture to a heavy medium nonaluminum saucepan. Add the butter and place over moderately low heat. Stirring or whisking constantly, bring to a boil; as the mixture thickens and clumps, remove it from the heat and beat vigorously with a stiff whisk; return to the heat. Add the wine, onion juice, lemon juice, salt, nutmeg, and pepper; cook, stirring constantly, for about 3 minutes, until very thick. Remove from the heat and stir in the chicken.

3. Line an 8-inch square pan with plastic wrap. Spread the chicken mixture into it; smooth the top, cover with plastic, and cool to room temperature. Chill for at least 4 hours, or overnight.

4. Coating and cooking: Invert the cold chicken mixture onto a work surface and peel off the plastic. Cut in thirds, then crosswise into 8 strips to make 24 sticks. If making balls, cut the sticks in half.

5. Put the flour, bread crumbs, and eggs in separate shallow dishes or pie pans. Using a fork, whisk 1 teaspoon cold water into the eggs to blend. If making balls, roll chicken mixture into balls with floured hands.

6. Working with 4 to 6 at a time, roll the sticks or balls in the flour to coat. Roll in egg so it adheres to the flour. Roll in crumbs to make an even coating. As they are coated put on a rack. When all are done, chill them for at least 30 minutes.

7. Pour 1½ inches of vegetable oil into a deep-fryer (this will be about 4 cups if your fryer is 6½ inches in diameter) and heat to 375°. Fry a few croquettes at a time until crisp and deep golden brown: 3 at a time will take about 2 minutes; 5 will take 2 to 2½ minutes and 7 to 8 at a time will take 2½ to 3 minutes. Balls will take 30 seconds to a minute less. Allow oil to return to 375° before adding each new batch. Scoop out finished croquettes with a slotted spoon and drain on absorbent paper. Lightly sprinkle with salt. Serve with lemon wedges.

NOTE: To make onion juice, grate a small onion onto a small piece of damp cheesecloth; wring out over a bowl to extract the juice.

Chicken-Potato Pirogi

These filled dumplings are East European comfort food. All the Slavic countries enjoy them in some form. They are something like a cross between ravioli and turnovers, and a little reminiscent of Chinese dim sum dumplings. The dough is softer than pasta dough, so it is easy to roll out.

MAKES ABOUT 4 DOZEN (4 SERVINGS)

Dough:
- 3½ cups all-purpose flour
- 1 teaspoon salt
- 3 large eggs

Filling:
- 1 large Idaho baking potato
- 1½ teaspoons salt
- 1 tablespoon butter
- 1 medium onion, peeled and finely chopped
- 1 7½-ounce package farmer cheese
- 1½ cups packed finely diced (¼-inch) cooked chicken breast
- 2 egg yolks
- 1 tablespoon lemon juice

For Serving:
- 3 tablespoons melted butter
- 1 cup sour cream, at room temperature
- ¼ cup chopped fresh parsley or 2 tablespoons snipped fresh dill

1. Prepare the dough: In a large bowl stir together the flour and salt. In another bowl stir the eggs with ½ cup cold water to blend. Make a well in the center of the flour and pour in the egg mixture. Stir with a fork to make a soft dough. Knead on a lightly floured surface, working in a little more flour if needed, just enough to prevent the dough from sticking but not so much as to make it stiff. Knead with floured hands for at least 5 minutes, until smooth. Cover and let stand at room temperature for 30 to 60 minutes.

2. Prepare the filling: Peel the potato and cut it into ¾-inch cubes. Put the cubes in a medium saucepan of cold water. Add ¼ teaspoon of the salt and bring to a boil, partially covered, over high heat. Lower the heat slightly and boil until tender when pierced with a fork, about 15 minutes. Drain well and turn into a large bowl; mash with a fork (you will have about 1 cup) and let cool to room temperature.

3. Melt the butter in a small skillet over moderate heat; add the onion and sauté to soften, 3 to 5 minutes. Scrape it into the bowl over the potato. Mash in the farmer cheese and chicken. Stir in the remaining 1¼ teaspoons salt, egg yolks, and lemon juice. Mix well.

4. Shape the pirogi: Divide the dough in thirds. Working on a floured surface and using a floured rolling pin, roll one-third of the dough to approximately a 12-inch round about ⅛ inch thick. Using a floured 3-inch biscuit cutter, cut out as many rounds as possible, making the cuts close together. Reserve any scraps of dough.

5. Spoon a scant tablespoon of the filling in the center of each round. Moisten half the edge of each with a pastry brush dipped in water. Bring 2 sides of one dough round up over the filling and press out the air, then press the seam to make a half-moon turnover shape. Repeat with all, placing them on floured baking sheets until ready to cook. If making ahead, cover with plastic.

6. To cook and serve: Bring a large pot of lightly salted water to a boil over high heat. One at a time, quickly add about one dozen pirogi. Stir gently with a slotted spoon so they don't stick together, and boil for about 2 minutes longer after they rise to the surface, or until tender (take one out and test one pointed seam). Drain and toss in a large bowl with the melted butter. Continue cooking the pirogi, then toss with the sour cream and parsley or dill. Serve hot.

Barbecued Chicken Quiche in Pepper Pastry

Who says real men don't eat quiche? Made big-boy barbecue-style with Cheddar cheese, this one always disappears quickly, pardner. You start with a deli-roasted chicken here and add commercially bottled barbecue sauce and mustard to make it nippy. The red and black pepper in the pastry add bite. If you want to start with a frozen prefab pie shell, you should fill the unbaked shell just to the brim with the custard (there will be a little left over) and bake it on a cookie sheet.

MAKES ONE 9-INCH PIE

Pepper Pastry:

- 1½ cups all-purpose flour
- ½ teaspoon black pepper
- ¼ teaspoon cayenne pepper
- ½ teaspoon salt
- ¼ cup vegetable shortening
- 4 tablespoons (½ stick) cold sliced butter
- 3 to 4 tablespoons ice water

Filling:

- 6 ounces (about 1½ cups) cooked chicken, breast and thigh, torn into large shreds
- ½ cup bottled barbecue sauce
- 2 tablespoons Dijon, brown, or yellow mustard
- 3 large eggs
- 1 cup light cream
- 2 tablespoons dry white wine
- ½ teaspoon salt
- ¾ cup (3 ounces) coarsely shredded sharp Cheddar cheese
- ½ teaspoon paprika

1. **Prepare the pepper pastry shell:** In a large bowl stir together the flour, black pepper, red pepper, and salt. Cut in the shortening and butter with a pastry blender or two knives, or quickly rub together with cool fingertips, until the particles are the size of rolled oats. Sprinkle with 2 tablespoons of the ice water and quickly stir with a fork. Stir in enough of

the remaining ice water to make a dough that can be gathered together (neither too moist nor too dry). Divide it into thirds, quickly flatten each piece, stack them on aluminum foil or waxed paper, and flatten into one 6-inch disk. Wrap and chill for at least 1 hour. (Pastry may be prepared a day or two ahead.)

2. Preheat the oven to 425°. Choose a 9-inch pie pan with a 4- to 4½-cup capacity; place on a small baking sheet.

3. On a lightly floured surface, roll out the pastry with a floured rolling pin to about 12 inches in diameter. Loosely drape it into the pan without stretching. Turn the overhanging pastry under all around and crimp decoratively or pinch to make a fluted edge. Line with aluminum foil (so ends extend about 4 inches) and fill with pie weights or with uncooked beans or rice. Bake on the sheet in the center of the oven for 10 to 12 minutes, until the edge has set and is light golden brown. Carefully remove the foil and weights and return the shell to the oven. Bake, pricking any bubbles that may form, about 5 minutes longer, until light brown. Lower the oven temperature to 350°.

4. Prepare the filling: Put the chicken in a medium bowl and stir in the barbecue sauce and mustard.

5. In another medium bowl whisk the eggs and then whisk in the cream, wine, and salt. Arrange the barbecued chicken in the shell and pour the egg mixture over it. Sprinkle with cheese and paprika. Bake on the sheet 40 to 45 minutes, until the quiche has puffed and become golden brown. Cool at least 30 minutes before cutting it into wedges. Serve hot, warm, or at room temperature.

Chicken Kreplach Soup

This is one of my very favorite soups. Kreplach are Jewish ravioli, usually served in chicken broth. You can also pan-fry them in chicken fat and serve them as an appetizer or hors d'oeuvre (see Note). They are best made from homemade pasta, but in a pinch wonton wrappers will do (see Note, page 129, under Chicken Ravioli).

MAKES 8 SERVINGS (4 DOZEN)

½ recipe Homemade Pasta (page 366), or 4 dozen wonton wrappers of medium thickness
1 tablespoon melted chicken fat (schmalz) or vegetable oil
⅓ cup finely chopped onion
⅓ cup finely chopped celery
1 medium garlic clove, peeled and minced or crushed through a press (optional)
1½ cups finely chopped cooked chicken thighs
1 large egg
¼ cup chopped parsley
1 teaspoon salt
⅛ teaspoon black pepper
⅛ teaspoon grated nutmeg
2 to 3 quarts Jewish Chicken Broth (page 50), or canned broth (see Note)

1. Make the pasta dough and let it stand, covered, at room temperature while you make the filling.

2. Spoon the chicken fat or vegetable oil into a heavy medium skillet. Add the onion, celery, and garlic and sauté over moderate heat to soften, about 3 minutes. Cool to room temperature.

3. In a food processor, combine the chicken with the sautéed vegetable mixture. Add the egg, 2 tablespoons of the parsley, salt, pepper, and nutmeg; process until smooth. Alternatively, you can mince very finely with a sharp knife before adding the egg. The filling will be slightly salty but will balance out later.

4. Referring to the pasta instructions on page 127 in the chicken ravioli recipe for the basic rolling technique and procedure, divide the pasta dough in half and roll each half very thin (about $1/16$ inch) so you have 2 long rectangles, each about 5 by 34 inches. Trim them to 5 by 30 inches and cut into $2\frac{1}{2}$-inch squares.

5. Spoon or pipe (with a pastry bag fitted with a plain round tip) about $1\frac{1}{2}$ teaspoons of the filling onto each square. One at a time, shape the kreplach: Pick one square up, dip a fingertip into water and run it along two sides of the pasta; fold over to make a triangle that encloses the filling. Pinch the two side points together (similar to a wonton) and place on a floured surface. Repeat with the remaining ingredients. If making ahead, cover and refrigerate.

6. Bring a large pot of lightly salted water to a boil over high heat. One at a time, quickly drop in the kreplach. Stir gently. When the boil returns, lower the heat, cover the pot, and simmer gently until tender. Traditionally kreplach are served well done, boiled 12 to 15 minutes. If you are making them ahead or they must sit in the broth for any length of time, cook them to the al dente stage, 8 to 10 minutes. Taste one for doneness. Drain in a colander and add to the broth. Sprinkle with the remaining 2 tablespoons parsley and serve hot.

NOTE: To freshen up canned broth, "doctor" it by adding a sliced carrot, celery rib, and onion and simmer 10 minutes.

To make pan-fried kreplach: Spoon 1 tablespoon melted chicken fat into a heavy medium-large skillet (such as cast-iron) and place over moderately high heat. Add 12 to 15 boiled kreplach and pan-fry, turning several times, until crisp and speckled golden brown, 3 to 5 minutes. Sprinkle with about 1 tablespoon chopped parsley and serve hot. If serving as an hors d'oeuvre, stick a toothpick into each.

Chicken Tacos

Tacos can be many different shapes and sizes, but there are only two basic categories: crisp (*tacos dorados*) or soft (*tacos suaves*). Instructions for making both are given below. Soft tacos are a good choice for a diet since they are considerably lower in calories than the crisp-fried ones. For soft tacos you should start with the freshest, tastiest corn tortillas available. Serve with cold beer.

MAKES 12

2 cups Shredded Chicken Filling (page 103)
12 6-inch corn tortillas
Vegetable oil (if making crisp tacos)
Salt
1¼ cups finely diced tomato
1¼ cups shredded romaine lettuce heart or iceberg lettuce
¾ cup to 1½ cups creamy Guacamole (half the recipe on page 328), or ¾ cup sour cream (both are optional)
¾ cup (3 ounces) shredded medium-mild Cheddar cheese, such as longhorn
Tomato-Jalapeño Salsa (page 382)
¼ cup finely chopped fresh cilantro (optional)

1. To make crisp tacos: Spoon about 2½ tablespoons of the chicken filling (it doesn't need to be hot for fried tacos) in a line across the center of one corn tortilla; repeat to have a second taco ready.

2. Pour enough of the vegetable oil into a heavy medium-sized skillet so it is ⅛ inch deep and place over moderately high heat until very hot. Pick up one tortilla, folding it loosely into a taco shape, lower just the fold into the oil, and hold for about 10 seconds to set, then place it on one side. Repeat with the second filled tortilla. Fry until crisp and golden brown, 2 to 3 minutes; turn with tongs and fry until the other side is crisp and golden, about 2 minutes longer. Drain on paper towels. Repeat with the remaining tortillas and filling, adding a little more oil when needed and always heating the oil before adding the tacos. Lightly sprinkle the tacos with salt as they drain.

3. In separate small bowls put the tomato, lettuce, optional guacamole or sour cream, cheese, salsa, and optional cilantro. Open each taco slightly and fill with about 1½ tablespoons tomato, 1½ tablespoons lettuce, 1 to 2 tablespoons guacamole or 1 tablespoon sour cream, 1 tablespoon cheese, about 1 tablespoon salsa (or to taste), and 1 teaspoon of the optional cilantro. Sprinkle with a bit more salt and serve.

4. To make soft tacos: Since soft tacos are best eaten promptly after assembling, heat only the number of tortillas you will be serving at once and then reheat for seconds. Place a large heavy dry skillet or griddle over moderate heat for about 5 minutes. Reheat the chicken filling in a small pan, adding a little water or broth if it seems dry. Unless your tortillas are extremely fresh, you will have to add moisture to them as they heat: Dip your fingers into water, flick drops of water across both sides of one tortilla, and place in the skillet. Turn several times, every 5 or 10 seconds, until the moisture has been absorbed and the tortilla is soft and pliable. Spoon about 2½ tablespoons of the chicken filling across the hot tortilla and fill with the remaining ingredients as in Step 3. Repeat with the remaining tortillas and ingredients.

Chicken Taquitos with Creamy Guacamole Dip

These can be called tacos (though tacos are usually somewhat fatter) or flautas (which are usually even skinnier and tighter so that they resemble the flute for which they are named). But in California, where I grew up, they were always called *taquitos* (little tacos). They are crisp and crunchy and can be picked up with the fingers and dipped into guacamole. They can be cut in half and served as an hors d'oeuvre. The creamy guacamole dip can be as mild or as hot as you like, depending on how many of the seeds from the

MAKES 18

Creamy Guacamole:

- **4** fresh jalapeño chile peppers
- **¼** cup finely chopped white onion
- **¼** cup chopped fresh cilantro leaves
- **1** teaspoon salt

Pinch of black pepper

- **1** tablespoon fresh lemon juice
- **2** large, firm, perfectly ripe California avocados, 8 to 10 ounces each
- **½** cup sour cream

Taquitos:

Vegetable oil

- **18** 5- to 6-inch-diameter corn tortillas
- **2** cups Shredded Chicken Filling (page 103), at room temperature

1. Prepare the creamy guacamole: If you have a Mexican *molcajete* and *tejolote*, by all means use them; otherwise a mortar and pestle or a food processor will do just fine. Slice off the stem ends from the chiles, then quarter the chiles lengthwise. Understand that the heat comes from the seeds and veins and that the rest of the chile gives great flavor without adding heat. With a knife, slice off the seeds and veins from each piece of pepper. Save about ½ teaspoon to add for hotness and discard the rest, unless you like fire-hot food; then save more, to taste. Cut the chiles lengthwise into thin strips, then crosswise to mince. Add to the *molcajete* or mortar along with the reserved seeds, onion, cilantro, salt, and pepper. (If using a processor, also add the lemon juice and the flesh from ½ avocado.) With the *tejolote* or pestle, pound the mixture until watery. If using a processor, purée until almost smooth and then scrape into a bowl. Halve the avocados lengthwise and take out the pits. Spoon the flesh into the mixture and coarsely mash with a fork. Stir in the sour cream. If desired, add more salt to taste.

2. Prepare the taquitos: Pour enough vegetable oil into a large heavy skillet so it is ⅛ to ¼ inch deep, and place over moderately high heat until the oil is just below the smoking point. Adjust the heat as necessary as you cook.

3. Meanwhile, place a medium skillet or griddle over moderate heat so you can warm and soften the tortillas as needed. Warm 1 tortilla, turning it several times, until it is soft and pliable, about 10 seconds (if dry, splash on a few drops of water to moisten). Spoon a scant 2 tablespoons of the chicken filling in a line across the lower third of the warm tortilla. Fold about 1 inch of the tortilla up over the filling and roll up tightly like a cigar (illustration A). Do not let go or it will unroll or loosen (illustration B). Carefully place in the hot oil, seam side down, pressing down with one finger; immediately use tongs to press the top and hold it in place (illustration C) until the seam has fried closed, about 30 seconds. Release it and fry until golden brown, 2 to 3 minutes longer. Turn and fry the other side until crisp and golden brown, 2 to 3 minutes longer. Meanwhile, continue assembling *taquitos* in the same manner, adding them to the pan as they are shaped. With practice you will find that you can fry about 6 at a time and they will all be at different cooking stages. As they are done, remove them with tongs and drain them on end in a colander lined with paper towels. Sprinkle them lightly with salt. Serve hot, with the guacamole for dipping, or spoon it over them on a plate.

jalapeños you add. If you want an authentic Mexican guacamole, simply leave out the sour cream.

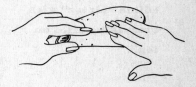

A.

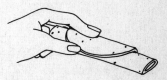

B.

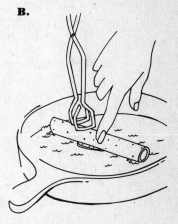

C.

Chicken Tostadas

Tostadas—those crisp, flat corn tortillas topped with beans, meat, and salad—are edible "plates" with everything piled on top.

MAKES 12

Vegetable oil
12 5- to 6-inch-diameter corn tortillas
3 cups mashed Pinto Beans with Bacon (page 375), or canned refried beans, heated
2 cups Shredded Chicken Filling (page 103), heated
3 cups shredded romaine lettuce heart or iceberg lettuce
1½ cups finely diced tomato
1½ cups Creamy Guacamole (page 328), or ¾ cup sour cream
Tomato-Jalapeño Salsa (page 382)
¼ cup chopped fresh cilantro leaves (optional)
2 tablespoons grated queso añejo or Romano cheese
Salt

1. Pour enough vegetable oil into a heavy medium skillet so it is ¼ inch deep. Place over moderately high heat. When oil is very hot, just below the smoking point, add 1 corn tortilla; with tongs, turn it several times and cook until crisp and medium golden brown. Drain on paper towels and sprinkle lightly with salt. Repeat to fry all the tortillas.

2. Spread 1 crisp tortilla with about ¼ cup of the mashed beans and strew about 2½ tablespoons of the chicken over the beans. Sprinkle with ¼ cup of lettuce and 2 tablespoons of tomato. Spoon on 2 tablespoons guacamole or 1 tablespoon sour cream and about 1 tablespoon of the salsa. Top with 1 teaspoon of the optional cilantro, ½ teaspoon of the grated cheese, and salt to taste. Repeat with remaining tortillas.

Smoked Chicken with Pasta, Sliced Tomatoes, and Mozzarella

MAKES 8 SERVINGS

Vinaigrette:

1 tablespoon Dijon mustard
1 teaspoon powdered mustard
1 tablespoon chopped fresh tarragon, or ½ teaspoon dried
1 tablespoon chopped fresh thyme, or ½ teaspoon dried
2 tablespoons chopped fresh basil, or 1 teaspoon dried
½ teaspoon celery salt
½ teaspoon freshly cracked black pepper
½ teaspoon salt
¼ cup red wine vinegar, or any flavored vinegar
⅔ cup olive oil

Layers:

½ pound thin spaghetti or linguine, broked in half
1 pound sliced smoked chicken
1 pound sliced fresh lightly salted mozzarella
4 medium tomatoes (1 pound), sliced
Fresh small basil and parsley sprigs for garnish
Coarsely cracked black pepper

This is a great cold marinated dish for a hot summer day. You can make it ahead and keep it in the refrigerator. It is best made with fresh herbs and fresh mozzarella cheese. Dried pasta, however, is best here because it holds up better during the marination. If you want to serve this *with* a pasta dish, simply omit the pasta here and it will be perfectly delicious on a bed of romaine lettuce hearts or Belgian endive. The smoked chicken can be sliced from a whole bird, or breasts, as you wish.

1. Make the vinaigrette: In a medium bowl combine the Dijon mustard, powdered mustard, tarragon, thyme, basil, celery salt, black pepper, and salt; mash with a fork and gradually add the vinegar, mashing with the fork. Gradually whisk in the olive oil to make a dressing.

2. Assemble the layers: Boil the pasta in a large pot of lightly salted boiling water until tender but firm to the bite.

Rinse under cold water and drain. Put the pasta in a large deep platter at least 9 by 12 inches and arrange the sliced smoked chicken over it. Drizzle with about a third of the dressing. Cut the rounds of sliced mozzarella in half and arrange over the chicken; drizzle with another third of the dressing. Cut the tomato slices in half and arrange over the cheese; drizzle with the remaining dressing. Cover with plastic and chill for 6 to 12 hours. Garnish with basil and parsley sprigs and top with freshly cracked black pepper. Serve cold.

Smoked Chicken and Sugar Snap Pea Salad

Sweet, crunchy, tender sugar snap peas may be the greatest vegetable hybrid to come along during my lifetime so far. Their season is short, so enjoy them while you can. They are best raw or quickly blanched in boiling water for 2 minutes. Do not overcook or

MAKES 8 TO 12 SERVINGS

Salad:

2 pounds fresh sugar snap peas, stems and strings pulled off

4 medium carrots, peeled and cut into ¼-by-2-inch matchsticks

4 large red bell peppers (1½ pounds)

4 small heads Belgian endive (½ pound)

1 pound smoked chicken, thinly sliced

Dressing:

1 tablespoon Dijon mustard

1½ teaspoons salt

1 teaspoon dried basil, crumbled

½ teaspoon dried oregano, crumbled
¼ teaspoon black pepper
½ cup olive oil

they will be ruined.
This salad is very
special.

1. Bring a large pot of lightly salted water to a boil over high heat. Drop in the sugar snap peas. Cover and cook for 2 minutes from the time they hit the water. Scoop out with a slotted spoon and rinse under cold water. Drop in the carrot sticks and boil for 1 minute after the boil returns. Drain and rinse under cold water.

2. Roast the red peppers by placing them directly on the burners of a gas stove or as close to the heat source as possible under an electric broiler. Turn the burners to high and roast, turning frequently with tongs, until peppers are blistered and black all over. Let them cool for a minute and then put them in a plastic bag, twisting the top to enclose. Chill for at least 10 minutes. Cut out the stems and cores, remove all seeds, and scrape away the charred skin. Cut the peppers into 1-inch squares.

3. Cut the Belgian endives in half lengthwise and cut out the small cores. Sliver the heads lengthwise into ¼-inch-wide shreds.

4. In a large bowl toss together the sugar snap peas, carrots, red peppers, endive, and smoked chicken.

5. Prepare the dressing: In a medium bowl stir together the Dijon mustard, salt, basil, oregano, and pepper; gradually whisk in the olive oil. (This may be done a day ahead.) Pour over the salad; toss and mound on an oval platter. Serve cold or at room temperature.

Smoked Chicken and Sour Cream with Buckwheat Blini

The little Russian pancakes (favored in Finland, too) known as blini are often served with caviar or with smoked salmon and sour cream. I discovered that they are exquisite with smoked chicken breast. There are two recipes for the buckwheat blini in this book: one made in the traditional manner with yeast, and a quick version for today's faster lifestyles.

MAKES 32 BLINI (4 TO 6 SERVINGS)

32 Traditional Buckwheat Blini or Quick Buckwheat Blini (pages 368, 369)
1½ cups sour cream, at room temperature
¾ pound smoked chicken breast, sliced 1½ by 2 by ⅛ inch thick

You can make the blini entirely ahead of time and reheat them in a microwave for about 20 seconds before adding the toppings, or assemble them and serve them as the Russians do, hot off the griddle. Place several blini on a plate; spoon 2 teaspoons of the sour cream onto each; top with one or two thin slices of smoked chicken and serve right away.

Odds and Ends 10

No part of a chicken should be wasted. Backs, necks and wing tips make perfect stocks, soups, and sauces; the skin can be transformed into crispy little golden gribenes and the fat rendered into schmalz. The hearts come back to life when skewered into teriyaki shish kebobs for a backyard barbecue or pan-fried with potatoes and herbs to create an elegant but homey brunch dish. The feet can be added to stocks or red-cooked the Chinese way and made into delicious dim sum. Gizzards can be deep-fried, pan-fried, double-cooked, and broiled or made into giblet gravy. I was going to include a recipe for hen's teeth but I couldn't find any.

Since chicken livers are by far the most popular giblet, there are plenty of recipes for them in this chapter. They are versatile indeed and can be chopped Jewish-style for an addictively delicious, rich spread for toasted rye bread, or wrapped with smoky bacon and crunchy water chestnuts for those Polynesian appetizers called rumaki. They can even be simmered in Italian tomato sauce to make spaghetti Caruso.

And last but not least, eggs are included in this chapter, too. Not many, just a few choice ways with perhaps nature's greatest culinary contribution of all.

New York Chopped Chicken Livers

This superb version of Jewish-style chopped liver is best when made with homemade rendered chicken fat (recipe follows). You might want to serve toasted triangles of caraway seed rye bread alongside for dipping, scooping, or spreading. The chopped liver also makes delicious sandwiches on rye bread with Russian or Thousand Island dressing. It is traditionally served for Rosh Hashanah but I've found that it disappears quickly no matter what the occasion.

MAKES ABOUT 5 CUPS

- **6** to 8 tablespoons rendered chicken fat (recipe follows)
- **1½** pounds chicken livers, halved
- **4** medium-large onions, chopped (5 cups)
- **½** cup dry sherry, or chicken stock or broth
- **5** large hard-cooked eggs (see page 352)
- **1** tablespoon coarse kosher salt, or 1½ teaspoons fine salt, or to taste
- **½** teaspoon coarse black pepper

1. Spoon 1 tablespoon of the chicken fat into a large heavy nonstick skillet or a well-seasoned cast-iron one and place over moderate heat. Add a third of the halved livers and brown well, turning 2 or 3 times until cooked through and no longer pink in the center (it may be necessary to regulate the heat between moderate and moderately high as you cook, to ensure browning). Take the livers out with a slotted spoon and transfer to a large plate. Repeat twice, adding 1 tablespoon chicken fat with each ½ pound of livers.

2. Spoon 2 tablespoons of the remaining chicken fat into the pan and add all of the onions; sauté, stirring occasionally over moderate heat, until soft, translucent, and lightly browned, 15 to 20 minutes. Scoop out half the onions and put them with the livers to cool. Increase the heat under the remaining onions to moderately high and sauté, stirring almost constantly, until deep caramel brown, 5 to 8 minutes longer; if they become dry, add 1 tablespoon of the remaining chicken fat. If they become dry again, add 2 to 3 tablespoons of water and let it boil away. The onions should be a deep color, but do not let them burn. Scrape them onto a small plate and reserve until needed. Pour the sherry or broth into the pan and boil it until reduced by half; pour over the livers and let cool.

3. Choose one of three ways to chop the livers and lightly browned onions: 1) Half at a time, coarsely chop them in a food processor using the pulse button; do not grind the livers too finely; 2) Use a sharp knife to finely chop on a cutting board; or 3), put them through the coarse blade of a meat grinder.

4. Put the chopped livers and onions in a large bowl; add the reserved well-browned onions. Peel the eggs. Using the coarse side of a cheese grater, grate 4 of the eggs over the livers (reserve the fifth for garnish). Stir in the salt, pepper, and remaining chicken fat to taste. Chill, covered. Mound on a serving plate and grate the remaining egg over the top for garnish. Serve cold.

Rendered Chicken Fat (Schmalz)

MAKES ABOUT ½ CUP

½ cup coarsely chopped chicken fat
½ cup coarsely chopped chicken skin
1 large onion, peeled and chopped
1 large garlic clove, peeled and sliced (optional)

1. In a heavy medium skillet combine the chicken fat, chicken skin, and ¼ cup water; bring to a boil over moderate heat. Lower the heat slightly and let simmer until the water evaporates and the fat begins to sizzle, 5 to 10 minutes.

2. Add the onion and garlic and cook slowly over low heat 45 minutes to an hour, until the fat, skin, and onions are deep golden brown. Watch very carefully during the last 15 minutes to avoid burning them. Strain into a small bowl and cool to room temperature. Cover and refrigerate or freeze until needed.

For a great flavor, chicken fat is browned with onions for a long time, until the fat has rendered. The onion and optional garlic contribute depth of flavor. You can pull pieces of fat from chickens when you have them and freeze until ½ cup accumulates.

Chinese Glazed Chicken Livers

This simple dish has a light sweet and sour flavor. It can be put together rapidly and is good served with noodles or rice and steamed broccoli or pan-fried watercress.

MAKES 2 TO 4 SERVINGS

- 2 tablespoons vegetable oil
- 1 pound chicken livers, halved
- 1 tablespoon minced fresh ginger
- 1 large garlic clove, peeled and minced or crushed through a press
- 8 to 10 medium scallions, cut on an angle into 1½-inch lengths
- ¼ cup chicken broth or canned stock
- 2 tablespoons dry sherry or Chinese rice wine
- 2 tablespoons thin or light soy sauce
- 1 tablespoon rice vinegar
- 1 tablespoon sugar
- 2 teaspoons cornstarch
- 2 teaspoons oriental sesame oil

1. Spoon the vegetable oil into a large heavy skillet and place over moderately high heat. Add the chicken livers and brown well (using a spatter screen if you have one), 3 to 4 minutes. Turn, lower the heat slightly, and cook to taste, 2 to 3 minutes longer if you like them slightly pink in the center. Take them out with a slotted spoon and reserve.

2. Add the ginger and garlic to the skillet and stir-fry 15 seconds. Add the scallions and stir-fry 10 seconds longer. Remove from the heat.

3. In a small bowl stir together the chicken stock, sherry, soy sauce, vinegar, sugar, and cornstarch until blended. Stir in the sesame oil. Return the pan to the heat. Pour in the sauce and stir constantly until thickened. Return the livers and toss to heat and glaze for 10 to 15 seconds. Serve hot.

Sherried Chicken Livers with Mushrooms

MAKES 4 SERVINGS

2 tablespoons olive oil
1 pound chicken livers, halved
2 medium onions, peeled, thinly sliced, and separated into rings
1/4 teaspoon dried thyme, crumbled
1 garlic clove, peeled and minced or crushed through a press
2 tablespoons butter
1/2 pound fresh mushrooms, thinly sliced
2 teaspoons all-purpose flour
1/2 cup dry sherry
About **1/2** teaspoon salt
1/8 teaspoon black pepper

These savory sherry-soaked livers and mushrooms are good with toast points or as an hors d'oeuvre on toothpicks.

1. Spoon 1½ tablespoons of the olive oil into a large heavy nonaluminum skillet and place over moderately high heat. Add the livers and brown well without stirring, about 3 minutes. Turn and brown the other side 1 minute longer. Take out with a slotted spoon and transfer to a plate.
2. Add the remaining ½ tablespoon olive oil to the skillet along with the onions and thyme; sauté to soften over moderate heat, about 3 to 5 minutes. Add the garlic and cook a minute longer; remove and hold with the livers.
3. Melt the butter in the skillet over low heat. Add the mushrooms and brown over moderately high heat for about 2 minutes. Sprinkle with the flour and stir to moisten it. Return the livers and onions and pour in the sherry. Bring to a boil, stirring, then simmer 2 to 3 minutes, until the livers are cooked to taste. Add ½ teaspoon salt, or more to taste, and the pepper.

Russian Chicken Livers with Sour Cream

A delicious sour cream and onion sauce for chicken livers keeps the livers tender and moist. For *zakuski* (hors d'oeuvres for a Russian cocktail party), serve with Smoked Chicken and Sour Cream with Buckwheat Blini (page 334), Chicken-Potato Pirogi (page 320), Devilish Eggs (page 352) topped with Russian caviar if you like, and plenty of iced vodka.

MAKES 6 APPETIZER SERVINGS

1 pound chicken livers, halved
3 tablespoons butter
2 medium onions, peeled, thinly sliced, and separated into rings
1/4 cup vodka
1 cup sour cream, at room temperature
1 teaspoon cider vinegar
1 teaspoon salt
1/4 teaspoon black pepper

1. Trim any stringy parts from the livers if you wish. Melt 1 tablespoon of the butter in a large heavy nonaluminum skillet over moderate heat. Add the livers and brown well, increasing the heat to moderately high, 4 to 5 minutes on the first side. Turn, reduce the heat to low, and cook to taste, 2 to 3 minutes longer (chicken livers are best just slightly pink in the center). Transfer with a slotted spoon to a plate and reserve.

2. Add the remaining 2 tablespoons butter to the pan and melt over moderate heat. Add the onions and sauté to soften and lightly brown, 5 to 6 minutes. Return the livers and increase the heat to moderately high. Standing back, carefully pour in the vodka and tilt the pan so the vodka flambés (or if using an electric stove, ignite with a match). When the flames die down, stir in the sour cream, vinegar, salt, and pepper. Serve hot or at room temperature, with forks or toothpicks.

Polynesian Rumaki

MAKES 24

12 whole chicken livers (1 pound), halved
¼ cup grated fresh ginger
3 tablespoons dry sherry
2 tablespoons soy sauce
2 tablespoons vegetable oil
1 tablespoon sugar
1 teaspoon curry powder
1 large garlic clove, peeled and minced or crushed through a press
12 slices bacon (½ pound), halved crosswise
12 pineapple chunks, halved
12 water chestnuts, halved horizontally

1. Trim away any stringy parts of each liver half, if you wish.
2. In a medium bowl stir together the ginger, sherry, soy sauce, vegetable oil, sugar, curry powder, and garlic; add the chicken livers and marinate 1 hour in the refrigerator.
3. Put the bacon slices in a large skillet and partially cook over moderate heat to melt off some of the fat, 3 to 4 minutes. Drain.
4. Assemble the rumaki onto toothpicks: Secure one end of a bacon strip on a toothpick. Add a slice of water chestnut, then a piece of pineapple. Jab a liver onto the pick and bring the other end of the bacon over it to wrap. If making ahead, cover and chill.
5. Preheat the broiler. Place the rumaki, best bacon side down, on broiler pan and broil until lightly browned, about 3 minutes. Turn and broil until the bacon is crisp and golden brown and the livers are cooked to taste, about 3 minutes longer. Serve hot.

This a popular choice for a hot hors d'oeuvre to serve at cocktail parties. Assemble the rumaki ahead but broil them during the party. The flavors of ginger, garlic, sherry, soy, smoky bacon, pineapple, and chicken livers come alive with the crunch of the water chestnuts.

Linguine Caruso

Opera stars love pasta, but then, who doesn't? This one, invented here in America and named for the great Italian tenor who was so popular around the turn of the century, is usually made with spaghetti but I prefer the thin flat ribbons of linguine. The chicken livers are complemented by the smoky bacon and there is a hint of heat from the hot red pepper flakes. A colorful sprinkling of green and white over red sauce make this a handsome and mouth-watering dish.

**MAKES 4 MAIN-COURSE OR
8 PASTA-COURSE SERVINGS**

- ½ pound lean smoked sliced bacon, cut into ½-inch pieces
- 3 medium onions, peeled, thinly sliced, and separated into rings
- 2 large garlic cloves, peeled and minced or crushed through a press
- 2 teaspoons dried oregano, crumbled
- 1 teaspoon dried basil, crumbled
- 1 bay leaf
- ¼ teaspoon hot red pepper flakes
- 2 teaspoons sugar
- 2 teaspoons salt
- ¼ teaspoon black pepper
- 1 35-ounce carton or can strained puréed Italian tomatoes
- 1¼ cups dry white wine
- 1 pound chicken livers, each cut into 6 pieces
- 1 pound linguine
- 1 tablespoon olive oil
- ½ cup chopped fresh parsley leaves
- ½ cup grated Parmesan cheese

1. Put the bacon in a large heavy skillet and cook over moderate heat until crisp and golden brown, 7 to 8 minutes. Spoon off all but 1 tablespoon of the fat, reserving 2 tablespoons for the livers. Add the onions and sauté to soften and lightly brown, adding 1 or 2 tablespoons water if they seem dry, about 5 minutes over moderate heat. Add the garlic, oregano, basil, bay leaf, and hot red pepper flakes; sauté for 1 minute. Transfer to a large heavy nonaluminum saucepan. Stir in the sugar, salt and black pepper.

2. Add to the saucepan the strained tomatoes, 1 cup of the wine, and 1 cup of water. Bring to a boil, then simmer over low heat for about 45 minutes. The sauce shouldn't be too thick.

3. Spoon the reserved 2 tablespoons bacon fat into a large heavy skillet and place over moderately high heat. Add the pieces of liver and brown well, shaking the pan occasionally, until they are cooked but slightly pink in the center (or well done if that is your preference), 2 to 3 minutes. Take out and add to the sauce. Deglaze the skillet by adding the remaining ¼ cup white wine and letting it boil for a minute over high heat; scrape into the sauce.

4. Bring a large pot of lightly salted water to a boil and add the linguine; stirring constantly, return the water to a boil. Boil, stirring occasionally, until the pasta is tender but firm to the bite. Drain in a colander and toss in a large bowl or platter with the olive oil and ¼ cup of the parsley. Ladle the sauce over the top and sprinkle with the remaining parsley and Parmesan cheese. Serve hot.

Soup of Chicken Liver Mousse

I first tasted a soup like this in China, but there it was made from squab. It's simple to make; the chicken livers are puréed in a food processor with eggs and seasonings and then steamed in a cake pan. The delicate custardlike mousse is soothing and delicious. You can make this well ahead of time and reheat it gently.

MAKES 6 SERVINGS

- ½ pound chicken livers
- 2 large whole eggs
- 3 egg whites
- 7 cups Basic Chicken Stock (page 47) or canned broth
- ¼ cup dry sherry
- 2 teaspoons oriental sesame oil
- 1 teaspoon salt
- 10 slices fresh ginger
- 2 medium scallions, thinly sliced

1. In a food processor or blender combine the chicken livers and the whole eggs; purée until smooth. Add the egg whites and blend briefly. Place a sieve over a bowl and strain the mixture. Stir in 1 cup of the chicken stock, the sherry, sesame oil, and salt.

2. Rig up a large steamer that will hold an 8-inch cake pan and pour in 1 inch of water. Cover and bring to a boil.

3. Coat an 8-inch cake pan with vegetable oil. Pour in the mousse mixture. Place in the steamer, cover, and steam over moderate heat until set, about 10 minutes. (Using tongs, jiggle the pan to see if the mousse has set; it will be soft but set in the center.) Remove it from the steamer and let cool slightly while you heat the broth.

4. Combine the remaining 6 cups of broth and the sliced ginger in a saucepan and bring to a boil. Remove from the heat and stir in the scallions.

5. Run a knife around the edge of the mousse and invert into a soup tureen. It doesn't matter if it breaks. Holding a ladle or large spoon over the mousse, pour in the hot broth (this so it does not pour directly onto the soft and delicate mousse). Serve hot. The soup can be reheated gently. To serve, ladle broth into soup bowls and spoon in a piece of the mousse.

Pâté Chinois

MAKES 2 1/2 CUPS

- **2** tablespoons vegetable oil
- **1** pound chicken livers, halved
- **1** medium onion, peeled and coarsely grated
- **1** medium garlic clove, peeled and minced or crushed through a press
- **1/3** cup dry sherry or Chinese rice wine
- **1/3** cup heavy cream
- **2** tablespoons light soy sauce
- **1** tablespoon fresh ginger juice (see Note)
- **1** tablespoon oriental sesame oil
- **8** tablespoons (1 stick) unsalted butter, softened

Here is a nice and easy chicken liver pâté that can be thrown together in practically no time at all. The flavorings are Chinese but the technique is French. Serve cool with crackers or crisp flatbread.

1. Place a large heavy skillet over moderately high heat; spoon in the vegetable oil and add the chicken livers; brown well, 1 to 2 minutes. Turn, lower the heat, and cook until slightly pink in the center, 1 to 2 minutes longer. Add the onion and garlic; sauté to soften, 1 to 2 minutes. Pour in the sherry, cream, and soy sauce; boil over moderate heat until the cream thickens, 3 to 4 minutes. Remove from the heat and stir in the ginger juice and sesame oil. Cool to room temperature.
2. Scrape into a food processor and purée until smooth. Add the butter and pulse until blended. Turn into a crock or a bowl.

Cover tightly with plastic wrap and chill for at least 3 hours. Serve cold, or allow to stand at room temperature for about 30 minutes to soften slightly.

NOTE: Coarsely grate ⅓ cup fresh ginger onto a square of damp cheesecloth; wring out very tightly over a bowl to squeeze out the juice. Discard the solids. You can also squeeze out the juice in small batches using a garlic press.

Quick and Easy Chicken Liver Pâté

Chicken livers are quickly cooked with bacon, onion, and garlic and flambéed with cognac to make a quick and easy pâté that is puréed in a food processor.

MAKES 3 CUPS

5 slices bacon, finely chopped
1 medium onion, peeled and coarsely grated
1 medium garlic clove, peeled and minced or crushed through a press
1 pound chicken livers, halved
¼ cup cognac or brandy
⅓ cup heavy cream
1 teaspoon salt
¼ teaspoon pepper
¼ teaspoon grated nutmeg
¼ teaspoon dried thyme, crumbled
2 hard-cooked eggs (see page 352)
8 tablespoons (1 stick) unsalted butter, softened

1. Warm a large heavy skillet over moderate heat. Add the bacon and cook, stirring frequently, until golden brown. Spoon off all but 1 tablespoon of the fat, reserving 2 tablespoons. Add the onion and garlic; sauté to soften and lightly color, about 3 minutes. Scrape into a bowl and reserve.

2. Return the 2 tablespoons reserved bacon fat to the skillet and place over moderately high heat. Add the chicken livers and brown well, 1 to 2 minutes. Lower the heat, turn the livers, and cook until just slightly pink in the centers, about 3 minutes.

3. Carefully pour in cognac with face averted and tilt pan to ignite (or use a match if cooking over an electric burner). Flambé, shaking the pan occasionally until the flames subside. Pour in the heavy cream. Add the salt, pepper, nutmeg, and thyme. Bring to a boil and cook for a minute or two until thickened. Cool to room temperature.

4. Turn into a food processor, add the eggs, and blend to a smooth purée. Add the butter and pulse until blended. Turn into a crock or bowl. Cover tightly and chill for at least 3 hours. Serve cold, or allow to stand at room temperature for about 30 minutes to soften slightly. Serve with crackers or crisp flatbread.

Pan-fried Potatoes and Chicken Hearts

In a way this dish reminds me of home-fried potatoes. It makes a hearty addition to a winter brunch.

MAKES 4 TO 6 SERVINGS

1½ tablespoons butter
4 medium red-skinned potatoes (1 pound), peeled and cut into 1-inch chunks
1 medium onion, peeled and chopped
1 pound chicken hearts
1 teaspoon salt
⅛ teaspoon black pepper

1. Melt the butter in a large heavy skillet over low heat. Add the potatoes and onion; sauté, adjusting the heat between low and moderate as needed, until golden brown, tossing or stirring occasionally, about 15 minutes, uncovered. Cover and cook over low heat until the potatoes are tender, about 5 minutes longer.
2. Push the potatoes to one side of the pan and add the chicken hearts; sauté over moderately high heat, adding the salt and pepper and tossing with the potatoes, 5 to 8 minutes longer, until crusty and golden. Serve hot.

Sautéed Chicken Hearts

MAKES 4 TO 8 SERVINGS

- **1** tablespoon olive oil
- **1** pound chicken hearts
- **1** small garlic clove, peeled and minced or crushed through a press
- **1** teaspoon dried basil, crumbled
- **¼** teaspoon dried oregano, crumbled
- **¼** teaspoon dried rosemary, crumbled
- **½** teaspoon salt
- **⅛** teaspoon black pepper

Spoon the olive oil into a large heavy skillet and place over moderately high heat. Add the chicken hearts, garlic, basil, oregano, rosemary, salt, and pepper; sauté, tossing the hearts in the pan, until cooked through, 5 to 7 minutes. Serve hot.

Good and juicy, these tender hearts with their herbal infusion make a good hors d'oeuvre, or you can serve them with buttered noodles.

Crunchy Fried Gizzards

These tasty morsels must marinate in fragrant yogurt for at least 12 hours before coating and frying, so plan your time accordingly. You can also add chicken hearts and livers if you desire (but marinate them only 30 minutes).

MAKES 4 SERVINGS

- **1** pound chicken gizzards
- **1** cup plain yogurt
- **2** tablespoons cider vinegar
- **1** large garlic clove, peeled and minced or crushed through a press

Vegetable oil

- **1** cup all-purpose flour
- **1½** teaspoons salt
- **½** teaspoon black pepper
- **1** teaspoon curry powder
- **½** teaspoon cayenne pepper

1. Rinse the chicken gizzards and let them drain on several layers of paper towels.

2. In a medium glass bowl stir together the yogurt, vinegar, and garlic. Add the gizzards; toss to coat, cover, and let marinate in the refrigerator for 12 to 36 hours.

3. The gizzards can be deep-fried or shallow-fried: they will cook quicker and become slightly crunchier when deep-fried, but the results will be just as special when they are shallow-fried, and you will need less oil. To deep-fry, pour 1½ inches of vegetable oil into a small deep fryer or heavy saucepan and place over moderately high heat until the temperature reaches 370°. At the first wisp of smoke, lower the heat so the temperature remains at 370°.

To shallow-fry, pour about ¼ inch of vegetable oil into a medium cast-iron or other heavy skillet and place over moderately high heat until just beginning to smoke. Lower the heat slightly to prevent the oil from smoking. Fry the gizzards in batches (coating them just before placing them in the hot oil) for about 4 minutes; turn with tongs and fry about 4 minutes longer, until crisp and golden brown. Drain on paper towels.

4. In a paper bag combine the flour, salt, pepper, curry powder and cayenne pepper; shake to blend. Take about one-fourth of the gizzards (or enough to fill the pan without crowding) from the marinade, letting the excess marinade run from them (but don't wipe the marinade from them) and put them in the bag of seasoned coating. Shake to evenly coat and place them in the hot oil. Fry, stirring several times with a slotted spoon, until crisp and deep golden brown, 4 to 5 minutes. Drain on paper towels and repeat until all the gizzards are cooked. Serve hot.

Chinese Chicken Feet

MAKES 4 TO 6 SERVINGS

- **2** pounds chicken feet (24 to 30 medium)
- **1/2** cup white vinegar
- **1** cup soy sauce
- **1** cup dry sherry or Chinese rice wine
- **1** 3-inch cinnamon stick
- **2** teaspoons Chinese five-spice powder, or 1 whole star anise and 1 teaspoon whole fennel seeds
- **1/2** cup sugar
- **5** slices fresh ginger, each the size of a half dollar
- **5** scallions, sliced
- **3** 1-by-2-inch strips orange peel or tangerine peel

The Chinese are perhaps the most practical of all the cooks in the world. This succulent Cantonese treatment for one of their favorite parts results in tender-spicy meat with a gelatinous quality. This is a red-cooking technique

and you can use the
braising broth over
and over again.

1. Put the chicken feet in a large bowl of cold water and add the vinegar. Wash well and rinse. If large yellow scales are present you'll have to sear the feet over a flame, holding them by tongs as you turn to soften them; then, use a paring knife to scrape upward to remove them. Most chicken feet bought in butcher shops in Chinatown nowadays don't require this step. With a cleaver or poultry shears, cut off the toenails at the first joint.

2. Put the feet in a large heavy pot and add 5 cups of cold water, along with the soy sauce, sherry, cinnamon, five-spice powder, sugar, ginger, scallions, and orange peel. Bring to a boil over moderate heat. Lower the heat and simmer until very tender, about 1½ hours. Take out and serve hot or warm. Strain the red-cooking liquid and reserve for cooking other chicken parts (see page 232).

Devilish Eggs

This is a damn good deviled egg recipe. A great variation is to add 3 tablespoons minced sweet pickle. If you want the stuffing hotter, add a pinch of cayenne pepper rather than more Tabasco sauce, which would thin it too much. Without the

MAKES 16

10 large eggs
¼ cup Mayonnaise (page 383)
2 tablespoons golden, brown, or yellow mustard
1 teaspoon Tabasco or other red hot pepper sauce
½ teaspoon salt
¼ teaspoon black pepper
½ teaspoon paprika

1. Put the eggs in a large saucepan with enough cold water to cover by 1 inch. Place over moderately high heat and bring to a boil. Immediately reduce the heat to low. Using a big spoon, carefully stir the eggs in a wide circle, spinning them faster and

faster for 10 seconds so centrifugal force pushes the yolks to the centers. Stop and keep the eggs at a bare simmer for 10 to 11 minutes, not a minute longer. Scoop out with a slotted spoon and put in a large bowl of cold water. Refill the bowl with cold water after 10 minutes and let cool completely. Crack, shell, and rinse the eggs. Slice them in half lengthwise and take out the yolks and put them in a medium bowl. Put the best 16 white halves on a platter; reserve the rest for another use.

2. Mash the yolks with a fork against the side of the bowl; mash in the mayonnaise, mustard, and Tabasco to make a smooth stuffing. Add the salt and pepper. If using sweet pickle as mentioned in the headnote, stir in.

3. Using a spoon (or pastry bag fitted with a ½-inch star tip), fill the egg white halves, mounding the stuffing generously. Sprinkle with paprika. Serve, or cover loosely with plastic and chill. For a party you might want to garnish each with a tiny leaf of parsley. Serve cold.

pickle, the stuffing can be piped decoratively. The stuffing is piled high because you make 16 halves from 10 eggs.

She-Deviled Eggs

MAKES 12

8 large eggs
6 slices bacon
½ teaspoon whole caraway seeds
¼ cup Mayonnaise (page 383)
1 tablespoon plus 1 teaspoon brown or golden mustard
Pinch of salt
¼ teaspoon black pepper
¼ teaspoon paprika

My best friend, the late, great Mary Ferguson, taught me to make deviled eggs this way. Crisp smoky bacon and caraway seeds flavor the filling and you start with two extra egg yolks so there is plenty.

1. Put the eggs in a large saucepan and add enough cold water to cover by 1 inch. Place over moderately high heat and bring to a boil. Immediately reduce the heat to low. Using a big spoon, carefully stir the eggs in a wide circle, spinning them faster and faster for 10 seconds so centrifugal force pushes the yolks to the centers of the whites. Keep the eggs at a bare simmer for 10 to 11 minutes, no longer. Scoop out with a slotted spoon and put in a large bowl of cold water. Refill the bowl with cold water after 10 minutes and let cool completely.

2. Put the bacon in a heavy skillet and cook over moderate heat until crisp and golden brown. Drain on paper towels; crumble fine.

3. Put the caraway seeds in a butter melter or small saucepan with ¼ cup water. Simmer over moderate heat until the water completely evaporates; as it nears that point, tilt the pan. Remove from the heat.

4. Crack, shell, and rinse the eggs. Slice them in half lengthwise; scoop out the yolks and put them in a medium bowl. Put the best 12 white halves on a platter and reserve the others for another use. Add the bacon and caraway seeds to the yolks along with the mayonnaise, mustard, salt, and pepper; mash with a fork until blended. Using a spoon, stuff the whites, mounding filling generously. Sprinkle with the paprika. Serve right away or cover loosely with plastic wrap and chill. Serve cold.

Old-fashioned Egg Salad

MAKES 3½ CUPS (ENOUGH FOR 6 TO 8 SANDWICHES)

- **1** dozen large eggs
- **1** tablespoon butter, softened to room temperature
- **½** cup Mayonnaise (page 383)
- **1½** tablespoons brown or golden mustard
- **½** teaspoon salt
- **¼** teaspoon black pepper

1. Put the eggs in a medium-large saucepan and add enough cold water to cover by 1 inch. Place over moderately high heat and bring just to a boil. Immediately reduce the heat to low and keep at a bare simmer for 10 to 11 minutes, not a second longer. Scoop out with a slotted spoon and put in a large bowl of cold water. Change the water in the bowl after 10 minutes (to make colder), and cool completely.

2. Crack and shell the eggs; rinse them under cold water and pat them dry. If you have an egg slicer, slice them one at a time, carefully reposition them so the slices run in the opposite direction, and slice again, this time letting them fall into a large bowl. Otherwise, finely chop with a knife. Add the butter and mash it in with a fork. Stir in the mayonnaise, mustard, salt, and pepper. Cover and chill for an hour or longer. If using for sandwiches, each sandwich will hold about ½ cup. Serve cold.

I just recently found out that most people don't know how to make a good egg salad. You must stay with the eggs during the entire cooking.

11 *Embellishments*
(Side Dishes and Basic Recipes)

Details. Sometimes it's what you put on the plate next to a piece of chicken that makes it extra-special. Other times it might be the sauce that you spoon over it, the pastry you wrap around it, or the dressing that you stuff inside.

Any of the embellishments in this chapter will certainly add excitement to your menus. But don't forget to contribute some condiments that may already be on hand in your refrigerator or on your pantry shelves: crunchy sweet or sour pickles, sweet-tart cranberry sauce, mild black or salty green olives, chutney, and corn relish are particularly good with chicken.

Certain flavors and textures complement chicken—for example, tomato and mayonnaise or green onions and cilantro. Mashed potatoes and gravy with biscuits on a plate next to chicken is mom's cooking at its best. Crunchy fried chicken tastes better and crunchier with creamy potato salad, and there's nothing as special as parsleyed potatoes, homemade creamed corn, and freshly stewed tomatoes with a roasted chicken that has just emerged from the oven.

Poultry and stuffing just go together. It's the American way. So, here you will find plenty of recipes for great stuffings— from whole wheat–bacon to apricot–brown rice (and be sure to check out the oyster stuffing on page 28 and the Hungarian cracker stuffing on page 26). This is the stuff that lip-smacking menus are made from.

Whole Wheat, Bacon, and Mushroom Stuffing

MAKES ABOUT 10 CUPS

- **1** 1-pound loaf sliced whole wheat bread or 8 cups toasted whole wheat croutons
- **½** pound sliced bacon (10 slices), cut into ½-inch pieces
- **2** medium onions, peeled and chopped
- **1** cup finely diced celery
- **3** tablespoons butter
- **1** pound fresh mushrooms, finely diced
- **½** cup dry white wine
- **½** cup chopped fresh parsley leaves
- **1** teaspoon salt
- **¼** teaspoon black pepper
- **2** large eggs, slightly beaten

About ½ cup Basic Chicken Stock (page 47) or canned broth

1. Preheat the oven to 350°. Cut or tear the bread into ½- to ¾-inch pieces and place on a large baking sheet. Bake, tossing and turning every 10 minutes, until dried and toasted deep golden brown, 30 to 40 minutes. Let cool. You will have about 8 cups toasted croutons.

2. Put the bacon in a large heavy skillet and place over moderate heat. Cook until crisp and golden brown, stirring occasionally. Pour off all but 3 tablespoons of the fat. Add the onions and celery and cook about 5 minutes to soften and lightly brown. Add the butter and diced mushrooms; sauté to brown lightly, 3 to 4 minutes.

3. Put the toasted croutons in a large bowl; add the bacon-mushroom mixture and toss to combine. Gradually sprinkle on the wine, tossing the croutons, so it absorbs evenly. Add the

This stuffing with its good smoky flavor and whole wheat texture makes enough to fill several chickens, but I like to bake the extra stuffing separately because everyone always wants more.

parsley, salt, and pepper. Add the eggs, tossing to coat. Gradually add enough of the chicken stock to make a moist stuffing, neither wet nor dry. Use fresh to stuff any roasted bird.

NOTE: Put any extra stuffing in a small generously buttered casserole. Top with 2 tablespoons butter, cut in bits; cover and bake at 325° 40 to 45 minutes, adding ½ to ¾ cup chicken broth and/or pan drippings as the stuffing becomes dry.

Apricot–Brown Rice Stuffing

Fruits steeped in white wine contribute a good flavor to the rice in this fresh-tasting stuffing. The chicken juices add even more. The dried fruit must soak for at least 8 hours, or overnight.

MAKES ABOUT 6 CUPS

- **4** ounces (½ cup packed) dried apricots
- **4** ounces (½ cup packed) pitted prunes
- **¼** cup dark seedless raisins
- **1** cup dry white wine
- **½** cup long-grain white rice
- **½** cup brown rice
- **1** tablespoon butter
- **1** large tart green apple, peeled and cut into ½-inch dice
- **1** medium orange, peeled and cut into ½-inch pieces
- **¼** cup chopped fresh parsley leaves
- **½** teaspoon salt
- **¼** teaspoon black pepper
- **⅛** teaspoon ground cloves

1. In a deep medium bowl combine the apricots, prunes, and raisins. Bring the wine to a boil in a small nonaluminum pan and pour over the fruit. Cover and let soak at least 8 hours or as long as 24. Do not drain.

2. Pour 2 quarts of water into each of two separate saucepans and place over high heat. When the water boils, slowly add the grains of white rice to one pot so the water does not stop boiling and the brown rice to the other. Boil the white rice until almost tender, about 12 minutes. Drain in a sieve and put in a large bowl. Boil the brown rice until almost tender, about 20 minutes. Drain and combine with the white rice. Add the butter and toss to coat.

3. Add the fruit, along with any wine in the bowl, to the rice. Add the diced apple, orange pieces, parsley, salt, pepper, and cloves. Toss to combine. Use to stuff a chicken.

NOTE: To roast in a casserole, top with chicken parts and bake at 325° for 1 hour. After 30 minutes, add about ½ cup canned chicken broth if the stuffing seems dry.

Kasha Stuffing

Kasha is the name for roasted buckwheat groats. The nutty flavor and texture make it one of my very favorite grains. It has an addictive taste and is perfect for stuffing chickens.

MAKES ABOUT 4½ CUPS

- **3** tablespoons butter
- **1** medium onion, peeled and chopped
- **1** cup finely diced celery
- **1** garlic clove, peeled and minced or crushed through a press (optional)
- **½** pound fresh mushrooms, finely diced
- **½** teaspoon dried thyme, crumbled
- **1** teaspoon salt

Pinch black pepper

- **1½** cups Basic Chicken Stock (page 47) or canned broth
- **3** large eggs
- **1** cup medium- or coarse-grain kasha
- **¼** cup chopped fresh parsley leaves
- **2** tablespoons plain dry bread crumbs

1. Melt the butter in a large heavy skillet over moderate heat. Add the onion and celery; sauté to soften, about 5 minutes. Add the garlic and cook a minute longer. Add the mushrooms and thyme; cook to brown the mushrooms lightly, 2 to 3 minutes over moderately high heat. Remove from the heat and add the salt, pepper, and chicken broth.

2. In a medium bowl stir 1 egg with the kasha. Transfer to a heavy medium ungreased saucepan and place over moderately high heat. Stirring constantly, and pressing occasionally, cook until the kasha kernels are dry and separated, 2 to 3 minutes. Stand back and carefully add the mushroom-broth mixture; it will boil up right away. Simmer, covered, for 8 to 10 minutes, until the liquid has been absorbed. Uncover and simmer 1 to 2 minutes longer, until dry.

3. Transfer to a bowl and let cool slightly. Stir in the remaining 2 eggs, parsley, and bread crumbs. Use to stuff any small bird.

NOTE: Place any extra stuffing in a small, generously buttered casserole. Cover and bake at 325° 30 to 40 minutes, adding 2 to 4 tablespoons pan drippings or chicken stock if the stuffing becomes dry.

Cornbread Stuffing

MAKES ABOUT 7 CUPS

6 cups toasted cornbread croutons (see page 370)
3/4 pound bulk sausage meat
1 1/2 cups finely diced celery
2 medium onions, peeled and chopped
1/4 cup chopped leaves from a celery heart
1 large garlic clove (optional), peeled and minced or crushed through a press
1/4 cup chopped fresh parsley leaves
1 1/2 teaspoons salt
2 large eggs, slightly beaten
1/4 teaspoon grated nutmeg (optional)
About 1 cup Basic Chicken Stock (page 47) or canned broth

Stuffing always tastes best when baked in the bird, so when you bake it separately in a casserole, be sure to add some of the pan drippings from a roasted bird. If you don't have any, bake some chicken parts (even backs) on top of the stuffing.

1. Make the cornbread a day ahead so it has time to dry before it is toasted.
2. Crumble the sausage into a large heavy skillet and place over moderate heat; cook, stirring, until no longer pink, 3 to 5 minutes. Add the celery, onions, celery leaves, and garlic; sauté

to brown lightly, about 5 minutes. Remove from the heat and stir in the parsley and salt.

3. Put the croutons in a large bowl; turn the sausage mixture over them. Add the eggs and optional nutmeg; toss to coat. Gradually stir in enough of the broth to make a moist (but neither wet nor dry) stuffing. Use to stuff any chicken.

NOTE: After filling the bird, put any extra stuffing into a generously buttered casserole and dot with a tablespoon of butter. Cover and bake at 325° for about 45 minutes, adding some of the pan drippings and/or some chicken stock or broth if it seems dry (you will need about ½ cup of broth).

Parsleyed Potatoes

MAKES 12 SERVINGS

3 quarts unsalted Basic Chicken Stock (page 47)
5 pounds (about 40) small new red-skinned potatoes of uniform size, washed and drained
4 tablespoons (½ stick) butter
½ cup chopped fresh parsley leaves

1. Pour the chicken stock into a large heavy pot or dutch oven.
2. Using a paring knife or vegetable peeler, remove and discard a 1-inch band of skin from around the center of each potato, dropping potatoes into the stock as they are pared.
3. Bring the stock to a boil over high heat. Partially cover the pot, reduce the heat slightly, and boil until the potatoes are tender when pierced with a fork, about 12 minutes; do not overcook. Remove the potatoes with a slotted spoon and transfer them to a warm platter. Cover with aluminum foil and set aside.
4. Increase the heat to high and boil the stock, uncovered, until reduced to 1¼ cups of concentrated stock, about 45 minutes. Watch carefully the last 10 minutes.
5. Return the reduced stock to the pan after measuring and stir in the butter over low heat. Add the potatoes and, tossing gently, heat until hot throughout, about 10 minutes. Add the parsley and salt and pepper to taste. Serve the potatoes in a warm covered serving dish, spooning some of the glaze and parsley over the top.

My mother made what she called "true parsleyed potatoes" by boiling small potatoes in plenty of chicken stock just until they were tender. Then the stock was boiled until it reduced to a glaze and tossed with the potatoes. All of this takes time, and canned stock just won't work here. Start early in the day or even a day ahead of time.

Mashed Potatoes and Gravy

This combination sits perfectly alongside many chicken dishes, from fried to roast. The gravy will be best if you have some pan juices from a roasted chicken.

MAKES 6 SERVINGS

Mashed Potatoes:

3 pounds (6 to 8 medium) Idaho baking potatoes
2½ teaspoons salt
3 tablespoons butter
¾ cup half and half or milk
¼ teaspoon grated nutmeg
¼ teaspoon black pepper

Gravy:

2 tablespoons butter
3 tablespoons all-purpose flour
2 cups Basic Chicken Stock (page 47), or canned broth mixed with any degreased chicken pan drippings you have to make 2 cups combined
¼ cup dry white wine
Salt to taste
Pinch black pepper

1. Make the mashed potatoes: Peel the potatoes and cut them into 1-inch chunks, dropping them into a large pot of cold water as they are cut. Add ½ teaspoon of the salt, partially cover, and place over high heat; bring to a boil. Adjust the heat to moderately high and keep at a steady boil until the potatoes are tender when pierced with a fork, about 20 minutes. Drain in a colander. Add the butter, half and half, nutmeg, pepper, and remaining 2 teaspoons salt to the hot pan; bring to a boil and then remove from the heat. Return the potatoes; mash with an electric mixer on low speed or a potato masher until fluffy. Cover to keep hot.

2. Make the gravy: Melt the butter in a large heavy skillet over moderate heat. Add the flour and stir with a fork or flat whisk for a minute or two. Pour in the stock or combined broth and drippings, and the wine. Stirring or whisking constantly, bring to a boil. Simmer 2 to 3 minutes, stirring, to make a light gravy. Add salt and pepper to taste (this will depend on the saltiness of the stock and drippings used). Serve hot.

Parsley-Scallion Rice

MAKES 6 CUPS

  3 tablespoons peanut oil or other vegetable oil
  2 cups long-grain white rice
3½ cups Basic Chicken Stock (page 47) or canned broth
  ½ teaspoon salt
  ¼ cup chopped parsley leaves
  4 medium scallions, minced

In this recipe you brown the grains of raw rice before adding the broth, as you would for Spanish rice. The technique ensures separate fluffy grains.

1. Spoon the oil into a large heavy saucepan and place over moderate heat. Add the rice and cook, stirring frequently, until the grains are toasted golden brown. Add the chicken broth and salt and increase the heat to moderately high. Bring to a boil. Cover tightly, reduce the heat to low, and simmer for 10 minutes. Uncover, stir in the parsley and scallions; fluff gently with a fork; cover and cook 5 to 8 minutes longer, until fluffy, tender, and almost dry. Serve hot.

Homemade Pasta

There's nothing quite so special as home-made pasta. If you don't have a pasta machine for rolling, keep the dough a bit on the soft side and you can roll it with a rolling pin, just as they have been doing for centuries in Italy and China. If you're not using it for stuffed pasta such as ravioli, omit the tablespoon of water and ¼ cup of the flour and use the pasta to make fettuccine or noodles.

MAKES ABOUT 1¼ POUNDS

3 to 3¼ cups all-purpose flour
4 large eggs
1 tablespoon cold water

1. Place 3 cups of the flour in a large shallow bowl and make a well in the center. Pour the eggs and water into the well.
2. Using a fork, stir the eggs and water together with a circular motion. As you stir, gradually incorporate the flour into the egg. Continue stirring with the circular motion until dough becomes too thick to stir. Then, with floured fingers, incorporate enough of the remaining flour to make a stiff but not dry dough. Remove the dough and knead it, adding some of the remaining flour if necessary to make a satin-smooth dough that is neither sticky nor dry. It will be best if it is on the soft side rather than dry. The kneading, which can be done on a lightly floured surface or in both hands while pinching and folding, should take 10 minutes. Cover and let rest 1 hour. If making ahead, wrap and chill in the refrigerator.

Corn Crêpes

Use these delicate corn crêpes to make Crepas ala Poblana (page 150). The crêpes can be made a day or two ahead, wrapped in plastic, and stored in the refrigerator, or frozen.

MAKES 18 TO 20

3 large eggs
1½ cups milk
¾ cup masa harina (see Note)
⅓ cup all-purpose flour
2 tablespoons melted butter
½ teaspoon salt

1. In a large bowl, lightly beat the eggs. Gradually whisk in the milk and masa harina. Whisk in the flour, melted butter, and salt. Let stand at room temperature for 30 minutes.

2. Lightly coat a heavy 6- to 7-inch crêpe pan with vegetable oil (a paper towel dipped in oil is a good way to apply it, wiping most of the oil away). Place over moderate heat. When the pan is hot, ladle in 2 tablespoons of the batter, quickly swirling to coat. Cook the crêpe until it's speckled brown on the bottom, 30 seconds to 1 minute. Flip and cook 15 to 20 seconds longer. Transfer the crêpe to a sheet of waxed paper. Repeat with the remaining batter, lightly oiling the pan between crêpes. Stack the crêpes between sheets of waxed paper and cover.

NOTE: Masa harina is a fine corn flour available in many supermarkets and most Latin American grocery stores.

Traditional Buckwheat Blini

Buckwheat blini are light little pancakes made from a yeast batter. The batter won't be ready for about 3 hours, so plan your time accordingly.

MAKES ABOUT THIRTY-TWO 3-INCH PANCAKES

- **¾** cup warm water (105° to 115°)
- **1** tablespoon sugar
- **1** ¼-ounce envelope active dry yeast
- **1** cup milk
- **2** tablespoons butter
- **1** cup all-purpose flour
- **1** cup buckwheat flour
- **2** eggs, separated
- **½** teaspoon salt

1. Pour ¼ cup of the water into a small warm bowl; stir in the sugar and yeast. Stir to dissolve and let proof in a warm draft-free place until foamy and doubled in volume, about 5 minutes. If this does not happen, throw out the mixture and start over with fresh ingredients.

2. Pour the milk into a small saucepan. Add the butter and heat to lukewarm. Stir to melt the butter.

3. Stir the all-purpose flour in a large bowl and add the warm milk mixture all at once as you stir. Stir in the proofed yeast. Cover and let rise in a warm place until doubled in volume, about 1 hour.

4. Whisk in the remaining ½ cup warm water and the buckwheat flour. Cover and let rise in a warm place until doubled in volume, about 1½ hours. Whisk in the egg yolks.

5. Place the egg whites in a deep medium bowl and beat with a handheld electric mixer or whisk until stiff peaks begin to form (do not overbeat or whites will become dry and lumpy). Fold the whites into the batter. Let batter rest, covered, for 20 to 30 minutes, until it begins to rise again (do not stir down).

6. Place a heavy griddle or skillet over moderate heat. When hot, lightly oil with a paper towel dipped in vegetable oil. To make the blini, carefully spoon off the fluffy batter from the top and do not stir the batter. Using a large spoon that holds about 2 tablespoons, spoon as many 3-inch pancakes onto the hot griddle as you can without crowding. Cook until bubbles appear and burst, and the edges begin to look dry, about 1½ minutes. Turn with a spatula and cook about 30 seconds longer. Lower the heat slightly if the blini are browning too quickly. Transfer to a platter. Continue making blini, lightly oiling the griddle as necessary. Serve hot. (You can make them all ahead of time and reheat in a microwave oven at full power for about 20 seconds.)

Quick Buckwheat Blini

MAKES ABOUT THIRTY-TWO 3-INCH PANCAKES

  4 large eggs
½ cup sour cream
  4 tablespoons (½ stick) butter, melted
½ cup buckwheat flour
½ cup all-purpose flour
  1 teaspoon baking powder
½ teaspoon salt
¼ cup milk

1. In a large bowl whisk together the eggs and sour cream to blend evenly. Whisk in the melted butter.
2. In a bowl or on a sheet of waxed paper, stir together the buckwheat flour, all-purpose flour, baking powder, and salt.

Usually buckwheat blini are made from yeast batter, which must rise for a long time (see previous recipe). If you are in a hurry, make this delicious version at a moment's notice. They have a good buckwheat flavor and a slight tang from the sour cream.

Gradually whisk it into the egg mixture until smooth. Stir in the milk and let stand 15 minutes.

3. Place a heavy griddle or well-seasoned skillet over moderate heat. When it is hot, lightly rub it with a paper towel dipped in vegetable oil. Ladle the batter onto the griddle, using 1 tablespoon for each pancake. Adjust the temperature as needed; moderately low should be just right once the griddle is heated to the proper temperature. Cook the pancakes until bubbles appear on the tops and the edges begin to look slightly dry, 1½ to 2 minutes. Turn with a spatula and cook the other side for 30 seconds. Serve hot. To reheat pancakes, place in a microwave at full power for about 20 seconds.

Cornbread

You can serve this directly from the cast-iron skillet, split, toasted, and slathered with butter, or use it to make croutons for cornbread stuffing.

MAKES A 9-INCH ROUND OR 6 CUPS TOASTED CUBES

1 cup all-purpose flour
1 cup coarse yellow cornmeal
1 tablespoon baking powder
2 tablespoons sugar
½ teaspoon salt
2 large eggs
1 cup milk
4 tablespoons (½ stick) butter, melted, or vegetable oil

1. Adjust a shelf to the center of the oven and preheat to 400°. Grease a 9-inch cast-iron skillet or round cake pan.

2. In a large bowl stir together the flour, cornmeal, baking powder, sugar, and salt. In a medium bowl stir together the eggs and milk; whisk in the melted butter. Make a well in the center of the dry ingredients and pour in the liquid ingredients. Stir just to blend, working quickly so the batter is slightly lumpy. Quickly turn into the prepared pan. Bake until the top springs back when lightly touched and the edges begin to pull away from the sides of the pan, about 20 minutes; when done, a toothpick inserted in the center will come out clean, without crumbs clinging to it. Cook on a rack.

3. To make croutons: Cut the bread in half horizontally and let air-dry on a rack 8 hours or overnight. Cut into ½- to ¾-inch cubes and bake on a sheet at 350°, tossing occasionally, until lightly toasted and dried out, about 30 minutes. Let cool.

Beautiful Biscuits

MAKES 8

- **2** cups all-purpose flour
- **1** tablespoon baking powder
- **½** teaspoon salt
- **⅓** cup white vegetable shortening, chilled
- **¾** cup cold milk

1. Adjust a shelf to the center of the oven and preheat to 425° for at least 15 minutes.
2. In a large bowl stir together the flour, baking powder, and salt until well blended.
3. Cut in the shortening with a pastry blender or two knives until it resembles petals the size of cornflakes. Pour in the milk all at once and stir quickly with a fork to make a moist dough.

Tender-flaky and delicate, these baking powder biscuits will always be successful if you follow the instructions carefully. It's wise to buy baking powder in small cans, because it can become inactive if it sits too long in your cupboard.

Knead on a lightly floured surface 4 or 5 times, folding dough as you work. Pat out so it is slightly less than 1 inch thick. Dip a 2-inch biscuit cutter into flour and cut out as many biscuits as possible, making the cuts close together. Place the biscuits 1 inch apart on an ungreased baking sheet. Quickly gather scraps and make more biscuits. Bake about 14 minutes, until puffed and light golden brown. Serve hot.

Croustades (Toast Cases)

These tasty toast cases make good containers for chicken à la king.

MAKES 6

2 evenly rectangular loaves unsliced firm white or whole wheat bread
2 tablespoons melted butter

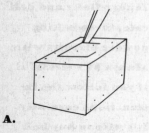

A.

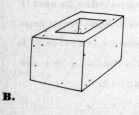

B.

1. Preheat the oven to 425°. Cut each loaf of bread into 3 crustless solid rectangles, each measuring approximately 2½ inches high, 2½ to 3 inches wide, and 3 to 3½ inches long. Use a knife to cut down in from the top (illustration A) to leave a half-inch shell around all four sides and the bottom. Pull out the soft centers (illustration B), making sure not to tear the bottoms of the cases.
2. Place cases on a baking sheet and bake for 5 minutes, or until lightly toasted. Dip a pastry brush into the melted butter and dab all over inside and out. Return to the oven and bake 5 to 8 minutes longer, until golden and well toasted. Serve hot or warm. You can reheat them for a few minutes in the oven, but do not put them in a microwave or they will become tough.

Roasted Shallots

MAKES 4 TO 6 SERVINGS

1 pound medium shallots
1 tablespoon butter
Salt and pepper

1. Preheat the oven to 400°. Put the whole shallots in a shallow roasting pan. Bake until soft and tender, 30 to 40 minutes.
2. To serve, slice lengthwise in half, dab with butter, and sprinkle lightly with salt and pepper.

Nothing could be simpler or more of a welcome surprise than roasted shallots. You don't even peel them; just roast them whole in their skins. Roast them ahead of time and reheat in the oven.

Creamed Corn

MAKES ABOUT 4 CUPS

4 cups fresh corn kernels, cut from 8 to 10 medium ears of sweet corn on the cob
2 tablespoons cornstarch
1 cup milk
3 tablespoons butter
1 tablespoon all-purpose flour
1/2 cup heavy cream
1 1/2 teaspoons salt
1/8 teaspoon black pepper
1/4 teaspoon grated nutmeg (optional)

1. Combine half of the corn kernels with the cornstarch and milk in a food processor or blender; grind to a coarse purée.
2. Melt the butter in a heavy medium saucepan. Add the whole

This is creamy, dreamy comfort food. No one ever thinks of making creamed corn from scratch anymore. After sampling this, who could ever eat the canned version again? Serve with roasted or fried chicken.

corn kernels, increase the heat to moderately high, and sauté to brown lightly, 2 to 3 minutes. Stir in the flour and cook a minute longer. Add the puréed corn and the heavy cream; cook over low heat, stirring, and bring to a simmer. Cook 2 to 3 minutes longer, to thicken. Stir in the salt, pepper, and nutmeg if you like. Serve hot.

Fresh Stewed Tomatoes

Good and simple, fresh-tasting and colorful, homemade stewed tomatoes bear little resemblance to canned ones. It's easy to cut this recipe in half.

MAKES ABOUT 8 CUPS

- **3** pounds (12 medium) firm ripe tomatoes
- **2** tablespoons olive oil
- **1** large onion, peeled and chopped.
- **2** small inner ribs celery, diced (½ cup)
- **1** large garlic clove, peeled and minced or crushed through a press
- **1** teaspoon celery salt
- **1** teaspoon dried basil, crumbled
- **¼** teaspoon dried oregano, crumbled
- **¼** teaspoon dried thyme, crumbled
- **1** bay leaf
- **1** cup dry white wine
- **2** to 3 tablespoons sugar
- **1** 8-ounce can tomato sauce
- **2** tablespoons chopped parsley
- **2** teaspoons salt
- **2** tablespoons butter

1. Bring a large kettle of lightly salted water to a boil over high heat. Drop in 3 or 4 of the tomatoes and scoop out after 20 seconds to a minute (depending on ripeness—the skin will begin to split and loosen when they are ready to take out). Rinse under cold water to refresh. Blanch the remaining tomatoes.

2. Working over a bowl to catch the juice and seeds, peel the tomatoes with a paring knife. Cut out the cores and discard them. Quarter the tomatoes.

3. Spoon the olive oil into a large heavy nonaluminum saucepan; add the onion and celery; sauté over moderate heat to soften, about 5 minutes. Add the garlic, celery salt, basil, oregano, thyme, and bay leaf; cook a minute longer. Add the wine and 2 tablespoons of the sugar and bring to a boil. Boil over moderately high heat until reduced by half, 3 to 5 minutes. Add the quartered tomatoes and tomato sauce and simmer for 15 minutes. Stir in the parsley and salt. Remove from the heat and swirl in the butter. Taste for sweetness and add the remaining 1 tablespoon sugar if desired. Serve hot or warm.

Pinto Beans with Bacon

MAKES 8 CUPS

8 to 10 slices smoked bacon, cut in small squares
1 pound dried pinto beans, rinsed and picked over to remove any grit
3 large garlic cloves, peeled and minced or crushed through a press
2 teaspoons salt

Sauté the bacon in a heavy 3-quart saucepan until crisp and deep golden brown. Add the beans and 2½ quarts cold water. Bring to a boil, stirring occasionally, over moderate heat. Lower

Pinto beans are my favorite beans. They are very tasty and easy to prepare. They need no initial soaking, contrary to what most instruct, and cook within an hour and a half. Whenever there is bacon that needs

using up, this is what
I make.

the heat and simmer, partially covered, for 1 hour. Add the garlic and simmer, uncovered, until very tender, 30 minutes to an hour longer. Add salt the last 15 minutes of cooking. Serve as is, or mash with a potato masher and use for tostadas and burritos.

Cole Slaw

No ordinary cole slaw, this nippy version is powerful, vigorously zesty, and almost hot with two kinds of mustard and horse-radish. The sour cream offsets the richness of the mayonnaise.

MAKES ABOUT 8 CUPS

3/4 cup Mayonnaise (page 383)
1/2 cup sour cream
3 tablespoons fresh lemon juice
2 tablespoons brown or golden mustard
1 tablespoon prepared white horseradish
1 teaspoon powdered mustard
1 tablespoon salt
1/2 teaspoon whole celery seeds
1/2 teaspoon black pepper
12 cups finely shredded green cabbage (about 2 pounds)

In a large bowl stir together the mayonnaise, sour cream, lemon juice, brown mustard, horseradish, powdered mustard, salt, celery seeds, and pepper. Add the cabbage and toss well. Cover and chill at least 4 hours, or overnight. Stir to blend the flavors and transfer to a serving dish (the quantity reduces as the cole slaw marinates). Serve cold.

Old-fashioned Potato Salad

MAKES ABOUT 7 CUPS

- **3** pounds (8 to 12 medium) red-skinned potatoes
- **1½** teaspoons salt, plus a pinch
- **3** large eggs
- **¾** cup Mayonnaise (page 383)
- **1** tablespoon brown or golden mustard
- **1** tablespoon cider vinegar
- **¼** teaspoon black pepper
- **¼** cup finely chopped fresh parsley leaves
- **4** medium scallions, minced, including green parts

Parsley sprigs for garnish

1. Put the unpeeled potatoes in a large heavy pot. Add a pinch of salt and enough cold water to cover by 1 inch. Partially cover and bring to a boil over high heat. Boil until tender when pierced with a fork, 30 to 40 minutes (if you have used small potatoes they will take 25 to 30 minutes). Do not test before 25 or 30 minutes and do not test often or potatoes will become soggy. Take out the potatoes and cool them. Do not chill.

2. Meanwhile, put the eggs in a small heavy saucepan and add enough cold water to cover by 1 inch. Place over moderately high heat and bring to a boil. Immediately reduce the heat to low and keep at a bare simmer for precisely 10 minutes from the time the water began to boil (if using an electric burner, have a second burner at the low temperature so you can switch burners at the right moment). Do not overcook or let the eggs boil. Rinse them under cold water and cool to room temperature.

3. Peel the eggs and grate them through the coarse side of a cheese grater into a large bowl. Stir in the mayonnaise, mus-

This simple country-style potato salad is perfect in flavor and texture. It's the version I always make. If it is too plain for your taste, add chopped sweet pickle and dill pickle and whole pitted black olives. This salad is best served on the day it is made.

tard, vinegar, salt, and pepper. Mash the eggs against the side of the bowl as you mix.

4. Peel the potatoes with a paring knife and cut them into 1-inch chunks, cutting this way and that rather than making uniform cubes. As you cut them, let them drop into the dressing. Toss all the potatoes and dressing with the chopped parsley and scallions. Cover and chill for about 2 hours. Mound onto a platter and garnish with parsley sprigs. Serve cold.

Flaky Pastry

The key to successful pastry, that is, pastry that's tender and flaky, is to use very cold ingredients and to work quickly, handling the dough and the rolled pastry as little as possible. If you have any hesitation, stop and chill the mixture at any time. If you are being conscientious about fat and calories, consider using only a top crust for your pies.

MAKES ENOUGH FOR 2 SINGLE-CRUST 9-INCH PIES,

OR 1 DOUBLE-CRUST 9-INCH PIE,

OR 8 SINGLE-CRUST INDIVIDUAL PIES

2¼ cups all-purpose flour
½ teaspoon salt
½ cup white vegetable shortening
4 tablespoons (½ stick) cold butter, thinly sliced
5 to 6 tablespoons ice water

1. In a large bowl stir together the flour and salt. Add the shortening and butter. Using a pastry blender or 2 knives (held as you would if cutting a steak), cut the fat into the flour until it resembles rolled oats or small flakes. If the mixture has warmed to room temperature, chill it until cold.

2. Sprinkle 3 tablespoons of the ice water over the top and stir quickly with a fork, just to moisten. Sprinkle on another 2 tablespoons water and quickly stir. Add just enough of the remaining water to make a dough that holds together. Divide into

2 pieces. Flatten each into a 6-inch round and wrap them in plastic wrap or waxed paper. Chill for an hour or as long as 2 days, or wrap well and freeze.

NOTE: To make enough pastry for 2 double-crust 9-inch pies or 8 double-crust individual pies, simply double all the ingredients here and proceed as directed, dividing the dough into 4 pieces rather than 2.

Orange-Basil Marinade

MAKES ABOUT 1¼ CUPS

½ cup frozen orange juice concentrate, thawed
½ cup cider vinegar
¼ cup olive oil
2 teaspoons dried basil, crumbled
1 teaspoon salt
½ teaspoon grated nutmeg
¼ teaspoon ground cloves

This fragrant marinade adds zest to barbecued or broiled chicken and is simple to stir together.

1. In a jar with a lid, combine the orange juice, vinegar, olive oil, basil, salt, nutmeg, and cloves; shake vigorously. Store in the refrigerator a week or more, or use right away.

2. Marinate chicken pieces in the marinade for 1 hour in the refrigerator, then 30 minutes at room temperature. Grill or broil.

Tangy Mustard Dipping Sauce

Make this tasty sauce at least a day before you want to serve it. It's particularly good with egg rolls and dumplings.

MAKES ABOUT ⅓ CUP

2 teaspoons powdered mustard
1 tablespoon rice vinegar
3 tablespoons Dijon mustard
1 tablespoon oriental sesame oil
2 teaspoons sugar

In a cup or small bowl, dissolve the powdered mustard with 1 tablespoon hot water and the rice vinegar. Stir in the Dijon mustard, sesame oil, and sugar. Cover and refrigerate for at least 1 day.

Salsa Verde

This addictive, slightly hot and somewhat acidic sauce is best when made with fresh tomatillos (little green tomatolike berries in papery husks) but if you can't find them, you might substitute canned. Note that the heat of chile

MAKES ABOUT 2 CUPS

1 pound (12 to 18 medium) fresh tomatillos (*tomates verdes*), husks removed, or two 13-ounce cans tomatillos
1 tablespoon vegetable oil
2 large garlic cloves, peeled and minced or crushed through a press
2 fresh medium-sized jalapeño chile peppers
¼ cup chopped fresh cilantro
1 teaspoon salt

1. Rinse the tomatillos and put them in a heavy medium non-aluminum pot with 1½ cups cold water. Place over moderate heat and bring to a boil. Lower the heat and simmer until they are soft but not bursting, 8 to 10 minutes; drain them in a strainer over a bowl and reserve the liquid. Let them cool to room temperature. If starting with canned, simply drain and discard the liquid.

2. Spoon the vegetable oil into a small skillet and place over low heat. Add the garlic and sizzle to soften but not brown, about 1 minute. Let cool.

3. Cut the jalapeño peppers lengthwise into quarters. Cut off the stems and slice off the seeds and ribs flush with the peppers. Reserve ½ teaspoon or more seeds, to taste, and discard the rest. Chop the jalapeños.

4. In the container of a blender or food processor, combine the tomatillos with ½ cup of the cooking liquid (or water if using canned) and the garlic, jalapeños (along with ½ teaspoon or more seeds), cilantro, and salt; blend to purée. If too thick, add a little more cooking liquid or water. If making ahead, cover and chill. The salsa sometimes sets upon chilling; simply add a little water to dilute it and stir.

peppers is contained in the seeds and ribs of fresh peppers, so you can add as many or as few as you like. To my taste, ½ teaspoon of seeds makes this hot enough. You add the flesh of the peppers for their good chile flavor without all the heat.

Tomato-Jalapeño Salsa

Here's a great way to make a fresh salsa all year long—long after the juicy summer tomatoes are in the market. You use 1 cup of canned tomatoes and 1 cup of fresh; the canned tomato adds the juiciness and the fresh the texture. The other ingredients add flavor and perk up the whole thing.

MAKES 2 CUPS

1 8-ounce can whole tomatoes, with juice, cut up
1 cup finely diced fresh tomato
¼ cup finely minced white onion
3 tablespoons chopped fresh cilantro leaves
2 fresh jalapeño chile peppers
¾ teaspoon salt

1. In a small bowl combine the canned tomatoes, fresh tomatoes, onion, and cilantro.
2. Slice the stem ends from the jalapeños and then quarter the chiles lengthwise. Slice off the seeds and veins (this is where the heat is contained). Reserve ½ teaspoon or more of the seeds for heat and finely chop them. Cut the chiles lengthwise into fine strips, then crosswise to mince. Stir into the sauce along with the reserved seeds and the salt. If making a day ahead, cover and chill.

NOTE: Chile peppers contain volatile oil that can burn your eyes or anything you touch, so wear rubber gloves when working with them.

Mayonnaise

MAKES ABOUT 1⅓ CUPS

- **2** large egg yolks, at room temperature
- **1½** tablespoons lemon juice
- **½** teaspoon salt
- **¾** cup vegetable oil
- **½** cup olive oil

1. Choose a deep 2½- to 3-quart glass or ceramic mixing bowl. Fill it with very warm tap water to warm it. Dry it thoroughly and add the egg yolks, lemon juice, and salt. Using a handheld electric mixer set at medium speed, or a whisk, beat the yolks until creamy, about 1 minute.

2. Combine the vegetable oil and olive oil in a cup with a pouring spout, or in a bowl. It is important to begin the emulsion by beating in tiny droplets of oil at first. Beating or whisking, add a droplet and continue beating. (I do this by dipping a spoon into the oil, letting most of it drip back into the cup; when the drips become small, I hold the spoon over the yolk mixture and let just one fall in. After a teaspoonful has been added this way the drops can become progressively larger.) As you beat in the droplets of oil, one at a time, beating well after each addition, occasionally scrape the mixture from the sides of the bowl with a rubber spatula toward the beaters or whisk. As soon as the emulsion has surely taken and the mixture is thick, beat in the remaining oil in a very thin steady stream, stopping once in a while to scrape the sides of the bowl and beat well. Scrape into a bowl or jar, cover, and refrigerate until needed.

NOTE: To repair broken or curdled mayonnaise (which sometimes happens if the ingredients are too cold or when the

Essentially, mayonnaise is an emulsion created by gradually beating oil into egg yolks to make a thick, creamy sauce. It is best made from ingredients at room temperature. By the way, you can freshen up 1 cup of commercially bottled mayonnaise by whisking in 1 to 2 tablespoons virgin olive oil and 2 to 3 teaspoons lemon juice.

oil has been added too quickly), my friend Julia Child recommends warming and drying a bowl, then whisking together 1 teaspoon prepared mustard and 1 tablespoon of the curdled mayonnaise until thick and creamy. The rest of the mayonnaise is then beaten in by teaspoonfuls, thickening each addition before adding the next.

Avocado Mayonnaise

If you love this simple concoction as much as I do, consider making a double batch. Besides being my favorite accompaniment to poule-au-pot, it's also exquisite on chicken and tomato sandwiches.

MAKES 1¼ CUPS

1 firm-ripe California avocado, such as Haas (about 10 ounces)
⅓ cup Mayonnaise (page 383)
2 tablespoons lemon juice
½ teaspoon salt

Combine all the ingredients in a food processor or blender and purée until smooth as velvet. Cover and chill if making ahead.

Cilantro Mayonnaise

MAKES ABOUT 1 CUP

- **1** cup Mayonnaise (page 383)
- **½** cup packed chopped cilantro (fresh coriander)
- **1** to 2 teaspoons freshly squeezed lime juice
- **½** teaspoon ground cumin
- **½** teaspoon salt
- **¼** teaspoon black pepper
- **⅛** teaspoon cayenne pepper
- **1** tablespoon olive oil

In the container of a food processor or blender combine the mayonnaise, cilantro, 1 teaspoon of the lime juice, cumin, salt, pepper, and cayenne pepper; process until blended. Slowly blend in the olive oil. Cover and chill. Serve cold. Taste for tartness and add the remaining teaspoon of lime juice if desired.

Use this fragrant, intensely flavored mayonnaise on chicken sandwiches or as a dip for strips of breaded chicken cutlets.

Index

Asparagus and chicken salad, Chinese, 130
Avocado:
  guacamole, 61, 63
    creamy, 328–29
  mayonnaise, 384
    poule-au-pot with, 30–33
Aztec pie, 164–66

Bacon:
  pinto beans with, 375–76
  whole wheat, and mushroom stuffing, 357–58
Baking powder (sidebar), 371
Barbecued chicken:
  citrus, spicy, 142–43
  kebobs; Tandoori, 168–69
  orange-basil marinade for, 379
  quiche in pepper pastry, 322–23
  satay with peanut sauce and pickled cucumbers;
      Thai, 178–80
  sticky-lick-it, 72–73
  with tabbouleh and hummus; Mid-eastern, 210–12
  teriyaki thighs, 207–8
  yakitori, 181–82
Basic chicken stock, 47
Basil-orange marinade, 379
Bean curd with chicken sauce, old pockmarked Mrs.
      Chen's, 276–77
Beans:
  black
    and guacamole tostadas; chicken ranchero with,
        60–63
  and chicken burritos, 76–77
  chicken chili and, 278–79
  garbanzo, in hummus, 212
  kidney
    and rice; drumsticks with, 236–38
  pinto
    with bacon, 375–76
    in smoky dal, 170–71
  white
    pasta shells with chicken, collard greens, and,
        158–60
Beans, green:
  and corn; chicken stew with, 209–10

Beautiful biscuits, 371–72
Biscuits:
  beautiful, 371–72
  cocks' combs, 297–99
Bleu cheese dressing, 223
Blini: *See* Buckwheat blini
Bonito shavings:
  in dashi, 174
Bread crumbs, homemade, 79, 235
Breads:
  biscuits, beautiful, 371–72
  cocks' combs, 297–99
  cornbread, 370–71
  garlic toast, 291
  pizza rustica, 118–21
Breasts, chicken, 87–174
  in Aztec pie, 164–66
  collard greens, and white beans; pasta shells with,
      158–60
  cooked
    in classic club sandwich, 306–7
    egg fu yung, 314–15
    grilled cheese sandwich, 305–6
    in Mexican club sandwich, 307–8
    potato pirogi, 320–21
    quiche in pepper pastry; barbecued, 322–23
    salad sandwiches with anchovies and eggs;
        Italian, 308–9
    and spinach cannelloni, 310–13
  cooking technique for, 88
  in crepas ala poblana, 150–52
  divan, 94–95
  enchiladas, 153–55
  filling; shredded, 103
  and green olive sauce; spaghetti with,
      113–14
  grilled citrus, spicy, 142–43
  hash, 111–12
  latkes, 110–11
  macaroni salad; crunchy, 90–91
  poached, simple, 88
  with potatoes and tomatoes; cold, 140–41
  and roasted peanuts; cold sesame noodles with,
      132–34

About the Author

A student of the late James Beard, JIM FOBEL is the award-winning author of six cookbooks including *Jim Fobel's Old-Fashioned Baking Book, Beautiful Food,* and *Jim Fobel's Diet Feasts.* He also writes frequently for *Bon Appetit, Family Circle, Cooking Light,* and *Food & Wine,* where he formerly served as Test Kitchen Director. He holds a BFA from Otis Art Institute in Los Angeles and currently lives in New York City.